Oliver Baldwin:
A Life of Dissent

'And thys meanewhyle com sir Palomdes, the good knyght, folowyng the questyng beste that had in shap lyke a serpentis hede and a body lyke a lybud, buttokked lyke a lyon and footed lyke an harte. And in hys body there was such a noyse as hit had bene twenty couple of houndys questynge, and suche noyse that beste made wheresomever he wente. And thys beste evermore sir Palomydes folowed, for hit was called hys queste.'

Sir Thomas Malory,
The Book of Sir Tristram de Lyones, IV

'We heartily pray thee to send thy holy Spirit into the hearts of them that possess the grounds and pastures of the earth, that they, remembering themselves to be thy tenants, may not rack or stretch out the rents of their houses or lands, nor yet take unreasonable fines or monies, after the manner of covetous worldlings, but so let them out that the inhabitants thereof may be able to pay the rents, and to live and assist their families and remember the poor.

'Give them grace also to consider that they are but strangers and pilgrims in this world, having here no dwelling place but seeking one to come; that they, remembering the short continuance of this life, may be content with that which is sufficient, and not join house to house or land to land to the impoverishment of others, but so behave themselves in letting their tenements, lands and pastures, that after this life they may be received into everlasting habitations.'

Thomas Becon,
'A Prayer for Landlords' (adapted),
The Flower of Godly Prayers, c. 1551,
copied out by Oliver Baldwin and found in his papers

Oliver Baldwin: A Life of Dissent

by

Christopher J. Walker

A

ARCADIA BOOKS
LONDON

Arcadia Books Ltd
15–16 Nassau Street
London W1W 7AB
www.arcadiabooks.co.uk

First published in the United Kingdom 2003
Copyright © Christopher J. Walker 2003

A catalogue record for this book is available from the British Library.

ISBN 1–900850–86–9

Typeset in Scala by Northern Phototypesetting Co. Ltd, Bolton
Printed in Finland by WS Bookwell

Arcadia Books distributors are as follows:

in the UK and elsewhere in Europe:
Turnaround Publishers Services
Unit 3, Olympia Trading Estate
Coburg Road
London N22 6TZ

in the USA and Canada:
Independent Publishers Group
814 N. Franklin Street
Chicago, IL 60610

in Australia:
Tower Books
PO Box 213
Brookvale, NSW 2100

in New Aealand:
Addenda
Box 78224
Grey Lynn
Auckland

in South Africa:
Quartet Sales and Marketing
PO Box 1218
Northcliffe
Johannesburg 2115

Arcadia Books: *Sunday Times* Small Publisher of the Year 2002/03

About the author:

Christopher J. Walker's books include *Armenia: The Survival of a Nation* and *Visions of Ararat.* Oliver Baldwin was an active witness to the nationalist/communist struggle in Armenia in 1920–21, and Walker came across his name while writing his first book. The idea of writing this book took shape when a friend directed him to an archive of Baldwin's letters. Christopher J. Walker lives in London.

Praise for *Armenia: The Survival of a Nation*

'Walker writes almost as if he were reporting a contemporary nightmare. Consular reports, eye-witness memoirs, local and vernacular sources, all are pressed into service and woven together marvellously. His book is a loving account of ancient Armenia and of its hideous destruction in modern times. He is passionate – at times almost incandescent – but scholarly'
Christopher Hitchens, *New Statesman*

Contents

Introduction

In 1929 Stanley Baldwin's wife Lucy was forced to abandon visiting the Distinguished Strangers' Gallery of the House of Commons, not because she found it painful to see her husband transformed from prime minister into leader of the opposition, but because the former premier and her son Oliver faced one another on the opposite sides of the House – as if acting out some ancient and primitive struggle between the generations, symbolic of the departure of the old and the emergence of the new. Oliver Baldwin had been elected as Labour member for Dudley on a resolutely socialist manifesto, and had thereby set a seal on his dissidence, which had been smouldering for six years. How this dissidence emerged, and how it coloured the rest of his life, is the subject of this study.

It is possible to imagine a deep antagonism between father and son, some unhealable wound resulting either from profound family dysfunctionality, or from an extreme form of the battle across the generations, humanity's 'first crude philosophy of life', in the words of Sir James Frazer. But personal relations between Stanley Baldwin and his elder son were marked by gentleness, good humour and essential tolerance. This human warmth – a manifestation of affectionate family values – reached a kind of culmination in the party given for the former prime minister by his son and his son's boyfriend in December 1938. Few more happy social events, or more fulfilling articulations of the notion of family, can be imagined than this reception given by Oliver Baldwin and his lifetime partner Johnnie Boyle for Oliver's father on the occasion of his taking leave of public life. As well as Oliver's parents, three of his sisters and his brother and sister-in-law were present. The happy party (as SB called it) was a celebration of a life, and also a triumph of inclusiveness, both political and personal.

Oliver had been born at the end of Queen Victoria's reign. His life was fashioned by service in the trenches of the Western Front in 1918, and by further military experience in Armenia in 1920. Bit by bit he moved to a socialist stance until, while living in a stable relationship with the man who would be his companion till death, he reached a moment of definition in November 1923 when he spoke on a Labour platform. Subsequently he stood as candidate for parliament – unsuccessfully in 1924, but winning a seat five years later. He refused financial help from his father except in the form of small gifts. Most of his income came from writing and speaking; and he poured much of his energy into speaking and raising spirits in areas depressed by wage cuts and unemployment. His socialist commitment did not derive from middle-class guilt; Oliver was largely free from guilt throughout his life, except as a reflection of his country's guilt at its bad faith in the conduct of foreign affairs. His conviction was rather that grinding poverty at home was, besides being ugly, plain wrong. It was a condition which derived from a misguided way of running society. There had to be a better way.

His radicalism was spurred by the fact that he discovered himself to be homosexual at about the age of 22. Since he had to create his own set of guidelines about love and sex and human relationships as he went along, so too he felt free to challenge and unsanctify the received wisdom of the necessity of capitalism.

The capitalism he attacked was largely the 'savage capitalism' (which sounds better in French as *capitalisme sauvage*), which existed before the establishment of the Welfare State. Socialism as he had envisaged it was achieved by the Beveridge reforms of the 1940s. He sought an end to the poverty, starvation, misery and unemployment of his youth. He remained thereafter on the left, and was a magnificently dissident colonial governor in 1948–50, but he never adopted any of the baggage of the ideological left. His political and personal friend was Clement Attlee, whose silver wedding dinner he organized in the House in 1948. Oliver Baldwin believed that capitalism would wither, and in his latter years did little except seek to cut its dried stems.

His journalism has been curiously overlooked, in the arena of leftist writing; at its best it was stirring and touched the core of the subject. His books were less successful, except where he had a personal narrative to relate, when the rawness of experience would find its way directly on to the page. The bitter cold and pain of his youthful journey in the east make a direct impact on the reader.

Even in his mature semi-squirearchical life in Oxfordshire, shared with his partner, where the two of them dispensed generous weekend hospitality in a relaxed country style, socialism was not entirely abandoned; the front door would be left unlocked in case a passing stranger might need shelter for the night. The pipe-smoking unaustere 2nd Earl might appear hardly a socialist – more a jovial old soldier; in London, with his love of the gossippy sleepy indifferent world of St James's clubs, there was little to identify him as belonging to the left: but beneath the enjoyment of ease and conventionality, his views remained radical, and his wit ready.

*

I became aware of Oliver Baldwin when writing about Armenia. His account of his time there, *Six Prisons and Two Revolutions* (Hodder, 1925), is an important text relating to the end of the first Republic of Armenia. The recollections of friends increased my interest, especially those of Sibylla Jane Flower, who told me of hospitable days spent in Wallingford in the company of Johnnie Boyle and Dickie Payne. I am grateful to her for introducing me to Dickie. I owe a special debt of gratitude to the Earl and the late Countess Baldwin of Bewdley. I am also grateful for the reminiscences of, or assistance from, the late Rt Hon Lord Jenkins of Hillhead, the late Lady Lorna Howard, the late Rachel Lady Redgrave, Sir Julian Ridsdale MP, Miles Huntington-Whiteley, Oswald Skilbeck, James Knox, Richard Davenport-Hines, Patrick Trevor-Roper, Ian Huish, Hugh Woodeson, John Sandoe, Stuart Jolley, David Tennant, John Bedding, and John Byrne. I am grateful to Leo Huntington-Whiteley for giving me a push to finish the book.

Prologue:
On the road to Cambrai, 1918

Resting briefly after the battle of the Canal du Nord, early in October 1918, the 19-year-old Oliver Baldwin pencilled the following letter:[1]

Darling Father,

At 5.15 a.m. on the 27th of September when you were asleep, your son (in command for the day of the 1st Guards Brigade Light Trench Mortar Battery) was crouching in a 3 foot trench with the Irish Guards, smoking one of his grandfather's cigars, waiting for 'zero' & under-going a slight German barrage. At 5.20 a.m. ('zero') a noise like six trains rushing through a narrow tunnel, coal being thrown downstairs, pots & pans being upset etc., etc rent the air. In other words our barrage of 9.2", 6" and 4.2" howitzers, 60 and 18 pounder, machine gun & every other gun on our sector tore 'No mans land' & the canal bank to pieces – & we (as they say in the paper) 'went over the top'. How we got through the wire & the German barrage of 'Minnies' I cannot tell, but we leapt into our first trench for a pause. This trench was receiving direct hits – one in the next bay to me & one on the parados wherein all went dark & I thought I was finished; but only covered with dirt. I thought it was time to get out so I led the battery to the canal.

Here for the infinitesimal second I stood on top, Henry Vth & Harfleur rushed to my mind. Below me a 100 ft chasm of concrete & earth, at the bottom helmeted English & on the other side scaling ladders!

We slid down one side & scrambled up the other. Here the shelling was not so bad but machine gun fire was knocking fellows over.

Here I pause because it strikes me that the rest of our engagement was so alike all the time & can only be explained verbally. However when our objective was reached we began to receive direct fire from guns on our left flank which had not yet come up & it was then I started to debate. The next traverse had a direct hit – shall I move or shall I not? – the traverse on my other side has a hit – if I stay here I may get it next – if I move fate might be annoyed – let's stay for a while. This sort of reasoning, then & earlier, with reference to machine gun fire, is very funny & I think everyone feels it. We had a lot of direct hits on people with shells which leaves rather a nasty residue. It makes one realise how foul the human body is & how much the soul creates the facial expression & when the soul is gone the face is so unlike what it was. I stood over young O'Farrell's body (Irish Guards) on the 27th for quite 3 minutes wondering who it was, it was so changed.

In the Irish O'Farrell & Close were killed, Bence-Jones (I think died of wounds) & Ogilvy, Boyle, Mathieson & O'Brien were wounded. I lost 5 out of the battery. Poor Eustace Chance was terribly mangled although he died at once & W. H. Gladstone (H. M.) was killed too. I haven't heard all the casualties; nevertheless Fate has been kind to me so far.[2]

Cheero.

O.R.B.

This letter vividly paints the horrors of trench warfare in 1918. But amidst the chaos and death, the young Oliver Baldwin was able to show maturity and competence. Until his military training and experience as an army officer, he had not known success or achievement. Public school had been a failure; he had left early, and sought every means by which to join up. As a 16 year old he had met only obstacles. Neither his father Stanley Baldwin, then Financial Secretary to the Treasury, nor his cousin Rudyard Kipling, could find a way round War Office regulations. Yet now, less than three years later, he had had experience of command, in pitiless conditions, and had found a level sense of capability. In this letter from the front there are pointers to themes which were to characterize the rest of his life.

The free and unabashed manner in which he relates the engagement to his 'Darling Father' has an informality and an equality of spirit, qualities which his friends would come to know and recognize. He reports the situation vividly, conveying the strange dark elation of battle; the slight roughness of the syntax is perhaps appropriate. He also has a perspective on English history, of which he feels he is part. The letter exudes confidence and enthusiasm. He relishes the danger, and the rapid decisions to be made in the field. His own leadership is not in doubt. His cadet training had led him to discover a possible vocation.

Death and mutilation were constant companions of serving men, and Baldwin – along with others – wrestled with the mysteries of soul and body, of Fate, and the beyond. Since childhood he had felt sceptical about conventional religion, holding that there was something hereafter, but rejecting ordinary English piety, or 'churchianity' as he dubbed it. Religious doubts paralleled those half-expressed towards the comfortable, conventional politics of the Conservative and Unionist Party, of which his father was a leading member. The pain and chaos of battle in 1918 confirmed within him his rejection of the respectabilities of English church-going, and gave him a transforming sense of the brotherhood of the men of the trenches – of the unity of all classes, artificially divided by the hard distinctions of society, of which the church often seemed a part. He found himself compelled to search for a new pattern which could accommodate what he had been through: being a soldier made him a searcher. Others might doubt that the garb of the seeker after truth was appropriate for one born to such upholstered material prosperity. Nevertheless Oliver knew and loved *Morte D'Arthur*, and of all the characters in the saga, the one he most closely identified with was the Questing Beast.

CHAPTER 1

1899–1908:
'Amazement, Question and Indignation'

The late-Victorian world into which Oliver Baldwin was born was burdened with a profusion of material objects. Interiors wilted as drooping curtains brought shadow to the brightest day, chairs sighed in arthritic sympathy with their occupants, and the decorative daintiness of children was reflected in plush plump pink cushions. Oliver had begun to ease himself into existence while his parents, Stanley and Cissie, were walking in the cloisters of Westminster Abbey. His father, in a gently humorous aside, said later that the splendour of the surroundings had made him decide on a sudden entrance into the world, and that it was an indication that he would end up a monk, as if it were pre-ordained that he would divest himself of the diffuse material abundance. His parents hastened back to their home at St Ermin's Mansions – the name seems cavernous with furnishings – and he was born, feet first, just after midnight on 1 March 1899.[1]

The Baldwins were a well-established West Country family. They originated from the Corve Dale in Shropshire; some of them had moved to Worcestershire in the late eighteenth century, as industrial opportunity beckoned. By the middle of the following century one of the family businesses was however in disarray, and it was only through the tenacity and hard work of Oliver's grandfather, Alfred Baldwin, that it was saved from collapse. Alfred became the leading local ironmaster, and ultimately chairman of the Great Western Railway: a letter to him from Oliver begins, 'My dear G.W.R.'. He was also Conservative MP for West Worcestershire.

Alfred Baldwin married Louisa Macdonald in 1866. She was one of seven children of a Wesleyan minister, George Browne Macdonald, four of whose daughters went on to marry distinguished husbands. A capable and literate woman in her own right, she was the author of several books, including a still-readable ghost story, 'The Shadow on the Blind' (1895). Through the Macdonald connection, Oliver gained his greatest childhood friend – John Kipling, the son of Rudyard, whose mother Alice was one of the sisters. Georgiana Macdonald became the wife of Edward Burne-Jones, the distinguished Pre-Raphaelite artist, and Agnes married Edward Poynter, later President of the Royal Academy. The Macdonalds – a Highland family who had left after the defeat of Bonnie Prince Charlie – prided themselves on their Celtic ancestry, in which themes of art and magic had not been entirely driven out by urban life and rational religion. They believed in spirits, in foretelling the future, and in a near-fatalistic destiny.

Stanley Baldwin was the only child of Alfred and Louisa. In many ways he did not have an ideal childhood. Though he was surrounded with affection and comfort, both his parents suffered from vague neurotic conditions. Alfred, despite his commercial success, was subject to anxiety attacks; and Louisa spent long hours on the sofa with the blinds drawn, partially immobilized by an ailment which to us looks like ME (or chronic fatigue syndrome). In the language of the time it could have been put down to an 'artistic temperament'. Stan was a humorous child, with a vivid historical imagination, conjuring up figures from England's past as playmates, and making his feelings known forcefully. But at some stage – probably in adolescence – he seems to have discovered a more indirect and self-deprecating approach, as he mused on the qualities of his country. He grew to express his developing patriotic feelings gently, affirming a belief in the brotherhood of mankind, and in the possibility of human self-improvement, especially by learning both from ancient classical literature and from the great writers of his native country. He also showed a devotion to his family, to his church, and to cricket.

It was cricket that led to the love-match in 1892 between him and Lucy (or Cissie) Ridsdale, of Rottingdean, Sussex. She was a lively and outspoken lady, of striking directness and modernity, and an excellent fast bowler, although it was her batting that initially captivated Stanley. The Ridsdales appear to have cultivated candour as a virtue. Theirs was the family of the fast delivery slogged to the boundary. Angela Thirkell, granddaughter of Burne-Jones, and daughter of Margaret Mackail, Stanley Baldwin's first cousin, wrote thus of them: 'The first characteristic of the Ridsdale family which struck an outsider was their alarming frankness of speech with each other. As children we used honestly to be a little afraid of being sent on a message to The Dene in the morning. The family . . . would be sitting at breakfast still. In any other family the torrent of criticism and plain speaking which burst out would have meant a violent family row. But with the Ridsdales it was merely a family conversation and though we knew it to be so, we were not the less alarmed and lived in some kind of expectation of immediate bloodshed, so that it was a relief when a diversion occurred.'[2]

Edward Lucas Jenks Ridsdale, Cissie's father and head of this discursive clan, was an assay master at the Royal Mint. He had married Esther Lucy Thacker, and they had had five children, three boys, Aurelian, Julian and Arthur, and two girls, Cissie and Lily. The eldest boy, Edward (later Sir Edward) Aurelian Ridsdale, GBE (1864–1923), was a scientist and an agnostic, and the author of *Cosmic Evolution* (1889); he was Liberal MP for Brighton in 1906–10. His book concerned the evolution of chemical substances from primordial matter, and it argued that inorganic bodies were subject to the same laws as the evolution of living things. It ended with a paean to 'the Goddess Science, whose features no man may see: her stature groweth with the years: her form changeth with the times: her person in the effulgence of its majesty no human thought can limn'.[3] Cissie by contrast was a devout traditional believer, but her Ridsdale background meant that she was not afraid to ask difficult and searching questions on social and moral issues. Sometimes it must have been hard for Cissie to suppress her natural outspokenness, in the interests of Stanley's public career; but her commitment to him was total (as was his to her, in a manner both generous and understated), and their shared religious faith acted as a bond which united them throughout their lives.

Already it is possible to discern some of the roots of the socialism which Oliver was to espouse. Cissie's background was one where it was quite normal to question accepted social attitudes. She was forthright, radical in her own way, and spoke her mind. Stanley's Conservatism was not in the rigidly class-structured or aggressively imperialist mould. He was never a Diehard. The Baldwins' Toryism had something pragmatic and even gentle about it. (A. J. P. Taylor mischievously said that Stanley Baldwin would have made an ideal Labour prime minister, and Oliver indeed once asked his father to become Labour leader.) One could easily see the family as Victorian Liberals, treating their workforce with benevolent patronage. Alfred Baldwin's father had actually been a Liberal. 'G. W. R' was the first Tory in the family.[4]

Industrial relations at the Baldwin family business, the Wilden Forge, were carried on in the old-fashioned spirit of 'master' and 'man', not of bosses and workers; this too looks like a kind of liberalism. Employees were all treated as individuals, and each had the right of access to the master. The spirit which informs this attitude may today be ridiculed as paternalistic, and devoid of legal back-up (there was no redress for the sack); but when – as at Wilden – the master was humane, the men would be given respect, so long as they worked. It treated employees as individual human beings, and it had within it an equality of spirit between all sections of the working community.[5]

Eight children were born to the union of Stanley and Cissie, of whom six lived; three daughters, Diana (Di, or Didi), Leonora (Lorna) and Pamela Margaret (Margot); then Oliver, the heir. Esther, known as Betty, followed. Last to be born was Arthur Windham, known among the family as Little, and later nicknamed Bloggs.

Oliver's birth was a cause of special rejoicing, in view of Cissie's loss of two children. Oliver was her first male child to survive. Cissie seems to have shown a very protective attitude towards him, an intuitive love which was strong, maybe over-strong, but not sugary. She often found it hard to criticize him in his childhood. Other members of the family felt, on reflection, that she spoilt him.[6]

There is a divergence of evidence here. On the one hand, part of the family believed Oliver almost always had his own way, and thereafter they felt deep, unhealable resentments towards him for his effortless power over his mother. But on the other hand, Oliver himself, in his autobiography, points out the pains and discomforts, and punishments, of childhood: a childhood which could perhaps be described as privileged, but not charmed. It seems that the true picture partakes of some of both of these versions: on the one hand Oliver did indeed hold a special place in his mother's affections, and, in comparison with her treatment of his sisters, she let him off lightly when he was naughty; but at the same time the established punishments of the time were still meted out to him.[7]

From 1902 the family lived at Astley Hall, near Stourport. It was comfortable, but not beautiful, situated in a perfect

West-Country setting, above the Severn, with a view of a great sweep of the Clee hills. (Oliver spent his earliest years at Dunley Hall, a smaller house just a few miles from Astley.) There were nurses and governesses, donkey-carts and gypsies, and in winter a footman leading a carriage though the fog with a lamp: things to stimulate imagination in childhood and create excitement. These elements were balanced by the bogeys of punishment and church. Both of these were, to the young Oliver, largely hateful and often incomprehensible. He was (he says) punished for doing wrong, although the nature of the wrongs he had committed was seldom explained to him; and he learnt that if he told the truth, he was often punished, but if he lied he escaped. Church was a routine, an outward form; something to be got out of, if at all possible. Apart from holding an indistinct belief in the soul and vague views on 'the other side', for most of his life Oliver believed only what reason taught him.[8]

His childhood was lively and action-packed; an accident, in which he fell out of his pram aged two, seems to have had no lasting effect. The early years were filled with games played mostly with his three elder sisters. Fierce battles were fought between the four of them, armed with stinging nettles, from which all would emerge bruised and stung and swollen. (Oliver says that the battles were fought against the nettles, but his sister Lorna has asserted that they were the instruments of warfare and not the enemy.) These vigorous, even violent, games would seem to have provided an outlet for the aggression and guilt which developed among the four of them over the issue of who was favourite. There were times of peace and childish heroism too; some years later Cissie's sister Lily Whittington reminded Oliver of the time he had, aged four, protected his sisters from a flock of noisy geese. But the other siblings had less favourable memories of these times. Lorna – the sister to whom he was closest – later said that only two people had any control over Oliver in his childhood: Aunt Lily, and John Kipling, the admired second cousin, two years older than Oliver, an idealized elder-brother-like figure. Lorna believed that their mother always capitulated to him. For his sisters and brother this favouritism built up resentment.[9]

Father took a kind but fairly remote interest in the turbulent games and other activities of his children. One senses that Stanley Baldwin did not feel at ease with children, and found it hard, or perhaps dangerous, to re-enter the world of childhood fantasy and make-believe. On one occasion the four elder children decided to play Roundheads and Cavaliers – the sisters, with their flowing locks, were Cavaliers, and Oliver was the solitary Roundhead. Checking that their father was in a good mood, they trooped down to the library to ask him which side he was on. Stanley, diplomatic and ironic, said he would have been like the squire who is alleged to have stood aloof from the conflict at Naseby (or Edgehill), and continued hunting, driving his hounds between the opposing armies.[10]

Shakespeare and Dickens made a deep impression on the boy. Shakespeare gave Oliver a colourful, pageant-filled view of English history, and a vision of the possibilities of history conveyed as poetry – a view drawn from the history plays above all. (Oliver recorded no opinions on *King Lear* or *Othello*). During his imprisonment in the east he was to crave a Shakespeare. Dickens was a favourite of all the Baldwins. His characters delighted them with their vigour and individuality. The novels stirred Oliver's youthful imagination, and were a powerful reference point in later life.

Perhaps the greatest childhood delight came from the stage which his mother had built for him at Astley. It induced a lifelong passion for the theatre. Even before the stage was constructed there had been the rudiments of theatre space at Astley, and here the younger members of the family used to perform Christmas shows. Oliver's first appearance was in December 1904, when he took the part of Prince Florizel in a piece called *The Two Princesses*. Other parts were taken by

Diana, Leonora and Pamela (that is, Margot – she later dropped her first name). Two years later the young Baldwin players, now calling themselves The Irresponsibles, performed a playlet entitled *The Magician and the Ring*. Oliver took the relatively minor parts of footmen, and gave a recitation. At Christmas 1907 they performed two short plays; in one of them, growing in confidence, he played 'Haroon, sultan of Baghdad'. Programmes were printed, and the plays were taken with increasing seriousness by Oliver. The actors gave themselves 'professional' names, an exciting exploration of the borderlands of identity and fantasy. Lorna called herself Ann Dromeda; Betty was E. d'Arcy; Little was Beecham Carter. Oliver gave himself two slightly sinister stage names: H. G. Mercurey, and Hanley Child. He once appeared *en travestie* in a burlesque called *Why Wives Wander*, taking the part of Little Winnie, and wearing a blonde wig. His female stage name, Clarice Lovibond, was more effective than either of his male ones. A note in the programme said 'This is Miss Lovibond's farewell performance to the stage which she has graced for more than 30 years.' Oliver was probably aged about 11.[11]

Lorna also appeared as a male impersonator; the young Baldwins were offered a remarkable range of personal identities to try out. Her music-hall song in male attire was worthy of Hetty King:

> First I flirt with Flora,
> Then I dote on Dora
> Then I cotton to Cora,
> Then I linger with Laura,
> Then I thirst for Thora
> Then I'm nuts on Nora,
> But tomorrow I'm Dora's adorer
> Once again.

Oliver later acknowledged that in spite of the excitement and stimulation, he was a sulky, even difficult, child, although in the example he gives his rage was fairly justified.

(Perhaps an enduring sense of childish superiority prevented him from recounting a more telling anecdote of those times.) Once, he says, when he was aged six, his mother returned from shopping and called out that she had something for the children. There was a rush from his three elder sisters and himself, only to discover that the shopping consisted of three cotton bonnets and nothing for him. He walked off in a sulky rage of disappointment, covering his eyes with his arms. He failed to realize how close he was to some stone steps, and fell forward against them, knocking his front teeth up behind his nose. His upper jaw remained slightly deformed as a result.[12]

Summer holidays in 1905 and 1906 were spent in France. Oliver remained a lifelong Francophile, speaking French fluently and feeling at home in cosmopolitan French society, and even more so, later on, in the relaxed atmosphere of Algeria. He felt all his life that he was a southerner by temperament, and claimed to have discovered a distant dash of Spanish ancestry. He believed that the Baldwin family originated, as 'Baodouin', from sunnier climes than the Welsh marches.[13]

The Baldwins also used to pay regular visits to Rottingdean. Angela Thirkell recalls: 'What with babies and nannies and luggage they were such a large party that Cousin Stan used to have a slip coach for them which shunted somehow from Stourport to Brighton.'[14] She used to sit by the window in Sussex and watch: 'Old Mr Ridsdale might be strolling down the road, looking like a patriarch with a white beard, velvet coat, and peculiar soft hat, shoulders a little bowed and hands clasped behind him, accompanied by his little grandson Oliver Baldwin who rejoiced the village by falling unconsciously into an exact reproduction of his father's gait as golden hair walked by white hair.'[15]

CHAPTER 2

Schooldays: love and hate

St Aubyn's: 'I love the school . . .'

In the summer of 1908 Oliver joined John Kipling (now aged 10) at St Aubyn's prep school, near Rottingdean. St Aubyn's had been founded in 1895 by C. E. F. Stanford, a gentleman who was known as Mr Stanford to people in the village, a style which indicated a certain regard for it and for him.[1] The young Baldwin's three years there proved to be happy and productive, and his friendship with John was one of those sunlit idylls which, though transient in temporal terms, seem eternal in their inner significance. In his first term Oliver (aged nine) wrote home, in May 1908:[2]

My dear F.
    Thank you very much for your letters. I love the school, & all its masters save one. Be quick & come down. F. is short for family, I am so happy here.
    With love to the F.
    from
    O.R.B. [with a drawing of an orb]

The school was fairly enlightened – there was no corporal punishment – and the rudiments of real knowledge were instilled. But writing with hindsight in 1931, Oliver described the place as 'essentially "patriotic"', meaning that it had a jingoistic side, upholding the imperial values of the day, teaching the boys 'that one Englishman was worth ten foreigners', and so forth. At the same time, being born to such cricketing parents, his early letters are full of match scores between local schools. Cricket in later life became very important for Baldwin – not as an emblem of 'playing the game', but as something valid, enthralling and relaxing in its own right, without external, establishment connotations. The Worcestershire Cricket Ground became almost a shrine to him, and his teens he became a member of the Viginti, a Worcestershire youth team.[3]

He was fortunate that his grandmother, Esther Lucy Ridsdale, and his great-aunt, Georgiana Burne-Jones, both lived in Rottingdean. (Georgiana's husband, Sir Edward Burne-Jones, had died in 1898.) Every other Sunday, John Kipling and he would visit Aunt Georgy, and he grew very attached to her. He also loved her house, which was filled with paintings and drawings by her husband Ned, and with other Pre-Raphaelite works of art. It was in some ways a fantasy house, for a Pre-Raphaelite carpenter had fashioned a table and a set of chairs as if they were to be the domestic accoutrements of one for the knights of the Round Table, depicted in a famous Burne-Jones tapestry which Oliver was one day to inherit. According to Angela Thirkell, these pieces of furniture were, despite their associations with romance, both impractical and uncomfortable. Oliver was also thrilled by Aunt Georgy's readings from a book he calls 'William Morris's Morte D'Arthur'; however no such volume exists, and he was probably referring to an edition of Malory's *Morte D'Arthur* with illustrations by Aubrey Beardsley. The idea of the Round Table, with its emblematic democracy, stayed with him for life, and the heroic deeds of its richly named knights – Sir Perin de Mountbeliard, Sir Bobart le Curé Hardy, Sir Meliot de Logres – cast a spell on him. The knights also became imaginary playmates; and as Aunt Georgy read of the heroic exploits of the world of Arthurian fantasy, the boy became stimulated by ideas of democracy and equality. Perhaps *Morte D'Arthur* provided the mixture of heroism, fantasy, quest, and shared earth truth discovered in our own day in the works of J. R. R. Tolkien.[4]

Georgiana Burne-Jones was a committed socialist. Her grand-daughter recalls her lecturing a local workman, sitting stiffly on the edge of a chair in his best clothes, on the subject of William Morris. Maids would be requested to spend the evening reading *The Distribution of Wealth* and Ruskin's *Early Italian Painters*, occasions which were uncomfortable for all except Georgiana herself. Angela Thirkell says that she appeared seriously to believe that the world would be significantly improved if Ruskin's *The Seven Lamps of Architecture* appeared on every working man's table. She supported the Boers wholeheartedly during the South African war.[5]

While he was at St Aubyn's, Oliver, perhaps following the example of his paternal grandmother, wrote and illustrated a ghost story, giving it the brilliant title 'The Hell-born Babe'. It passed rapidly among the boys, until it was confiscated by a mistress. She handed it over to Stanford, the headmaster, who summoned Oliver to his study. How dare he write such stuff?, Stanford raged. Had he got the idea from the servants? He had to promise never to write again. Oliver, in tears of misery at this outburst, agreed. It seems curious, even by the most philistine standards, that writing a story could be considered wicked; and even odder that a nine year old, coming from a literate background, could be assumed to have got the idea of writing from the servants. It is odd too that this came from Stanford, held in high regard by the village. During the holidays Oliver told Rudyard Kipling about the story and its title. Kipling was delighted, and gave the young author all encouragement.[6]

'The Hell-Born Babe' has not survived; but what has survived is an imaginative autobiographical fable written in an exercise book, illustrated with pictures cut from newspapers and magazines, which gives other insights into his personal world at this time. Oliver would have been about ten at the time he wrote it. 'I was born in London at Kensington Palace Mansions' he begins; 'I' is illustrated with a cut-out of a delightful girl-child in a longish dress with a ruffed collar tied with a bow. 'After a few years I left my residence for Dunley Hall butt we left on account of its smallness & as it had 2 chimneys. 3 sisters were born and lived here with me they were a great hand-full & although they were very nice they gave their dear mother a lot of bother.' There are pictures of the three sisters; the eldest and youngest are represented by pleasant line-drawings taken from advertisements for children's clothes, while the middle one is a frightening voodoo doll, merely a grinning head smoking a pipe with a sinister circlet hanging from the pipe's stem, and in place of a body an arrangement of feathers pointing downwards; the whole image stuck on a stick. Was this how Oliver saw Margot, the sister with whom in his childhood he had least sympathy?

Mother is illustrated as a captivating and charming lady, whose warm and generous presence is fully expressed in her richly waved hair. 'Our new residence was very nice as it had some very fine chimneys.' One hardly need to have read anything of Freud to sense that there might be a hidden meaning to the young lad's emphasis on chimneys. 'The house Astley Hall has as you perceive a very nice chimney. My Father having an attack of gout was confined to his bed, & accordingly took pills.' The language is a baroque take on adult discourse. 'On my 5 birthday I was given a camera of the latest type. My Father after many years of bother, in order to travel quickly bought a motor. I went to school which I liked very much. Here is my room. In a few years I went, with a lot more of my friends, into the army & was a very good shot. But in a battle in India my head was bashed in by a drum, so as soon as [possible] it was bound up with a rag. I was escorted home on an elephant to the barracks, & for the rest of the time I was carried about in my buggie, drawn by a very powerful horse.

'On my return I was engaged to a pretty young girl.' Here
the illustration is of a young girl facing away, showing no
part of her face, only giving us a glimpse of her elegantly
coiffed hair. 'My head soon got right & I was able to write for
the Edinburgh Review on India. But since we had no
children I went to parties. Cigarettes I smoked in abundance,
especially when I went in a balloon.' (The boy author moves
effortlessly into English nonsense territory.) 'The other day I
found my old baby bottles which brought back many childish
remembrances. One day I sent for a horoscope of my life
which told me I should die tomorrow which I accordingly
did. But my wife cried herself to death with her new hand-
kerchief.' As a tailpiece there are pictures of two tombstones,
one with the inscription, 'Here lies a poor buffer below', and
the other, 'Here lies a poor bufferess below'. 'THE END'.[7]

What would St Aubyn's have made of this childish fantasy,
combining as it does a slyly individual wit with a Daisy
Ashford-like imitation of grown-up talk? And the analyst?
(Not only the chimneys, but the sickness of father.) Despite
the imitation of adult slowness, it is a pacey text too, and the
child author shows no fear of death.

One other detail from Oliver's time at St Aubyn's is of
interest. He was caught reading *The Hill*, H. A. Vachell's
highly-wrought 1905 'romance of friendship', whose subject
matter Isabel Quigly has described as 'a long amorous
struggle that lasts for years and ends in death'. Oliver had
been given this novel by his father, who evidently thought it
most suitable. But the school did not think so, and confiscated it. As a result, Oliver says, every boy who could get hold
of it read it in the holidays.[8]

Nevertheless St Aubyn's was a good environment for
Oliver, and he benefited intellectually and socially from his
time there. He left in the summer of 1911, in, as he puts it, a
riotous week of happiness and hope, tinged only with the
regrets of not seeing again some of the friends he had made.
John Kipling was bound for Wellington. Oliver was going to

Eton. Stanley Baldwin had been to Harrow, an experience which had not been a success; so it seemed that the best thing to do was to put his son down for 'the other one'.[9]

Eton: 'A complete waste of time'

Unfortunately Eton was a disaster for Oliver. He says that this was not so much because he was unhappy there (although he was almost certainly far from happy for much of the time), but because he 'learnt nothing of the slightest use to me in after-life, except to dislike the system that goes by the name of the Public School system most intensely'. Hints of loneliness and alienation edge the picture, and there is a sense of being lost in a maze, and subject to lingering threats of sadistic punishment on the whim of a senior boy; these things appear as an undercurrent to the severely objective reasons which he gives for disliking the school. He really loathed it. He was given a place in Hugh Macnaghten's house, no. 7, Jordley's Place. Macnaghten (later vice-provost of Eton) was a translator of some poems of Catullus, and the author of a volume entitled *Fifty Years of Eton in Prose and Verse*, a work containing minor religious/sentimental verse, interleaved with reflections and anecdotes which are not to today's taste. He was otherwise undistinguished. Oliver mentions him nowhere in his memoirs. The curious rules which governed – and may still govern – Eton, he found puzzling and finally ridiculous. The seven points, which he called the key to the whole system, he described, with engaging subversiveness, thus:

1. No one, other than members of 'Pop' (the Eton society composed of the chief athletes of the school and the Head of the school – who was a scholarship boy – and the Captain of Oppidans – the Head of the non-scholarship part of the school) was allowed to roll up his umbrella.

2. No one but a member of 'Pop', the Sixth Form, the 'Upper Boat Choices' (2nd rowing eight) and the 'Twenty-two' (or

2nd cricket eleven) was allowed to turn down the collar of his blazer or overcoat.

3. No one was to walk arm-in-arm except 'Pop'.

4. No one could walk on the left side of the Eton High Street on the way to Windsor.

5. No one could put sealing wax on his top hat except members of 'Pop'. (Why anyone should want to is somewhat extraordinary, but 'Pop' did.)

6. No one outside of 'Pop' or the Sixth Form could wear soft shirts with his 'tails'. This was altered during the war.

7. No one was allowed to button the bottom button of his waistcoat. This was most important.[10]

Once a boy had learnt these seven points, Oliver concluded, he was considered suitable to be a member of the ruling classes and qualified to see that the lower orders behaved themselves. Work was not considered to be of significance. Anyone who worked was apt to be set upon and bullied.

Oliver also believed that while at school he had cracked the code of 'playing the game'. 'Playing the game', he concluded, was simply the dead upper classes' view of what the living upper classes should do at all times. He enumerated seven rules of this game:

1. *Noblesse oblige*, which, being interpreted, means when you have £10,000 a year you can give twopence to a beggar, but if he asks a second time he is not 'playing the game', so you win.

2. Never kick a man when he is down. You can push him down if you like and sit on him, or get someone else to do the kicking, but you must not do it yourself or you lose.

3. Never shoot a fox. They prefer being hunted by dogs and torn to pieces. [*Footnote to the original*: You are in danger of losing a point or two here. You should say 'hounds' not 'dogs'.]

4. *Esprit de corps.* Has nothing to do with the body or the OTC. It means thinking a hell of a lot about this 'game' business.

5. Always thrash a man if he runs after your wife. If you run after his, be a co-respondent.

6. Anyone who runs down your 'game' (which includes the Public School system) is not playing the 'game', and as in your 'game' everyone ought to play it if he is a gentleman, you win by sheer weight of numbers.

7. Don't hit anyone smaller than yourself unless he is alone and you are three or four to one. This is important when ragging smaller boys' rooms at school.[11]

Baldwin could not discern any real value or inner truth in either the day-to-day life and work (such as it was) of his school, nor in its arcane traditions; so he escaped the most pervasive spell of the conventional upper-class world of the time. The 'mystique of schooldays', the self-referential folklore of the chaps at school, which has obsessed and, arguably, enfeebled generations of young Englishmen, just did not exist for him. He saw no point in school traditions, and since there was almost no learning, the whole thing was a waste of time. Tradition has to be accepted before it can be given meaning, and Oliver Baldwin took on board none of Eton's traditions. Their esoteric language and arcane symbolism were an empty shell to him. This was not because he had no desire to join in, or because he was a cynical outsider: on the contrary, his later regimental experience, and his enjoyment of the world of gentlemen's clubs, show that he found great importance in belonging to valid institutions. However, Eton at this time had nothing of significance or inner worth to offer him, despite the presence of an enlightened headmaster, Edward Lyttelton. The exotic rituals of exclusivity and elitism were there, but to Oliver they were forms of nothing; and since the symbols were somewhat bizarre and narcissistic, they only emphasized the nullity of the residue beneath the glittering surface.

One of the few things he found to have some point was the OTC (Officers' Training Corps). He was genuinely keen on the corps; but promotion depended on prowess at games, so it was closed to him, since he was no good at competitive sports. He attended a camp in the summer of 1914, and found the experience full of soldierly excitement, tinged with despondency that the war with Germany would be over by Christmas, and therefore he and the others would not get out to see 'this great football match'.[12]

When he was fourteen, he was told by his housemaster that he was to be confirmed. He objected, and in a spirit of defiance said he was an unbeliever. The only effect, he notes, that confirmation had on his acquaintances (for he had no actual friends in his house) was to make them 'temporarily prudish and afterwards desirous of making up for it'.[13]

Oliver received his sexual initiation from other boys while at Eton, but when and how are matters only for conjecture. Of his first experience, he later said to a colleague, 'I had no idea what was happening, but it was very pleasurable, so I didn't object.'[14]

The last year at even the most barren school can be worthwhile, and this proved to be partially true for Baldwin at Eton. He gathered a few friends around him at the library – one of them was Sacheverell Sitwell – and together some of them produced a volume of war verse. Baldwin seems in some measure to have admired Lyttelton, in spite of the system that he presided over.

Many of those he knew were dead before they were twenty-one, and he could not help reflecting on how bad some of them had been at games, which had been held to be so important. One who was awarded the Military Cross, and who was among the first to die, had not even received his 'shorts' (house football team colours) while at Eton. This was a mystery to the school. The system did not predict that anything like this could happen.

By the summer of 1915 Oliver Baldwin felt he had had enough of school, learning nothing. So he begged his parents for permission to leave. And if permission was denied, he had formulated a plan to run away and join up. But permission was granted, and Oliver left Eton aged sixteen. The headmaster told him that he would always regret his decision, and that Eton would be recollected as the happiest time of his life. Lyttelton was wrong on both counts. Baldwin was never happier to leave anywhere, except prison, and the four years spent he had spent at his public school were 'the most useless and unhappy years of my life up till then'.[15]

On leaving Eton, Oliver took leave of his childhood. His boyhood had been an interesting mixture. Within the family, father was kindly but rather remote. Mother was of a voluble and passionate nature, and devoted to Oliver as her first boy to survive. To him she extended a tough uncritical defensive protective shell. The mother-and-son relationship had developed in a complex manner, with the boundaries between each unclearly marked. With his sisters, on the other hand, in their tumultuous games, he learnt to express direct feelings of hate and love, and not to be ashamed or frightened of acting them out boldly. Relations with the older generation were obscure, unclear, and a bit shrouded. But with his own generation, anger and jealousy, and sometimes protectiveness and affection, were given their full rein. These feelings were powerfully present. As a result Oliver felt strongly that he belonged to the present, not to some make-believe world of the past. To him there was something evasive about the past and the old; something akin to the shadow on the blind of which his grandmother had written. The present might be full of danger, and anger, and pain; but it was entirely alive and real. Given the alternatives of the obscurity of the past, or the raw reality of the present, Oliver unreservedly chose the present.

His experience of his public school, with its clutter of strange tradition, had only reinforced this desire to live in the present, and not to be a servant of outworn totemistic ideas and prejudices. His conclusion at the age of sixteen was that the present was all that we have, and that class barriers are meaningless contrivances. While most of his contemporaries clung to the ideas of the past for safety, he sought to move on.

Maybe it is odd that one so favoured within the family should look to ideas of equality, eventually adopting socialism as a political creed, rather than emerge as an effete snob, a superior person perpetually seeking in real life a place parallel to that he had held in his mother's affections. But Oliver did have a strong if sometimes wrong-headed moral sense. Confusion, laced with a measure of adolescent angst, was around owing to his family experience; this and the negative experience of his public school were powerful determinants of his attitude towards society. A way out of confusion is to live fully in the present. He was led to work out a social system which could accommodate all people (including himself). The privileged place that his mother had given him not only left him with ambivalent feelings; it was also intellectually untenable. She might have spoilt him, but he was determined, so far as he could, to unspoil himself. Favouritism is not a universalizable ethical principle. The basis of justice cannot be an appeal to an authority figure. Something new had to be worked out, from first principles.

Astley Hall, too, played its part in the development of his political thinking, compelling him to look at relations between the different classes. Real life and industrial relations existed all around him. Family life at Astley was not just an introverted, self-referring game, but something that reached out to the broader horizons of industrial society in the West Midlands. Astley meant present reality, not fossilized traditions. That is not to say that it was without moments of imagination and poetry; since it was situated in a perfect country setting, its inhabitants were receptive to powerful pre-industrial ideas derived from English rural society, history and literature. Astley, part industrial and part rural, was no retreat from the world. On this basis, Oliver could move away from childhood and adolescence, and establish his own guidelines, casting a critical eye on his schools, accepting one and rejecting the other; and he could also look without fear at phenomena such as the rituals and class antagonisms which were the basis of so much of English life at the time. In future, he would look outward to the real world around him, rather than to the dangerous and ill-defined world of family relationships, or the questionable superiority of callow youths who took upon themselves the mantles of imperial proconsuls.

CHAPTER 3

War and Post-war

In the summer of 1915 it seemed to Oliver Baldwin that there was no point in enlisting, because the war would soon be over. So he thought vaguely of a career as a diplomat, and went down to Brighton to study German and work on English literature. He enjoyed the south coast; in his spare time he rode over the Downs, and bought a motor-bike, on which he sped across the country.[1] But a tragic event turned his mind again towards the war. In early October he received a letter from his mother:[2]

My precious Olly
    I am afraid that you will already have seen that our dear John is missing & believed killed in this last attack. – I wanted to tell you myself as I knew how fond you were of him, but I am afraid that you will already have heard, poor poor Uncle Ruddy & Aunt Carrie & poor Elsie too. It is all too dreadful. – Fondest love
        Thine own most loving
            Mother

John Kipling had been reported missing in action at Loos, on 27 September 1915. Oliver experienced a steeling of determination rather than a surge of grief at the loss of his cousin and childhood friend. 'One of the family had fallen; I was the avenger.'[3]

But at 16 he was too young to enlist. This was a cause of great frustration. He visited Uncle Ruddy and Aunt Carrie at the time of their distress. Kipling at once recognized Oliver's potential, and noted how he had developed. He wrote to Stanley Baldwin in October, saying how Oliver had within him the making of a real soldier. Kipling described Cousin Stan's son in a positive and physical manner, and his enthusiasm for the lad's keenness seems to indicate that it was, in part, a compensation for – or at least a distraction from – the appalling loss of John. Oliver, Kipling wrote, had an ideal frame on which to hang muscle, and strong feet. A month later, Kipling wrote again to SB, voicing the boy's frustration at not being able to join up. He was a big lad – over six feet tall now – and he bore himself like a man. Kipling, expressing himself with careful understatement, begged the father to allow Oliver to join up at the first opportunity.[4]

To Oliver, Kipling wrote an equally tactful letter, urging restraint: in the first and second and third place he should keep his head and not fly off the handle. If he was being stopped in his career, then, as a man, the obstacle had to be met with patience and dignity. Kipling would do all he could to smooth the road to enlistment, and Oliver had to promise not to sulk or storm. Relations with a father were the most precious thing in the world, and once broken were hard to re-establish. If Oliver showed uncontrolled disappointment, this would just add weight to the conclusion that he was too young to go forward to training.[5]

Oliver remained impatient. Kipling stressed his own sympathy, and believed the same would be true of SB also. Eventually he would be freed from the indignities which size rather than age exposed him.

Oliver looked everywhere for a way to obtain a commission. A chance came when he had turned 17, since the War Office had a policy of accepting 17 year olds for training. But as he applied the age limit was raised. He thought of trying for the Sandhurst examination, but again he was too young. Finally he learnt that the Cambridge OTC had become a kind of Cadet Battalion, and that unenlisted youths could train to become commissioned officers by serving in it. So in May 1916 he left for Cambridge, where he received the uniform that he had sought, to begin the career that he most wanted.[6]

Oliver surprised himself by his keenness and bellicosity. He was assigned rooms in Trinity College, and his company paraded on the grounds of Pembroke. Physical training was done at the Leys School, and trench-digging in the Gog and Magog Hills. He revelled in it all; no one attacked straw men with a bayonet more fiercely than he, or did a 'full knees bend, on the hands, down' with greater enthusiasm.[7]

He also adopted a pro-war position, he later admitted somewhat wryly. His rooms in Trinity belonged to an under-graduate who was a conscientious objector. Anti-war posters and pamphlets were strewn around the room. Oliver angrily burnt them. He also learnt that one of the dons – quite con-ceivably Bertrand Russell – objected to the war. How, the young private asked the college dean, could such a creature be allowed to remain within the precincts of the college? He was not mollified to be told that the man in question had been brave enough to save an undergraduate from drowning in the Cam. Oliver could not understand this. However, the Master of Trinity used to doff his mortar-board at the young soldiers, showing that he at least knew his place.[8]

Oliver seems, throughout his life, to have felt an ambiguity about war that he never really resolved. On the one hand he admits to disliking the crude militaristic positions of the jingos, and he claims, later on at least, to have come to under-stand the economic and imperial reasons for the 1914–18 war, and thereby to have rejected the postures of the pro-war party. But he never became anything like a pacifist. War rather seems to have been to him a job that had to be done, whatever the theoretical objections. He fought shy of being too dogmatic about understanding any really theoretical 'reasons for war'. Was it fought for the honour of Britain, for the defence of British interests, for international justice, or for the millionaire arms dealers? These questions were part of the discussion, but no final decision was reached, where theory and practice could unite. Oliver Baldwin was a good soldier, so, although he mulled over the underlying issues of war indirectly, he did not address them head on. He got on with the job in hand.

Of the studies that he had to undertake in 1916, map-reading he found the hardest. But one day a group of cadets was told that the battalion was short of instructors, since a new batch of recruits was arriving the next day. Did any of them know about map-reading? There was silence. Oliver took a pace forward. 'I do, sir,' he said. Right, he was told; he would be instructing the recruits at map-reading at ten the next morning. That evening he worked at the subject for six hours, reading and reading, and memorizing anything he did not understand. When he took the class the next morning, he found that he was in command of the subject; and the following day he received the two stripes of a corporal. Soon he was training recruits in all subjects: drill, musketry, bayonet fighting, PT, trench-digging, and so forth. That winter he found that he enjoyed playing football for the first time; it was now a game played for its own sake.[9]

The Kiplings visited him in Cambridge in October 1916. RK was astonished by the progress Ollie had made: he had no idea that a lad could come on as he had. It was, he wrote to SB, simply beautiful to see and hear and watch. Kipling said that Oliver had grasped an essential point: that when one saves the other fellow trouble, one is the other fellow's master. Oliver had a natural instinct for drill, and could lecture on anything at a minute's notice, and make it interesting. Oliver was smart and well turned out, and he was saluted as an officer. He showed sheer determination to get on, and a keen interest in the drama and the human nature of it all. Carrie and he were pleased beyond words to see him happy and competent. Their letter reinforces the idea that Oliver's determination and calm maturity mitigated their grief in some small measure.[10]

Promotion came quite rapidly. By December 1916 Oliver was a staff sergeant instructor, with three stripes and a crown. This meant the end of the OTC, and joining the 2nd Cadet Battalion. He played in the battalion's hockey team, and once drilled the entire battalion on Parker's Piece. He recalls them as 'the finest collection of fellows I ever had to deal with'.[11]

His course ended in February 1917, when he left to join the Household Brigade Cadet Battalion at Bushey, near Watford, for the final part of officer training. Further fairly intensive training followed – digging entire trench systems, and going for long route marches in wet weather – which was alleviated by visits to London at weekends. Oliver showed a continuing love of the theatre. He recalled a show called *Pell Mell* at the Ambassadors Theatre, and visits to The Bing Boys.[12]

To his surprise and chagrin he failed his passing-out examination the first time, unfairly, he believed. He passed it at the second attempt. His commission is dated 27 June 1917. Aged 18, as an officer he faced a new world and a new social environment. This was his first taste of real achievement. He started to feel confident; in the opinion of some people, he admits, it looked like over-confidence.[13]

Baldwin was gazetted, following the example of John Kipling, into the Irish Guards. The memory of his cousin was still strong with him. He joined the Irish Guards Special Reserve of Officers, first at Tadworth, then at Warley. From September 1917 to May 1918 he took part in courses on almost every military subject, including sanitation and wiring, but specializing in signalling. One course was held at Chelsea Barracks, and he was dining at the Savoy on 4 September when a bomb fell on the Embankment, shattering a tram and killing many of its passengers.[14]

In May 1918 he left with first-class honours, and was then granted 'leave prior to embarkation'. He travelled to the Kiplings at Burwash. With his enthusiasm and competence, they were more than glad to have him as their guest. For him, Bateman's was a second home, if not a first.

One day in high summer the telegram calling him to the front arrived. Oliver danced for joy at the prospect of the 'great adventure'. He left for London at once, and gathered his kit in preparation for the departure. His father asked him what kind of memorial he would like if he did not come back. The prospect of being killed had not occurred to him. After expressing surprise, he suggested that some almshouses might be built, or a working men's club. Stanley Baldwin promised that this would be done.[15]

Early in the morning of Friday, 31 May, after saying good-bye to his mother in bed, he left from Victoria. He dined at Boulogne, and later passed by Etaples, where he heard the sound of exploding bombs. He left the troop train at Saulty, and made his way to Pommier, where the Irish Guards Reserve Battalion was stationed. Oliver was curious to know just what war was like. He used to travel up to the line (which was quiet in that region) and watch shells bursting in the distance.[16]

Throughout June he was stationed at Berles-au-Bois, awaiting a German offensive. The Guards regiments comprised the VI and XVII corps of the Third Army, under the overall command of General Sir Julian Byng. There were two battalions of Irish Guards; on leaving the Reserve, 2nd Lieutenant Baldwin served in the First. In the spring the Germans had made substantial gains, without achieving a breakthrough. By June the front was slack again. Much of Baldwin's work was recreational; he took part in divisional sports, and on one occasion he produced a concert (in which officers were not permitted to perform). Then the Allies began a slow counter-attack. During this period, as second-in-command to No. 1 Company, Baldwin spent the best part of five months in the front line or battalion reserve. It became a joke in the company, he says, that senior officers wanted to get him killed.[17]

In his first experience of battle – he does not say where – the rain was pelting down. As he neared the support line, he heard what he thought was the hiss of escaping gas. He remarked on this noise to Captain Arthur Paget, his company commander, who replied that the noise was the swish of machine-gun bullets.[18]

Transatlantic troops joined the British for the advance on this sector in August 1918. Oliver experienced some (largely good-humoured) conflicts with them over tactics – in particular, their apparent difficulty at staying still and quiet when the Germans were within earshot. In August he was transferred to the 1st Guards Trench Mortar Battery, and was again at the front line. A major Allied offensive began on 21 August; the Guards were in the thick of it, and Baldwin lost the seat of his trousers as a result of a shell landing close as they captured St Leger.[19]

2nd Lieutenant Baldwin then returned to No. 1 Company, for a grim period of trench duty outside Moeuvres, which was actually on the front line, since the town had been captured from the Germans on 3 September. During it, lax security arrangements allowed a German patrol to enter the village and take ten prisoners in broad daylight. Baldwin does not say whether or not he was to blame.

But this was a period of solid and continuous Allied gains. Bapaume had been captured by Byng's New Zealanders on 29 August. The Germans were back defending the Hindenburg Line. To General Ludendorff the main defence in that sector remained the Canal du Nord, west of the Scheldt canal, situated between Cambrai and Bapaume; Ludendorff doubted that tanks would attempt to cross it. Throughout early September a massive amount of armour was built up along either side of the canal.

The battalion advanced towards the Canal du Nord. A major assault was planned for 27 September, with an attack of fourteen divisions across the canal along a twelve-mile front in which Scots, Grenadier and Irish Guards would all take part. It was a fearsome engagement, vividly recounted in Oliver's letter quoted in the Prologue. The Canal du Nord was crossed in every sector, and the Allied troops moved close to the next major obstacle on the road to Cambrai, the Scheldt Canal. One old soldier described the fighting as 'so terrible, that even the worms got up and cried for mercy'. Baldwin sums up the whole engagement as a 'ghastly muddle'; but the war was virtually won by then, with Ludendorff begging to resign, and Germany's allies suing for peace in eastern Europe. There is no question that he acquitted himself with remarkable bravery in crossing the canal.[20]

Baldwin, still only 19, was beginning to feel the strain. His nerves were 'in none too good a state'.[21] Even before the battle of the Canal du Nord, letters home indicated a half-jesting hope for leave – 'It's about time I got wounded; it seems to be the best way of getting home these days'.[22] Progress was slow in October. Oliver was again in command of the battery at Bevillers on 8 and 9 October, when the Hindenburg Line finally disintegrated.[23] He sustained a minor injury, and speaks of his second sight at knowing that it would occur, just as he 'knew' that he would not be killed. Oliver believed – a legacy of the Celtic Macdonalds – that he was gifted with second sight.

On 16 October he was told that he was to command No. 4 Company for the forthcoming battle, for St. Python, just outside Solesmes. Oliver was cursed by his men for telling them to dig and re-dig their trenches three times, each time higher up the hill where they were stationed, before he was satisfied with the position. This they did, throughout a night of pouring rain. He himself was frightened and in a foul temper; and the rain froze in his boots. But the next day the men thanked him, since the German shelling had blown to bits all unprotected trenches on the low ground.[24] In the engagement No. 4 Company crossed the River Selle. The 2nd Lieutenant remembered little beyond the exhaustion, the cold and the pools of mustard gas lying on the roads, which tempted him to kneel down and so get evacuated. He managed to pencil another letter to his father, postmarked 25 October, which is indicative of his state of mind:[25]

Darling Father

Just finished my fourth 'show'; in other words I've been in every attack since the advance began. In the last show (20th) I had the honour and the appalling worry of commanding No 4 Coy in the attack. I must say this last show was the worst as far as nerves are concerned & towards the end I'm afraid my nerves were completely 'dissed'. There can be no greater strain in this world than commanding a coy. in the attack & on top of that we had to hold the line for two days after, which meant digging in little posts & not daring to stir by day. I've never been so badly shelled before & I don't want to be again. I suppose it was an honour but I'd rather do without.

For the first time now I've had enough war: all the other officers have only done 1, 2 or 3 'shows' but I've done 4 & j'en ai eu assez, enfin. Oh for London again. What about a job in M.I.15 now – that's what I feel like. If they leave us to rest for a few days I shall be better soon. Talk about self-control & acting – in the last show 'myself' was non-existent & I was acting, acting the whole time to save my going off it. My Sergeant Major went 'gagga' & ceased to be of further use, so things were worse than ever. I must say my two officers were wonderful – Hutchinson & Barnewall. My leave ought to be along in the next few weeks I hope. My two orderlies were both knocked out by a shell which landed in a post I had vacated a minute before. Something told me to go to another spot & I went, damned quick. I had half the side of a trench in on top of me as well.

However, furious conceit & rampant self-confidence restores nerves well.

Heavens, how one realises there is a God out there & how one prays & what satisfaction & renewed courage after it.

This seems a pessimistic letter but this sort of thing takes the gilt of the ginger-bread for the moment.

Cheero.

O.R.B.

He was soon released from the front. From St. Python he travelled by lorry to Carnières, which was a paradise of rest and relaxation. Here he worked on matters of decorations and promotions for the men under his command. Leave was granted for 2 November and he returned to England; he was among the crowd that wept outside Buckingham Palace at the time of the armistice on the 11th.[26]

But the war was not quite over for him. He returned to the battalion, joined them at Charleroi, and marched with them all the way to Cologne. Here he began to express the defiant, radical views which were characteristic of the way his opinions were moving. It was as though the ending of the war had allowed these views and feelings to break through, into new ground. To his superiors he was beginning to look dangerous. They removed him to the relatively safe position of the command of a steamer on the Rhine, which was taking Allied prisoners to Rotterdam. From his deck he saw the skirmishing between the German government troops and the Spartacists.[27]

Revolution was in the air in Britain, too; and the whole division was ordered home to be ready to put it down. There had been minor mutinies in some of the other Guards regiments, so the plan was of doubtful point. Baldwin was sent back to square-bashing at Warley, which was itself conducive to nothing except a spirit of revolt, until May 1919, when he was demobilized.

The war had shaped Oliver's life to a remarkable degree. He had proved himself a man in the most extreme conditions, showing competence and bravery. War is the most testing of rites of passage for a youth. He had passed through with distinction. His men respected him. He had learnt, too, respect for the men he commanded. But perhaps most of all he had gained the comradeship of the trenches: he later remarked on the strange gap between those who knew what it was like and those who came after – that those who had not experienced the war would never know how it felt, and that those who had been in thick of it were united by an indissoluble bond. The bonds between serving men were exceptionally strong; in his own case, he grew deeply attached to Private Jim Brady, who survived the war only to die in the Spanish flu epidemic.

After demobilization he went to stay in Scotland with a wartime comrade, Captain W. C. Mumford, MC. The two soldiers argued, and grumbled, and did nothing in particular. But they liked one another's company, and appeared to need each other. So they stayed together for a bit.

Returning to Worcestershire, he threw himself into the Comrades of the Great War movement (which was later one of the constituents which formed the British Legion), which sought some sort of reform for the country in the aftermath of the war; but with a predominance of generals and colonels it became a movement for confirming, and not challenging, the status quo. This he found depressing.[28] Now more than ever he felt the need for change. The end of a war is both the practical and the symbolic moment for a new dispensation.

Oliver at this time lived a strange life of a drifter, almost of a drop-out. He would wander, oblivious of class or origin, from pub to pub, in a vague and almost distracted way, observing, talking to anyone prepared to listen, saying what he thought, without reserve, 'in the old army spirit', and generally idling time away: feeling, despite an outward appearance of being one of those who had had experience of the trenches, and who was in a sense one of the heroes of the time, an overpowering sense of futility and let-down, now that the war was over. Maybe he still carried a bit of shell-shock with him, although his competence in other fields of life would rule out any real damage. It is possible that, deprived of the tension and activity and stimulation of war, he, along with others, found it hard to adjust to civilian life. Or perhaps there is a hint of a disturbed personality, a kind of temporary schizoid evasion of, or drifting away from, reality: a minor break-down. It is not hard too to see that the smugness and self-congratulation of the non-combative politicians and well-upholstered generals had created a sense of suppressed fury among combatants such as him. He poured his anger into a hatred of the English class system, and of the artificiality and patronage that pervaded English life.[29]

Oliver soon tired of doing nothing, and met a man he describes as 'the famous Captain C., the head of the Secret Service'.[30] This would have been Mansfield Cumming, a figure with more than a whiff of absurdity about him. Thus Oliver joined Intelligence: or at least, he said he did. We have only his word to go on. His father had secret service connections, having sat on the Aliens or Internment Committee in 1915–16. Captain C. gave Oliver a job as acting vice-consul in Boulogne, a post he took up on 1 October 1919. His 'cover' job there was to give out visas and other matters; what his secret job was we are not told. However the job did not last long. On one occasion (he says) he had a row with a French lady asking for visas for herself and her servants. Baldwin stuck to the regulations, and said she could not have a visa. She became angry. A week later the Foreign Office sent him a report of their conversation, and asked him for his comments. He replied that it was accurate. He was recalled at once, and sacked without explanation. Wherever the truth about the story lies (and it is possible that it was subject to autobiographical embroidery, since a search of the Consular files for Boulogne in the Public Record Office reveals nothing about the incident with the lady – just a reference to a complaint about the obstructiveness of a young official), he certainly appears to have been a most undiplomatic diplomat; in his post-war state he was hardly the person to whom matters connected with security should have been entrusted.[31] On his return from Boulogne he took part in a charity matinee at the Apollo Theatre, which he enjoyed.

It was time for a break. Oliver decided to take a holiday in Algeria with a fellow Irish Guards officer, Captain George Bambridge, M.C., who had commanded No. 3 Company at the battle of St. Python when 2nd Lieut. Baldwin had been in command of No. 4 Company. George Bambridge became a close friend, eventually marrying Elsie Kipling, Rudyard's daughter and Oliver's second cousin, and settling at Wimpole Hall, a fine Queen Anne house not far from Cambridge.[32]

Oliver was immediately delighted by Algeria. Here was the freedom and peace that he had longed for: he was thrilled by the climate, the marvellous light, the quiet, and the orange blossom, eucalyptus and mimosa. He delighted in the variety of the countryside – alternately sea, mountains and desert. No greater contrast could be imagined to the climate of the industrial English Midlands, or of gloom-chilled London, sheeting black rain. It confirmed his belief that spiritually he belonged to the south. Here in Algeria it seemed he was rediscovering a land which held the feel of his primal, pre-conscious habitat. After a month in Algiers, Bambridge went to Morocco. Oliver went further south to live as an Arab and learn the language and explore the Arab way of life.

Life in Algeria impressed Oliver on account of the superiority of French over British colonialism. Neither with him, nor indeed with most other semi-radicals of the period, was there any suggestion of decolonization. He just saw a better and fairer form of colonialism. French colonialism, he noted, was more flexible and less racist than its British counterpart. Europeans and Arabs worked together on enterprises, and there were no signs saying 'Europeans only' on public transport. Arabs could go to hotels and restaurants unimpeded. This was in great contrast to British Africa.[33]

Oliver travelled with some friends to Bou Saada, 120 miles (200 kilometres) south-east of Algiers, a journey he found magical. His travelling companions stayed a few days. After their departure he met a young French painter, Roger Duval, who had just rented a house there, and the two teamed up together. From February to June 1920 Oliver's life here was an idyll; he lived cheaply and imbibed deeply the atmosphere and way of life. He celebrated his twenty-first birthday with a bottle of champagne at the local hotel, presumably with Roger. Why should he go home to celebrate that anniversary, when he had found his true home, and a deep peace, in the climate, sounds, sights and scents of Algeria? There seemed little point in moving from this sensual paradise. He wrote and travelled, and improved his Arabic, while Roger painted. Together they climbed the hills and explored the rivers, and watched the sunsets of Bou Saada; of unsurpassable brilliance, according to Oliver, yet as with every sunset, conveying to him not a sense of exhilaration, but rather a feeling of profound poetic sadness. Oliver describes the time spent with his French friend so richly that it is hard to avoid the conclusion that the two young lads were deeply in love.[34]

They also met at Bou Saada another French artist, Etienne Dinet, an accomplished painter of Oriental and North African scenes, who died in 1930. Today his paintings are much valued by collectors. He lived with a Mzabite called Sliman, who had rescued him when he had been set upon by a gang of thugs. Dinet actually became a Muslim, and married one of Sliman's sisters.

In June 1920 Oliver left for Tipaza, west of Algiers, famous for its Roman ruins. There he met a third French artist, Eugène Deshayes, and together they explored the ruins. On some days he would sit with an Arab schoolmaster and his pupils under a tree, and they would all recite the Koran together. Like a devotee of the southern sun, Oliver was letting the fruits of the senses weaken any tendency towards structure or direction in his life. How far away now were determination and dynamism, as well as the military competence and instinct for drill that had so impressed Kipling. Algeria was a profound and wonderful relaxation after the stresses of European war and peace; here every sense was awakened, soothed and burnished to a dull gold. But might the warm and sensuous south be granting more than balm to his soul? Might it not, in its subtle radiant bliss and quietly resonant harmony, be bearing away all resolve and ambition from his existence, and substituting an endless purposeless delicious drift?

CHAPTER 4

Armenia, 1920–21:
'Fate is a sea without shore'

In Algiers, as he sat beneath the tree reciting the Koran, Oliver Baldwin appeared to be living in a world defined entirely by the senses: the agreeable, passive, unhurried existence of a Mediterranean lotos-eater. But he had not entirely lost the active desire to achieve and to carve out a life of significance, and this impulse proved stronger than the lure of doing nothing beautifully. He developed a vague wish to go to Russia: or so he says; it is possible that Mansfield Cumming had indicated to him that his participation in the struggle against Bolshevism would be welcome. (Bolshevism was more often seen as 'Germanic' or 'Hun-like' rather than Leninist and Russian in circles of intelligence and extreme militarism.) So he shook off the pleasant inertia of Islamic Africa, and on 3 August 1920 caught a Dutch cargo vessel bound for Malta, Athens and Alexandria. In Athens the marvel of Hellenic civilization filled his soul with joy and peace. As in Algeria, he contrasted the warm, open Mediterranean society, with its unforgettable echoes of antiquity, its bright colours and strong scents, and the bold, emotionally frank natures of the people, with the cold, grey and repressed nature of society at home in England.[1]

Alexandria was rocked by riots against the British occupation; this was the period of the intellectual and political ascendancy of Saad Zaghlul, the Egyptian nationalist (that is, the reasonable defender of his people against foreign occupation). Oliver says that he found himself staying at the same hotel – the Savoy Palace – as Alexander Khatisian, a former prime minister of Armenia, who had led that country from June 1919 to May 1920, and who was now touring the Armenian communities abroad in an effort to raise money for his country. However, we are faced by another conflict of evidence: Khatisian says that he met Baldwin in Cairo, not Alexandria, and that they decided to confirm arrangements a month later in Constantinople.[2]

Armenia had been an independent republic since May 1918. The dominant political party since then had been the Armenian Revolutionary Federation, or *Hai Heghapokhakan Dashnaktsutiun*, whose policies were partly socialist and partly nationalist. Supporters of this party are known as Dashnaks, and Alexander Khatisian was one of their leaders. Pious words had been offered by European and American statesmen on behalf of Armenia, which had suffered a genocide at the hands of the Ottoman Turkish Ittihadist party during the war, and had still managed to put up a critical defensive line against the Central Powers for five months in 1917 after the defection of Russia. But little of substance had actually been delivered to her. From mid 1919 the economic priorities of European industry and defence had favoured Azerbaijan, then (as in the post-Soviet world) a country hostile to Armenia. Only the Bolshevik gains in late 1919 and early 1920 made the European powers take note and enquire what Armenia needed to avoid social and economic collapse. It is not unreasonable (although there is no proof, and Oliver vigorously denied that his visit to Transcaucasia was at the request of a spymaster) to see the hand of an intelligence department in putting the young British adventurer in the same hotel as the representative of threatened independent Armenia.

Khatisian offered Baldwin the job of infantry instructor with the Armenian army, an offer which was readily accepted. Oliver boarded a boat for Constantinople. It was, he recalled, a glorious voyage; as thrilling as that to Alexandria. Yet while now (as in Algeria) he relished the colour and light, there was, following his meeting with Khatisian, no longer any risk that he would be a mere servant of the sights and sounds of the Mediterranean. He had been given a purpose, which was in line with his achievements. Thereafter, he retained an objective grip on the external world of politics and society; he allowed the delights of the senses to exist at the edge of his consciousness, but not to occupy its central area.[3]

As he was travelling to the still-Ottoman capital he noted that the Italian soldiers were 'doing a roaring trade by selling their arms and ammunition to Mustafa Kemal's agents'. This was at a time when there existed, on paper, a united front of the Allied nations (of which Italy was one) towards the defeated Ottoman Empire; indeed, Italy had just itself signed the Treaty of Sèvres, by which the Allies sought to dismantle and decolonize the defeated empire. The practice of selling arms to Turkish nationalist rebels (who in the east behaved more like imperialists than nationalists, and of whom Mustafa Kemal was the leader) was entirely inconsistent with the signature on that treaty.[4]

From Constantinople, at that time a city of beauty and magic, he boarded an Italian boat for Batum, the chief port of the independent Republic of Georgia. Now a sense of lurking anxiety invaded his hitherto happy consciousness. He experienced terrifying waves of doubt and depression, amounting almost to panic, as he sailed eastwards in the Black Sea. But his belief in Destiny – a legacy of the Macdonalds – made him continue: Destiny to him was a figure more remote, but at the same time more potent, than the Trinitarian God of the English Church, an establishment whose comfortable yet class-ridden traditions he found irrelevant. Destiny was congenial, in harmony with the experiences of his life, and a good companion in the remote places where he was travelling. Destiny was a kind of deist God, who had started the machinery of the universe and then left it to run. An absentee divine power. Moreover, Oliver wanted to see what Bolshevism was like.[5]

After a delay for a cholera inoculation, he left for Tiflis (Tbilisi today), the Georgian capital. Initially he was forced to travel in the corridor, sitting on his suitcase: 'I don't know when I have felt so unutterably alone,' he noted wretchedly. Things improved when a kind traveller, speaking to him in French, offered him a place in a compartment. Now he could see the fine landscape: 'Glorious leaves on trees I had never seen before: little cascades that thundered with the pride of strength: arid lands that lay cracked and parched with the late summer's heat, and ruined castles that told of ancient and unhappy far-off days.'[6] Squeezed in the compartment for the 16-hour journey, he was soon conversing with a socialist editor, analysing the benefits of land nationalization, and discussing the visit a few weeks earlier of a British Labour Party delegation, which had included Ramsay MacDonald and Philip Snowden.

Baldwin remained for two days in Tiflis, imbibing the heady and diverse atmosphere of the greatest city of the South Caucasus, a region then more usually known as Transcaucasia. He spent one evening at a fashionable cabaret, and later at a performance of Maeterlinck's *Sister Beatrice*. An attempt to get into the Opera House failed, because it was the workers' free night and the house was full.[7]

Then he left for Armenia. The sense of impending doom returned to him, and he slept badly before his departure, rising early to get to Tiflis station. Here there were 'Indescribable smells. Human forms asleep on the floor; baggage thickly piled; wet clothes sending fumes of musty dampness into every corner of the large booking-hall. Tartars, Georgians, Armenians; poor, starving, helpless; moving, ever moving, unsettled by the past, harassed by the present, fearful of what was to come.'[8]

During the journey to Yerevan, the Armenian capital – in those days it was known as Erivan – the anxieties continued.

The motion of the train seemed to say to him, 'Go back, go back. Now don't go on.' Fellow-passengers included 'Armenian volunteers from America, Constantinople and Tiflis. Armenian officers from Tiflis. Much wearing of the Armenian national colours, much talk, much sadness. Not a cheerful company.'[9]

As the train, with its brave but downcast company, rattled through Transcaucasia, he again drew strength and a sense of calm from the landscape, glimpsed through the broken windows. It seemed untouched and untroubled by the miseries of the region.

Oliver Baldwin was, in all his writings, careless about giving dates. But the probable date of his arrival in Transcaucasia is mid to late September 1920. This was a grim time for Armenia. Despite the paper guarantees of the Treaty of Sèvres of August 1920, which acknowledged the country's independent existence, and declared that its borders would be determined by the decision of the American president Woodrow Wilson, Armenia was menaced on all sides. None of its borders was in any way fixed. Azerbaijan, eastern Transcaucasia, had fallen to the Bolsheviks in April 1920. From the Soviet city of Baku, Armenian Bolsheviks were launching assaults on independent Armenia, a country which they saw not as their homeland but as an agent of imperialism. However, no 'imperialism' had ever appeared in Armenia, since Britain held back from supporting Armenia for a variety of reasons: support for Russian monarchists, favour to Azerbaijan for its raw materials, and dislike of Armenian political adventurism. France, the other main 'imperialist' power, was engaged (like Italy) in negotiating corporate deals and concessions with the enemies of Armenia, the Turkish Nationalists, who, led in the east by Kiazim Karabekir, could scarcely be restrained from attacking the struggling republic.

A further factor which threatened Armenia was the alliance between the Kemalist Turks and the Bolsheviks – a strange alliance, often very powerful, but then sometimes off, like a stormy passion. Until well into the 1930s Bolshevism and Kemalism were quite close. This alliance, and the bemused and deferential way in which Stalin (and Lenin himself) looked to Kemal, led to the unjust territorial arrangement in the Transcaucasus for Armenia, giving her the worst deal of the three major nationalities, the others being the Georgians and the Azerbaijanis.

Baldwin's train journey from Tiflis to Yerevan took three days and two nights. Despite the shaking discomfort and showers of sparks, it was unforgettable. After a day and a night in the train he was out of Georgia, 'and the beauty of Armenia came down to look at us. Trees and trees, multi-coloured and sun-kissed, sheltering little villages and peasants' huts. Then the trees thinned and the hills grew taller and bleaker, mountain streams appeared, and the fall of water was audible amid the snorts of our straining train.'[10]

Alexandropol, the first stop inside Armenia, later called Leninakan, and today Gumri or Gumayri, was teeming with refugees fleeing from the Turks. They were starving and half-clothed, 'full of memories of the massacres that they had seen and wondering where the rest of their families could be; but the rivers are deep and the snow of western Ararat covers Turkish warfare very carefully. The great plain of Alexandropol looked wide and bare of comfort to the poor wretches who were in search of new homes and peace. There was no note of cheerfulness at this great station; just a confused babel of voices and the hungry, hopeless look of a broken people.'[11] Whatever his shortcomings as a novelist or dramatist, Baldwin was an able journalist, aptly describing the desolation of warfare.

On his first day in Yerevan Oliver Baldwin went to confer with his original contact from Egypt, Alexander Khatisian, and the Minister of War Ruben Ter-Minasian. He was to be given the rank of lieutenant colonel, and was to instruct troops in the Yerevan sector. He worked in close association with the Yerevan town commandant, Lieut-Col. A. V.

Shakhkhatuni (whose name can also be spelt 'Chachatouni'), a former star of the Armenian stage and the Russian silent film industry, who had enlisted in 1914 and fought bravely on the Caucasian front, being twice wounded. (Later Shakhkhatuni was to star in Abel Gance's *Napoleon*.) His interpreter was Jacob Kayalian, known later as Jacques Kayaloff, a military historian of great knowledge and a man of generous charm and hospitality.[12]

He also met the head of the British Military Mission in Yerevan, Captain H. D. Court, who treated him hospitably but with great reserve. Court did not like Armenians much, nor care for their supporters, and he believed him to be a Bolshevik spy.[13]

There were major problems in training the Armenian army at that time. In the first place, the country was exhausted by six years of almost continuous warfare. This exacerbated the differences in the aspirations among the people. The activists who sought to continue the war were convinced that somehow 'the West' would one day show its hand; while a broad spectrum of the people saw that Allied promises were insubstantial, and looked for the re-establishment of the country's connection with Russia, which had been severed in 1917. In his job, Baldwin found that the techniques of military instruction veered between two extremes: one was old-fashioned, where the officers bellowed at their men, expecting total discipline; the other was that of the new 'democratic' officers, who let all standards slide. Britain had sent a few uniforms; also a consignment of Canadian Ross rifles, 'guaranteed to explode at first shot', and boots which were too small for the Armenian peasantry. All that Armenia really had was, he mused, 'a blind, strange faith in Great Britain, who had made so many promises to help her and who had once beaten the Turks'.[14]

Oliver Baldwin acknowledged that the army raised to resist the Kemalist attack was a failure. Disaster occurred after about a month. The Nationalist Turks seized the fortress of

Kars, Armenia's second city, on 30 October 1920. The Armenian army was exhausted and demoralized. The Turks occupied this hitherto impregnable fortress under cover of darkness and thick mist, before the General Officer Commanding, Daniel Bek Pirumian, was awake. Bolshevik propaganda had weakened the morale of the troops; promises of peace were too powerful for the war-weary Armenian troops. One theory for the rapid and catastrophic collapse at Kars is that the defenders thought that the Turks with their red flags were in fact Russian Bolsheviks. Large numbers of the Armenian inhabitants fled eastward to Alexandropol. The GOC of the Alexandropol district, General Silikov, saw that further fighting was impossible, and started negotiations. Baldwin notes bitterly that Britain did nothing to assist Armenia at this critical time, despite having signed the Treaty of Sèvres three months earlier. Neither was the League of Nations of any practical help.[15]

At this time Baldwin was drilling the town guard of Yerevan, just 20 km (12.5 miles) from enemy lines. On one occasion, following his instruction, he watched a battalion do an imaginary night attack. Afterwards the men listened to his criticisms of the manoeuvres in an atmosphere of calm and determination. There was no failure of nerve in this sector.[16]

One day, accompanied by one of the town adjutants, he went to the Bolshevik mission in Yerevan. Boris V. Legrand, of French-Russian-Jewish extraction, headed the mission; his second-in-command, Otto Silin, was a former commercial traveller in Scandinavia, and the secretary, Schieffers, was a young student. The visit proved pointless. Apart from predicting imminent revolution in England and South Africa, his hosts' conversation seldom rose above the level of saying, 'We know. Anything you may say against us is capitalist propaganda.'[17] The visits of British trade unionists to Russia were a similar deception. These people were capitalist spies dressed in peasants' clothes.

About this time he says he met a sinister young officer in the Armenian army, named Joseph Markossian. Markossian, initially from Marseille, was a plausible and unscrupulous villain, according to Baldwin a former member of both the English and French secret services, a cocaine user (or 'fiend' in Baldwin's glamourized language), who was to end up in jail in Moscow in 1923. He is referred to alternately as a good friend, or as an evil rogue. It seems that the two somehow became entangled in one another's lives.[18]

All the time the military situation was worsening. Armenia was being driven into humiliating capitulation by the ruthless advance of the Kemalist Turks. The British Mission was planning to leave on 14 November. Captain Court offerred Oliver a lift in the British government lorry which was going to the Georgian frontier.

He thought the matter over. If he stayed, and the government changed, would a new government, made up of enemies of Britain, dare to arrest a British representative? And was it not cowardice, and betrayal of trust, for him to disappear from the country he had agreed to serve, just when things started to get tough? The Armenian people themselves had a deep trust in Britain. This trust surely could not be betrayed.[19]

So the next day he wrote to Court, saying that he would stay. Court said he was a fool, and that Britain would not be able to do anything if he got into trouble. Some hours later, the Mission, and representatives of the main British charitable relief fund, departed for Georgia. For the first time since his arrival Baldwin felt cut off from the world.[20]

On 2 December, amid a swirl of rumours, Baldwin learnt that the Armenian government had resigned, and power had passed to a coalition made up of Left nationalists and Bolsheviks. Earlier he had been round to the Georgian consulate, who had given him a visa and advised him to get out while he could; and now too his former colleague, Colonel

Shakhkhatuni, discussed the possibilities of escape. The Turks were solidly entrenched to the west; the Bolsheviks were advancing from the east. A possible escape route lay southward to Persia; but the route, over the mountains of Zangezur, was long and hazardous. Baldwin however wanted to see what would happen. He was keen to have experience of Bolshevism at first hand. So he chose to stay.

At the American charitable mission, Near East Relief, some of the staff left too. Baldwin was again given the option of getting out, but declined. By 5 December there were only five foreign representatives in Armenia: two American relief workers, Dr Clarence D. Ussher and Mr Charles Peers; Signor Parmigiani, an Italian merchant; the Persian consul; and Lieutenant-Colonel Baldwin. They waited expectantly. The Armenian government departed, under the terms of the agreement to allow the Red Army in. Would Bolshevism arrive with liberty, equality and fraternity, and with peace and bread, or with the Red Terror?[21]

By midday the executive of the Armenian Communist Party had arrived in Yerevan, and were lunching in macho style at the Hotel Orient, with their weapons left very visibly on the table, 'making them look very dreadful and wicked'. Their average age was probably eighteen.[22] At 2.30 the Bolshevik cavalry of the 11th Red Army arrived. They were expecting trouble, but were received in silence. The exhausted populace hung the buildings with red flags, and all wore red rosettes. There were speeches, punctuated by a band playing the Internationale. Comrade this and comrade that spoke. '*Quelle blague!*' murmured someone in Oliver's ear. But he did not think so. He felt a hint of enthusiasm, and he liked the talk of brotherhood.

But on 6 December the arrests began. Members of the old regime, doctors, lawyers and journalists, army officers and academics: anyone who might be likely to voice opposition to the new regime. Wholesale confiscations of goods from the populace followed. Even the milk sent to starving Armenian refugees by Near East Relief was requisitioned. Ox-carts took the spoils away. Baldwin's enthusiasm turned to fury at what he saw; but his anger was nevertheless tempered by the attitudes of the one or two military commissars who seemed to express true notions of fraternity. He appears to have had a genuine intention to see good in Bolshevism if at all possible.[23]

On 8 December he got wind that he might be arrested by the new regime. He had criticized the wholesale seizures of goods by the Bolsheviks, and had been denounced as a capitalist spy by the cocaine-addict Joseph Markossian, who had (he says) informed the new rulers that he had large sums of money which he was using to benefit British interests.[24] Baldwin entrusted his money to J. V. Arakelian, Shakhkhatuni's former adjutant, and his silver Caucasian sword to Mme Khansorian – in Russian the name is Yablokov – the Russian mother of his aide-de-camp. Again he was urged to escape, this time to take to the hills. But no. To be caught there would be to invite a brutal death. The following day he was escorted to jail, to begin his first term of imprisonment. His fellow prisoners, 'cheerful and interesting', were two elderly educated anti-Bolshevik Armenians, Ishkhanian, a professor of statistics, and Ter-Mikaelian, a former doctor in the Russian army. The food was frightful, dust and pebbles were to be found in the bread, but fortunately relatives of Baldwin's fellow captives brought them edible items, which they generously shared with him. His captors were considerate. He felt largely resigned, doing little more than waiting to see what would happen. He was depressed when his fellow-captives had visitors, and his spirits rose when they were gloomy. It added up to 'seeing life', with a vengeance! He mused that at this rate he would be worn out by the age of 30. He looked back: at 17 he had been a corporal and a staff-sergeant; at 18 a cadet and 2nd lieutenant. At 19 he had been a lieutenant leading a company of Irish Guards in battle. At 20 he was a vice consul and at 21 a lieutenant-colonel and a prisoner of the Soviets.[25]

After two days he was moved to the town prison, 'the real thing', according to his diary: 'four dirty stone walls, one tiny barred window and a door with a slot in it.' Some of his possessions were taken from him, but he was allowed to keep his watch. Again his fellow prisoners shared their food with him. He grew depressed, and felt he would go mad if he stayed there long. He wrote an epitaph for himself:

Here lies Oliver aged twenty-one
Who ended his life where others had begun
If any poor prisoner loses cheer
Just think of me ere you shed a tear[26]

The weather turned to the fearsome cold characteristic of the Armenian winter. The prisoners became preoccupied by the matter of the seating arrangement around the stove. Oliver, moving his seat to try to keep warm, thought of his old comrades, especially George Bambridge, 'the apostle of luxury'. As he ate the black prison bread, he imagined Bambridge dining at the Berkeley. 'Oh, when shall I see Piccadilly again?' he wondered gloomily, The English prisoner was not allowed any reading matter, which left him acutely deprived.

The next day, 11 December, he stayed in bed till the fire was lit – 'The sort of thing Di would have done in the circumstances.' He thought more of what people at home were doing – 'bad thing to do', he noted. He hoped mother was not worrying, but he expected she was. She never need, he confided to his prison diary, since 'if I am dead, I shall come and see her if I can'. His morale was rather better; he felt he could tolerate prison in Yerevan, though he could not face the idea of being taken to Baku or Moscow. He wished Georgia would declare itself soviet and 'end all this stupidity' – expel the British representative Colonel Stokes and free a Bolshevik mission in Tiflis held captive by the Menshevik government. Again he remembered days at Astley: 'Oh, the thought of the billiard room fire.'[27]

The 12th was bitterly cold, and he felt desperate for something to read. 'If only I had a William [Shakespeare].' His thoughts, and his memories, turned to England, especially to the Kiplings at Bateman's; Uncle Ruddy would be gathering brushwood for a bonfire, and Aunt Carrie would be bustling in and out of her room, while Elsie was preparing her clothes for Astley. Amid this reverie, Arakelian came in bringing milk, apples, pears, white bread and cheese, which he had bought with his own money, an act of kindness which touched Oliver. He told Oliver he would be out in a few days, but the prisoner was sceptical. And he was feeling irritable. The doctor, Ter-Mikaelian, would whistle just one tune, the waltz from Gounod's *Faust*. Baldwin found him a dull old stick, and could understand why, with such officials, independent Armenia had failed as a state. They had another quarrel about the seating around the stove. Oliver refused to accept a plan offered by Ter-Mikaelian.[28]

Trivia passed the time, alternating with anguished self-questioning addressed to the diary: 'If I do get out of this, how on earth am I going to get to Georgia?'. Thoughts drifted back home: 'It is now nearly 5, I can see George [Bambridge] having his tea and a bun at the Bath Club, Baby Alex writing in the Mess, Lorna ogling Derrick, Betty with a bosom friend playing the piano "ensemble". Mother handing a cup of tea to Jack Battye, & he saying, "Oh, thank you, Mrs Baldwin". A cackle from Joan Sturgess, & her voice: "Aunt Cissie's worrying about her little Olly. Don't do it dear, he's alright." Alex [Carlsen] is downstairs knitting & humming "kind, kind & gentle is she". I wonder who is Lorna's latest & whether Betty has hooked any one yet.'[29]

Days passed; vacant days, filled alternately with hope and despair. Oliver worked on ideas for his plays. In his teens he had written a number of adolescent plays for the Astley theatre, mostly one-act crime fiction dramas of the Grand Guignol type. Titles included 'The Fog', 'Two's Company', 'Walpurgis Nacht' and 'Dr Chachia'; though none was remarkable, the best were respectable, and he was proud of them. (Six years later 'The Fog' was performed as a radio play by the BBC.) In prison his thoughts turned to a summer week of drama, to be held at the home theatre, and he became engrossed in details about casting, and moves for the characters, which he worked out with the aid of drawings. This passed the time, creatively.[30]

Joseph Markossian turned up as a convicted prisoner, probably following a theft. He said that the Cheka (the precursor of the KGB) had been informed that Baldwin had £150 Turkish and £65 sterling, and that he was a friend of Captain Court and of Colonel Rawlinson, the British officer held prisoner by the Kemalist Turks at Erzerum. Wonderful, he thought. Only later did he learn that Markossian had himself informed the Cheka of these details. The doctor was freed on the 15th, and the statistician on the 17th. Oliver was now alone, except for some pestering visits from Joseph. His spirits were low. Despairing thoughts, like the fibres of dry rot, multiplied in his consciousness. The fire went out – the wood was damp – and he felt he would freeze to death – 'a good job too'.[31]

He tried to get statements of his innocence put before the authorities via both the doctor and the statistician. But nothing seemed to happen. He was roused to anger by the theft of half a loaf of bread, and by the arrival of four prisoners in his cell, whose convictions were for playing cards. 'One is like a typical stage villain and the others are ordinary. They spit and blow their noses all over the room; and they call themselves *bourgeoisie*. One, it appears, was inspector of prisons, and the stage villain with the beery eyes and whisky voice is cashier in the bank.'[32]

Markossian was freed on 20 December. He went to the Khansorians, and said that the prisoner wanted his silver sword; whereupon he took it and sold it, while protesting that he would do anything for its owner. Oliver saw him the next day, and questioned him about it; Joseph said that it was with one of the Bolshevik leaders. But Oliver was forgiving: 'it is impossible to be angry with the man.'[33] As Christmas approached, and as other prisoners began to be freed, a note of desperation is found in Baldwin's diary entries. The fleas and the mice drove him to distraction. A mouse was caught by a man from Karabagh, and drowned in the slopping-out bucket; another in apparent revenge spent the night running over Oliver's bed.

Christmas Day, 1920, dawned darkly for the English prisoner. The others had been released. There was no fire and no wood, though the room had kept its heat. Christmas dinner consisted of sausage and Tatar bread. He made himself a Christmas present of tobacco and a box of matches. Later, when he had managed to get hold of some wood, and had made a fire, some small seasonal good-will extended itself over him.[34]

On Boxing Day he received 'a host of good things' from Dr Clarence Ussher, the famed American missionary and relief worker. One of the presents was an apple, with the words 'Don't worry – cheer up' pricked out on the skin. Oliver replied with a note stuffed into the pepper pot.

There were small signs of improvement. On the 27th, a boy made a roaring fire, and actually gave him hot water, the first he had known since leaving Egypt. He felt that he was getting used to prison, and was thinking less of liberty. But things were back to the usual on the following day; no fire, and the mouse mistaking his bed for the Champs Elysées. It became clear to him that Dr Ussher was working for his liberty. On the 31st he summed up his hope for the new year: 'May it bring me peace and happiness, and may I get out of this damned country.' Over the next few day Ussher was permitted to send him some books, and Baldwin wrote a ten-stanza piece of sub-Housman doggerel about Ludlow, Clee and Tenbury, which he was unwise enough to reproduce in his memoir of the time, *Six Prisons and Two Revolutions*, but which nevertheless indicated an anguished longing for home and roots.[35]

More prisoners started appearing; with the addition of two members of the old government, there were five in the jail, 'a collection of bourgeois', Oliver observed.

In his prison diary, he wrote another verse at this time, but he put a blue pencil through it when he published *Six Prisons*. It is however rather better than the Ludlow verses written two days earlier. Its muscular rhythm is effective, and it is revealing of his general state of mind:

If some wise man to me should say,
'You've but an hour to live!'
Should I be filled with dark dismay,
Or signs of sorrow give?
I rather think I should not mind,
(My hopes on earth are few;)
In other worlds I'm sure to find
Those friends that I once knew.
Of late grim death has come to be
A most persistent friend,
And now in him I'm sure to see
A means unto an end.
For in this world I did not live
In all ways as I should
But in the next world they might give
More chance of doing good.
So I will answer that wise man
Next time he passes by:
'If sudden death should be thy plan,
I do not fear to die!'[36]

Baldwin's last entry in his prison diary was for 12 January; he was then released on parole, the condition of his parole being that he would not leave Yerevan without the authorities' permission. Dr Ussher offered him the use of his house. His reflections on prison, and military Bolshevism, make clear his loathing of the system, especially of the leech-like manner in which the Bolshevik rulers preyed on the starving

Armenian people, exemplified by their requisitioning of the stores of the American charity Near East Relief.

It was the arrogance of the young Bolshevik rulers which led to the counter-revolution in Armenia. They increased the misery and starvation which was current in the country. The mountainous districts of Karabagh and Zangezur had remained unconquered by Lenin's people. Yerevan grew thick with rumours. The Bolshevik authorities in Moscow sent the sinister, leather-clad Cheka chief Gevorg Atarbekian to crush the brimming insurgency. He imposed a series of drastic, sadistic regulations on the people; but nothing stopped the surge of revolution. In an act of pitiless cruelty, 1500 officers from the Armenian army were force-marched, in appalling weather and without proper clothing, from Yerevan eastwards to Azerbaijan. (This action was similar, on a much smaller scale, to the death-march deportations of Armenians conducted by the Ottoman Turks six years earlier.) Wives and mothers followed their loved ones, in spite of the terrible conditions, and in spite of the whips of the Red guards. Rather than stifle revolution, the action gave strength to it. In Baldwin's words: 'Under the hard exterior of Soviet rule could be heard the first rumblings of awakening Liberty.'[37]

How did Oliver hold on to his socialism, amid the terror and darkness of Bolshevism, which called itself socialism? Was Bolshevism socialism? His experience told him otherwise. In *Six Prisons*, he relates, of this time:

> Another poster showed a crowd of men, bare-footed, working in a field under the supervision of a man with a whip. In the distance arose a red sun out of which stepped a Red soldier bearing a red flag inscribed 'Liberty'. Underneath: 'The Red Army brings liberty to the English proletariat'.
>
> A little Social Revolutionary who translated the inscription to me remarked: 'It's enough to make you a damned capitalist.' And certainly, for a Socialist to see how his hopes and ideals have been rendered ludicrous and trampled out of recognition,

is a distinct push down the hill of Disillusion. But then those Socialists who have seen Bolshevism as ordinary mortals, and not as Government tourists, do not see Socialism in Bolshevism. We hold the latter to be the monstrosity produced by premature birth.[38]

In an aside, Oliver noted that his opponents in Britain had used the same tactics as the Bolsheviks against him: right-wing black propagandists had accused him of having been a conscientious objector, and having been imprisoned for forgery. In Oliver's experience, right-wingers could be as mendacious as Bolsheviks.[39]

All the time the plans for overthrowing the Bolshevik regime were maturing. Baldwin was doubtful about the chances of success. The geographical situation of Armenia was bad. But on 14 February the spirit of the people improved. Nods were exchanged in the streets; and the leading Bolsheviks appeared uneasy. Oliver thought of escaping; but he was still on parole, and Dr Ussher was his guarantee.[40]

On 15 February a number of armed Commissars left for the south; the following day the official press spoke of 'slight trouble with robber bands in the hills behind Yerevan'. At lunchtime that day Oliver Baldwin and Dr Ussher heard one rifle shot, then another; then machine-gun fire. The insurgents were closing in. By 3.00 the noise had become louder; there were troop movements.

That evening a crowd gathered silently to read a decree signed by the commissar for war, Avis Nurijanian, and countersigned by the Cheka chief. It said that if the counter-revolution did not stop, the imprisoned Armenian leaders whose names were listed would be shot. There followed a roll-call of distinguished names from the pre-Bolshevik period. Soldiers, former ministers, parliamentarians, doctors, journalists, peasant leaders. Dashnaktsutiun, the Armenian Revolutionary Federation, which had handed power over to the Bolsheviks, now had a terrible choice to make: to continue the revolt, and see those men die; or to call it off, and see savage retribution fall on the people for being the vehicle for counter-revolution.[41]

Deep into the night representatives of different groups discussed the matter; and Baldwin says to their eternal credit they decided to continue the revolt; in his own words, using language resonant with religious reference, 'It was held that where the freedom of the people lies in the death of individuals, it is always expedient that a man die for the people, and therefore the fight should continue.'[42] This decision was unanimous, the more so since the party realized that logistically it would be impossible to order the insurgents to stop fighting. It was also a decision of great significance and meaning for Oliver Baldwin, and one which he honoured, and remembered all his life.

Firing grew closer on the 17th; bursts of fire could be seen in the hills. At midnight there was a lull.

At 6.30 on 18 February Oliver was wakened by Dr Ussher shaking his shoulder. 'Listen . . .,' he said. Rifle shots, Lewis guns, Vickers guns, rattling and pounding as Oliver had heard them in the trenches; and through the air, across the hills, the call 'Hayastan, Hayastan' (Armenia, Armenia). He dressed in five minutes, grabbed a revolver, and went out into the street. Firing was continuous all around; the insurgents were coming from the north. Baldwin noticed the discipline of the people; everyone was in place. The united call was 'Hayastan, Hayastan.' Cheering, kissing; Oliver placed Vickers guns in place and opened fire. Then someone called out, 'To the prison, to the prison.' Armenian snipers were on every housetop, and in the town centre two companies of Bolshevik troops were captured and marched away. The crowd reached the prison, the gates were unlocked. Inside there was a deathly silence.[43]

Cells were opened, and prisoners stumbled out, emaciated, weak, crying. They pointed feverishly to the centre block, and there the crowd went. Blood was half an inch thick on the floor. At the top of a flight of stairs the sight they saw was truly terrible: 20–30 naked or half-clothed bodies, hacked to pieces; and more in a cell. A freshly dug pit was also located. Seventy-five bodies in all were discovered. 'Sickened, appalled, we stumbled back into the light. The other cells were opened, but in silence. They had heard the whole massacre extending through two nights.'[44]

Fifty prisoners had been shot on the first night; the rest had been machine-gunned to death by non-Armenian Bolsheviks, since the Armenian Reds had refused to fire on their co-nationals. Even that did not kill them all, and the same extremists had to go in with axes to finish them off.

The battle for Yerevan was not yet over; Bolshevik detachments were everywhere being arrested, but a number of escapers fled to the railway station, at the time some way outside Yerevan. Only later did the insurgents realize the significance of the flight to the station: that an armoured train was ready there, prepared by the Bolshevik leadership, stacked with provisions, capable of being used either for warfare or a hasty departure. With their lack of organization, the insurgents (of whom Baldwin considered himself one) had not thought of derailing the train. Nevertheless the town was free, and the people savoured freedom. The banned national anthem was sung again, and the red, blue and orange tricolour of Armenia was unfurled and waved. A new government was formed, under an emergency committee known as the Committee for the Salvation of the Fatherland, and headed by Simon Vratsian, a Dashnak revolutionary who had been the last prime minister of Armenia before the hand-over of power in December 1920. Baldwin calls him 'a man of high principle, courage and resource'.[45]

Bolshevik agents were rounded up and imprisoned; they included Joseph Markossian, jailed again, this time for betraying Baldwin. Some of the rebels recommended that he should have been shot, but Baldwin says he persuaded them to spare him, and indeed to release him after a few days since he was such a hopeless case and a coward. He adds that he would probably have been better off shot, 'but there it was'.

A few days later the people paid special thanks to Dr Ussher and Baldwin. Both were asked to speak in reply; Ussher spoke in Armenian, and Baldwin in English, which Ussher translated. In his speech Oliver said he was glad to see that Armenia had taken the Bolshevik slogan 'Workers of the world, unite' to heart. Perhaps this was not the most appropriate comment to make in the circumstances, but it was one which Oliver, who sometimes had a penchant for heavy irony, could not resist.[46]

The prisons grew full of Bolsheviks; and at the instigation of Dr Ussher, and with Vratsian's permission, a prison inspection team was formed, one of whose members was Baldwin. They checked that conditions were more humane than they had been under the ousted regime.

Social and political circumstances became more settled, and Ussher and Baldwin arranged a dinner party to celebrate the re-birth of Armenian liberty. It coincided with Vartanants, a great feast of the Armenian church, which commemorates the sacrifice of St Vartan and his comrades for the faith in Armenia in AD 451. Throughout the evening people carried candles to and fro, and men fired salvoes in the air in celebration. At one stage, Armenian cavalry were seen galloping along the street; to Baldwin it appeared to be part of the festivities. The meal, which was splendid, was accompanied by music, toasts and speeches. The serious question of the evening was: what was the geographical limit, beyond Yerevan, of the counter-revolution? Had it reached Dilidjan and Karakilisa? The news was unclear. Oliver says he was only waiting for accurate information before leaving for Georgia.[47]

Dinner was interrupted at about 11.00 by the arrival of a breathless visitor, with a message from Simon Vratsian. He brought the grim news that there had been panic among Armenian troops to the south of Yerevan, and that Bolshevik forces were on the outskirts of the town and might be in Yerevan before dawn. Vratsian wished to entrust his wife and young child to Ussher, as he prepared to escape through Zangezur to Persia. Oliver now understood the significance of the cavalry movements earlier that evening. The guests were plunged into depression and gloom.[48]

The Bolsheviks were entrenched on the town side of the armoured train. Baldwin wanted to destroy the train with artillery; but an old Russian colonel believed that a night action by cavalry would be preferable. A dawn attack two days later compelled the rail-wagon communists to speed off; and the battle line was pushed out to ten miles south of Yerevan.[49]

The re-established Armenian government had sent a telegram to Moscow which had urged an exchange of prisoners. It had received no reply. The silence indicated to the Armenians the revenge that the Bolsheviks would exact when they retook Yerevan. Baldwin, and many inhabitants of Yerevan, were in no doubt that they would retake Armenia. But that knowledge was not depressing, and the people remained cheerful. Freedom was marvellous, and savoured to the full; the people lived in the present, because it was such a contrast to the past.

Baldwin knew that as an Englishman he had to make plans; he was beginning to feel like a rat in a trap. Anxiety hovered like a miasmic cloud above Yerevan; popular insecurity led to a man-hunt for Bolsheviks and their sympathizers. The town was shelled again on 26 February; thereafter a major effort was needed to boost morale. Despite the success of the counter-revolution, the general situation was deteriorating all the time. The rebels were outnumbered five to one, and with the arrival of reinforcements from Baku the proportion would grow to ten to one, Baldwin estimated. Free Yerevan was a cul-de-sac. He had to escape.

The representative of Kemalist Turkey, Behaeddin Bey, had recommended that he pass through Turkey (rather than take the longer and more perilous journey through the mountains of Zangezur to the Persian frontier). This seemed good advice. He thought it would only be a matter of days before Bolshevik pressure would force the Dashnaks out of Yerevan, so he had no qualms of conscience now about quitting Armenia.

Simon Vratsian gave him an Armenian passport, and he obtained a Turkish visa from the consul. Baldwin could not read Turkish, so he had no idea what the visa said. But the consul had been charming. He was to travel with his former aide-de-camp, Shura Khansorian; they would take with them some letters for Near East Relief. The horses were made ready, and they left on the evening of 1 March 1921, Oliver's twenty-second birthday. As they left, Shura's horse cast a shoe, and they had to wait while a new one was fitted. This was a bad omen; Oliver regretted that he did not heed it, and later chided himself for being too materialist. Unsettled by the portent, he left the Armenian capital, never to return.[50]

CHAPTER 5

Armenia (II): 'How completely can snow cover all traces of a stranger in a foreign land'

The two riders set off for Ashtarak, about ten miles north-west of Yerevan, to stay the night at Shura's grandmother's. Oliver felt a sense of freedom and space in the course of the journey, drawing deeply on the peace of the winter landscape after the close-booming guns of Yerevan. Ashtarak was full of fruit trees; snow on the rocks gleamed pink in the dying sunlight.[1]

Up early the next morning, they left with an escort. The route to their next halt, Bash Abaran, was almost due north; the road climbs all the time, and in winter the mercury sinks to a shrivelled seed. Drifting snow had created softly treacherous ice mounds. In places it was up to the horse's belly, and when Oliver was dismounted snow reached his waist. Guns could be heard in the distance. The travellers met a battery of fieldgunners on their doomed way to Yerevan to join the anti-Bolshevik forces; and they passed hamlets half-hidden amid snow and rocks. Here too they were given food: bread, mutton, goat's cheese and wine.

Brilliant sun shone down on the universal snow, and Oliver's eyes began to hurt. He pulled his Caucasian hat well down over his eyes. Each step brought more pain. Nevertheless by late afternoon the riders and their escort had to hurry, since darkness was looming and they had some distance to go; and on either side in the fading light they saw the circling grey forms of hungry wolves. For the final few miles they travelled with revolvers in hand. By now Oliver could hardly make out the form of the rider in front of him.

Finally they reached their halt at Bash Abaran. Oliver climbed a ladder to enter a room lit by an oil lamp. He could now see nothing, and realized than he was snow blind. After a meal, he slept, and the pain left him. But the next morning he was still weak. He had some vision, but his eyes hurt if he kept them open. He held snow to them, a folk remedy, which made them no better. As he rode out of the village next day, Shura led his horse, for he could not see.[2]

The snow again grew deep, and Oliver was forced to dismount and walk, holding his horse's tail for direction. He was, he admits, helpless, and in a foul temper. Shura by contrast showed great patience. Oliver knew he was the worst of companions. At one stage he accused Shura of leading him the wrong way. Towards evening he heard the wolves again, and in a gesture of hopelessness (which he admits was childish) he urged Shura to make his way by himself to Georgia, and to abandon him to the circling predators. The howling drew nearer. Oliver often asked Shura the where-abouts of the wolves: 'Some way off,' was the invariable reply. Later he was told that two of them had approached quite close.

Finally they reached Norashen, about half way between Bash Abaran and Alexandropol/Gumri. This was the last village under Armenian control, before Turkish-occupied lands began. It is a measure of the extent of the advance of Turkish 'Nationalist' – in fact, imperialist – forces, unrelated to the national composition of the people of the territory, that the Turkish army had advanced so far into purely Armenian territory. Here the village headman bathed Oliver's eyes in vodka, and made him gaze into a white bowl full of still snow water, and apparently these remedies benefited him, for he could dimly make out his surroundings. He lay on a bench in a barn, warmed by a small fire and by the presence of the cattle on the other side of a low partition. Here the entire village assembled at night. After food and drink, he slept well, in the warm hay-filled atmosphere. The steady cud-chewing of the cows infused itself pleasantly into his dreams.[3]

Next day, despite continuing eye problems, he felt pleased to be crossing Turkish lines and probably meeting a doctor with eye-lotion. A guide led them for about four miles, but no further, fearful of roving Turkish soldiers. They left their weapons with him – all except for a Mauser pistol, which Baldwin kept in his coat pocket. After two miles they sighted Turkish outposts. Baldwin held up his passport, hoping that its whiteness would indicate that their purpose was peaceful. Three Turkish soldiers rode out to meet them, and they fetched a serjeant who could read. What was their business, Shura and Oliver were asked in Russian. They had come from Near East Relief, and were bound for Alexandropol, Baldwin replied, and thence for Batum so as to escape the Bolsheviks.

They were taken to a village about a mile from the outpost, for further questioning. Oliver was given relief for his eyes, and was told that sores on his face were frost-bite. He gave his interrogators details of the former Bolshevik regime in Armenia and pointed out to them that he could not now escape the returning wrath of Moscow's men. After some conferring by telephone he was told that he could proceed to Alexandropol, and that he would be given an officer as a guide. It was all quite amicable. He asked the officer commanding if he wanted to see the bag of letters addressed to Near East Relief, but the offer was declined. A decent meal followed. In late afternoon, they turned their horses to the setting sun, trotted down the slope, and made for the great plain of Alexandropol.

It was a wonderful ride, and my healed eyes took in the beauty of the sun-streaked plain and rose to see the summit of Mount Alagöz [known in Armenian as Aragats], blushing with a soft pink colour tingeing the whiteness of her face.

There are two distinct mountains on the western side of Armenia – Ararat and Alagöz, but for colouring alone the latter is by far the most impressive, since her contours are so perfectly formed and her slender neck widens out till it reaches the plain, where the shoulders take shape and stretch away into the beginning of sight.

My first clear view of wolves came to me in the plain, and I saw them hugging the mountain and running out towards us and then retreating, uncertain. At one place my horse stumbled badly, and, on looking down, I saw half buried in the snow the body of a woman and baby, and I knew they would lie till the wolves tugged them out and left but the skeletons to show the fate of refugees from Turkish invasions.[4]

At Alexandropol brigade headquarters they were ushered into the presence of Osman Bey, a security officer. After being questioned, Oliver asked him if he could leave for Batum the next day. Osman replied that the road was impassable, and told him that he had better aim for Trebizond via Erzerum. Only later did Baldwin realize that Turkish troops were then marching on Batum, a town which they held thereafter for some months. Baldwin asked if he could spend the night at the Near East Relief hostel. This request was granted, and he was given a guide.

'Who's there?' 'A messenger from Yerevan, and thank God I've got here.' The travellers' hosts were Martin Brown and Clark Martin, two charming Americans who had worked for NER in Salonika, Romania and Georgia before coming to Armenia. Their warmth, kindness and hospitality were much appreciated by the visitors. After a meal, Brown suggested that the interpreter should read the letters addressed to individual Armenians in Alexandropol, since sooner or later Turkish censors would read them. This was a fortunate decision, since a perusal of the letters made it clear that they had to be burnt (which they were), since they contained denunciations of the Bolsheviks, and even more of the Turks. Oliver was lucky that they had not been read earlier.[5]

A Turkish private soldier, attached to the commissariat, entered in the middle of the proceedings. His activities cast a curious light on the dealings of Near East Relief. In exchange for blankets given by the NER, he gave them a sheep. Maybe aid agencies have sometimes to engage in a bit of dealing. But the blankets he received were made into uniforms, and thereby the NER can be said to have helped kit out the Kemalist army, which was occupying Armenia with ferocious determination, with no regard for the lives of those it controlled. The soldier was nevertheless an agreeable individual, conversation flowed easily, and the company retired to bed late.

In the morning a message was waiting from Osman Bey asking Baldwin to bring round the letters. When he reached headquarters, he was questioned about his service in the Great War, and the Turkish officer was sceptical when he said he had not served in Mesopotamia. He asked when he would be leaving, and was told that it was being ascertained whether or not the road was clear.[6]

Oliver was shown round the work of Near East Relief in Alexandropol, and was impressed by the organization and its equipment, all of which had been financed through the generosity of United States citizens. ($30 million had been raised in the months following the 1918 armistice.[7]) Nevertheless he reflected: 'There should have been no need for this vast private enterprise if only the Allies had kept their promises and settled an enduring state in a wider Armenia.' Next day he went the short distance into Turkish-occupied Alexandropol itself, and described what he saw.

> The streets were dirty, and the town almost empty of inhabitants. Here and there an aged Armenian tailored for the Turkish soldiery or baked Turkish cakes or cobbled shoes, but the rest of the population were scattered, massacred, or living in caves by the side of Alagöz, waiting for death. The silence of the town was enhanced by the snow in the streets, and our

rumbling wheels were the only sounds, except for the soft patter of a Turkish soldier's feet on the pavement.[8]

The two were not permitted to ride on the next stage of their journey, to Kars; they were taken to the station, and put in a freezing goods wagon, accompanied by two armed guards. There was no light except that from a small slot. When Oliver asked about this mode of travel, he was told that it was for their own safety. Through that little aperture they observed what they could of the countryside. It made a powerful impression on him by reason of its vast loneliness and silence. 'On these plains a nation died,' he said to Shura. 'On these plains a nation was betrayed,' came back the reply. They travelled with four or five merchant Turks, one of whom showed immense pleasure when Oliver recited three *suras* from the Koran in Arabic, which he had learnt in Algeria.[9]

Arriving in Kars, they were taken first to a guard-room full of soldiers, and then to the town commandant's; here, after a meal, they slept the night in their coats. His hosts found the pistol which Oliver carried in his coat, and took possession of it 'as a precaution'. Oliver slept well that night; nevertheless, he felt some anxieties. Kars 'had a bad name for prisons and strange happenings'. They were completely cut off from the world. And what of half-Armenian Shura? Oliver reassured himself by recalling that he spoke Russian without any accent, and could not speak Armenian.

At 10.00 the next morning they were taken to see not Kiazim Karabekir Pasha, the commander of the Eastern Front, whom they had expected to see, but Roufat Bey, the head of intelligence. (The correct spelling of his name may have been Refet, but Roufat is the manner in which Baldwin spelled the name.) He had a reputation as a capable and perceptive man.

Oliver had to disguise the fact that his presence in Yerevan had been on account of his job of training the Armenian army for action against the Turks. Such an admission might have indicated that he had been sent there as a British spy.[10]

Roufat Bey questioned him at length. Baldwin described his journey, saying that he had travelled from Algeria via Egypt. Roufat seemed not to know where Algeria (or 'Alger' as Baldwin would have pronounced it) was situated, so the prisoner called it by its Arabic name, El Djezair. This might have been a mistake, he later realized, since there is an area of northern Mesopotamia also known as El Djezair. (Today it is largely in south-eastern Turkey, and appears on maps as Cizre.) Had he after all fought with the Mesopotamian army? Roufat made a note.

The interrogation was conducted with subtlety and flexibility. Roufat posed as a Bolshevik sympathizer, to see if Baldwin was a Leninist spy, and his questions roamed widely over many of the ideologies, movements and activities current in the area: Islam, British imperialism, Turanianism, Armenian revolutionary activity, Bolshevism, NER work. Despite the ignorance of Algiers (which might have been feigned) Roufat showed a thorough knowledge of political and ideological matters, typical of Turkish military intelligence. It gave the lie to any stereotype of incompetence.

Shura had replied, in answer to Roufat, that his father was Russian, and mother Armenian, whereas his parentage was the reverse; but the interrogator seemed less interested in 'Aleksandr Yablokov' (Shura's name in Russian). He asked Oliver what political views he held. 'I am a Social Democrat,' he replied. He asked Shura the same question. 'I am a Social Revolutionary,' was the reply. This was another mistake, since he might be considered to be a Dashnak revolutionary.

Roufat rose and shook hands with Oliver, who felt relieved. He looked at him and spoke slowly: 'You will go to Erzerum and be imprisoned.' Oliver was stunned. 'And my friend?', he asked. 'He is an Armenian. *Guten Tag.*'[11] But the destinies of the two friends were not yet to diverge. An easy-going NCO took charge of them both. They were led upstairs, and shown into a room, papered but bare, with two beds, two large windows and a Russian stove in the corner. Here they were left, with a sentry with rifle and bayonet posted outside. Baldwin thought it his best prison so far.

They sat down and took stock of the situation. Remarkably, they had not been searched, and they rapidly burnt incriminating items, such as Baldwin's Armenian military badge. Anxious thoughts crowded in on them. A gun boomed from the fortress. They started. It was only the midday gun, but loud sounds heard in prison take on significance, and shake the spirit like portents.

Food was less of a problem; they were allowed to have dishes brought in from the local Turkish restaurant, if they paid for them; so they ate quite well of various ragouts and tasty baklavas.

Boredom and the routine of prison life became the most difficult issues. To counter the tedium, they talked, paced up and down, and invented fairy tales in various languages. Oliver gave Shura French lessons, and Shura taught Oliver Russian. Things grew worse in the evening, when thoughts turned to their plight, and they grew morose; ears strained for sounds that they were not meant to hear, such as faint rifle shots and running footsteps on the pavement outside.

Oliver wrote a number of essays in the prison, which he then burnt in the stove. One of them concerned ambition. Ambition seemed empty; once an ambition is fulfilled, it loses its savour, and the human animal casts about for another thing to strive after. The ultimate rewards of ambition seemed to be only emptiness and disillusion. These thoughts were comforting and protective to the young prisoner.

One item they did not burn was a large map of the region. Shura had taken it from Bolshevik headquarters in Yerevan. They were looking at it one evening when the friendly Turkish NCO came in for a chat. He didn't mention it when he was with them, but took it as he left. Shura and Oliver looked and one another, sensing trouble.

Oliver was almost at once summoned to Roufat Bey's presence. The intelligence chief declared it was an Armenian Dashnak map, showing the boundaries of Armenia as laid down by President Wilson. He enquired how they had got hold it. Oliver told him of its provenance, and said they intended to use it for their journey onwards. Roufat was not impressed. It was the kind of map a spy would carry, he said. He asked Baldwin if he had any other items. The prisoner obligingly fetched the photographs of the massacre in Yerevan prison. 'Someone knows how to deal with the Dashnaktsutiun' was Roufat's reply. Oliver was angered by this response, and said a similar fate was awaiting him if Russia should manage to take Kars. 'Prisoner, sir, you won't deceive us,' was Roufat's answer.[12]

The two prisoners tried to get in touch with Near East Relief representatives in Kars, but without success. Oliver thought that the failure was deliberate, but it is possible that their message went astray. Whichever, the failure to make contact increased their sense of isolation, and made the future seem bleak. Days dragged into weeks. The routine consisted of 'walking, talking, eating, drinking, thinking, sleeping, and the more we thought the worse it was for us, and the more we talked the worse we made our position out to be'. They played games such as noughts and crosses, and wrote essays. They tried spelling their names in different languages; Oliver argued furiously with Shura about the letter B in modern Greek, saying that there was no such letter; he used a P instead for his surname. For exercise they engaged in wrestling bouts; this too would have helped them work off tension and aggression. The booming of the midday gun in the fortress ceased to stimulate anxiety, and became a daily diversion. When the Turks gained a victory in March 1921 over the Greeks, the prison authorities handed them a handful of tobacco each.[13]

An Armenian peasant brought them wood for their stove: tall, powerful and black-bearded, he had stayed behind after the Turkish Nationalists had seized Kars, and was being used by the occupying forces as a general slave, obtaining food in exchange but nothing else. He was a man of cheerful disposition, and his easy temperament created a good atmosphere for the two prisoners. One day they noticed that he no longer had his beard. He told them he had been ordered by a Turkish officer to shave it off, since it was not proper for a Christian to carry the mark of respect, age and wisdom. They had another Armenian visitor, an old man, 'of the much-suffering sort'. He would crave tobacco, and slowly shuffle his feet in imitation of an Armenian popular dance, humming the tune as he moved. Then one day he did not come any more; dead, from cold, old age, and hard work.

They managed to make contact, by tapping on the wall, with their fellow-prisoners, and the next morning they opened the door as soon as they heard their neighbours' open. The guard was some way away. A small piece of paper was thrown in. The neighbour was a young lawyer from Rostov and Tiflis, whom Shura had known. Soon they were given a volume of Pushkin's plays in the original, a book entitled *Crimes célèbres*, and an American magazine. From their fellow prisoners they learnt that there were many Armenians imprisoned in Kars and Erzerum, and that their number was diminishing by execution. (They also heard that a number of them had been repatriated, but this was false.) This lowered their morale somewhat. From the formerly bearded Armenian they heard of the indignities and brutalities that the Turks were visiting on the occupied Armenians of Kars, and the entire absence of the rule of law that accompanied the presence of the Turkish army.

Oliver took stock of the effect of prison on Shura, who beforehand (he says) had been carefree and somewhat ambitious and selfish. It is possible that the writer was obliquely referring to himself, but even if we doubt that, it shows the values which were uppermost in his mind at the time.

'In Kars I was able to watch a change: a quieter outlook, an interest in those less fortunate, a slight knowledge of the brotherhood of man and the inhumanity of man, the give and take back of Fate, the comfort of literature and the desire for knowledge, the superiority of mind over body, the bearing of disappointment after disappointment and the terror of hoping too much.'[14]

It was now early April. One day they were summoned out with the single word '*hammam*', and given the unheard-of luxury of a session in the public baths, revelling in the warm water in the tiled room. It was also a chance to pick off the many lice from the seams of their clothes. Did the bath signify a change in their circumstances? They felt happy, and looked forward to the move to Erzerum. They yearned for a change; anything would be better than the present. Optimistically they sang, on the way back to the prison:

Mit hohen Kopf' und grossem Ruhm,
Fahren wir nach Erzerum.

Finally the day of departure came, and they were taken to Kars station. In their wagon were two other men, who were also prisoners. One was a Kurd, aged about 38, named Mustapha Maksout; the other was a Circassian, tall, young and good-looking, with blue eyes and a sad preoccupied expression, a former officer in the Turkish army. His name was Yusuf Adil Kemal. Maksout had been captured by the Russians in 1916, and in the following year had become a Bolshevik, working on propaganda in Baku, but had been arrested as a spy in Nakhichevan. Kemal too had become a Bolshevik, but became disillusioned with the behaviour of the Communists, and deserted to White forces in Northern Mongolia. Recaptured by Reds, he escaped with the advance of Kolchak's Whites, and after many adventures ended up editing a Turkish Communist paper in Baku. He hated the new Turkey of Mustafa Kemal, and did not have a high opinion of Turks in general. Both Kemal and Maksout had been, they learned, condemned to death, a point which did not give them much cause for cheer. Oliver asked Kemal if he had heard any opinions of them. 'Yes,' he replied, 'you are a spy, and your companion is the interpreter. Maps were found on you. Maybe – a shot in the dark.'

They spent the night at Sarikamish, where they had to change trains owing to the different gauge in use west of that town. A local khan was their overnight lodging. Oliver notes wryly of his companions, 'They did not think much of Europeans except that they were very kind and built railways and roads for the Turks to occupy at the end of each war.' His observations on the Turks' Armenian prisoners, seen from the train, showed deep compassion for them, and clearly delineate the horror of their situation:

'Eventually our train snorted and creaked and we started slowly on the last stage of our journey, rolling through high banks of snow that had been made by the clearing of the track by poor Armenian peasants who stood waist-deep in the snow and watched us with hungry eyes, clutching their rags round their shoulders, their teeth chattering with the cold, their shovels held loosely in their yellow hands. Kemal broke off and watched them. "Ah," he said, "the poor devils. See what the Turk does to his prisoners. They die in hundreds and nobody cares." . . . The sight of these little gangs of prisoners made one's heart bleed. Here and there a body in the snow; here and there we saw a man drop as he shovelled the snow, whilst his colleagues worked on, making curious whimpering sounds, like starving dogs.'[15]

They spent three hungry days on the move through the icy landscape – 'I remember bleak bouldered stretches of land and ruined huts of stone', he says – before arriving at Erzerum.[16] Here they were shown to a low bare room, where the rain lay in pools allowing only two small dry spots to remain, each about two square feet. The prisoners were searched. A number of Baldwin's possessions were taken from him, letters and writing materials, but he managed to keep his wristwatch, a ring, and a fire opal on a chain, which he persuaded them was a religious symbol. Two men entered carrying a hammer and sets of chains. His heart sank; the chains were put in place, but, just as the iron was about to be fixed around his ankle, the order was countermanded, and the blacksmiths left. The prisoners chose the driest patch of the floor, laid down coats and blankets, and slept as well as they could, despite a steady drip, drip from the roof. Food was loaves of black bread, consisting largely of sharp pieces of grit, almost inedible except for the crust.[17]

On the fourth day, a soldier came and took away Shura. Kemal and Maksout thought it would be the end for him; but he was taken to work with other Armenians in a munitions factory. Oliver, with great generosity, gave him one of the two English £5 notes he still had. He felt Shura's absence deeply. He had been a fine companion.

Their windows looked out on to a courtyard, and there they would watch about 30 Armenian officers exercising. These motioned them to throw down a message, which, with care, they did. However, Baldwin believed that it might have been detected, for soon afterwards a soldier came in and ordered them to prepare to move. They were taken to the barracks, and after a conversation between their soldier and 'a very bejew-elled officer' they were led to a first-floor room, nine paces by four, with two broken windows, ivy'd over with strands of barbed wire, looking on to the barrack square. The plaster of the walls was mostly broken, and so were some of the floor-boards. Three dirty-looking paliasses were the only furniture.

This was a grim prison. To Oliver it was the worst. Boredom, lack of exercise, no sight of the sky, little warmth, and feverish uncertainty at their situation took their toll.[18]

Fifty other prisoners were locked up in the barracks, whom they used to watch exercising in the courtyard. Four of them were in chains; one of them was a fair-haired boy. Oliver wondered what his nationality was. One day Oliver found himself next to him at the latrine. Speaking low, in French, he found out that he was a French Armenian who had been a driver in Kars; he was in chains because he had tried to escape while driving for the Turks at Erzerum. The visits to the latrines provided a daily renewing sense of freedom, even though the prisoner was prodded by a Turkish soldier's bayonet if he walked too fast or slow.

Relations between the three prisoners became difficult. Oliver himself cannot have been an easy person to share a cell with, but he points out the faults of the others: the changeableness of Kemal, who believed his wife would come and rescue him; and the irritable atheism of Maksout, who believed that the Red Army would be his salvation. They could be generous companions too, sharing the occasional drink of yoghurt or warm milk with him, which provided a needed addition to the starvation ration of black bread. (One week Oliver stored up some of his bread ration and hid it, in order to give himself a Sunday treat. Alas, when Sunday came, there was no bread; the mice had got to it first, and nothing remained. The lesson he learnt was to enjoy what was present, and to keep none for the morrow, an economic principle he adhered to all his life.)[19]

One day Oliver noticed Charles Peers, the Irish-American NER worker who had been his friend in Yerevan, with a Turkish officer. He tried to call out to him, but he did not hear. Peers' presence in Erzerum – presumably he was en route for Constantinople – was proof that Yerevan had fallen to the Bolsheviks. Maksout was thrilled. Oliver also saw the figures of Joseph Markossian and another Yerevan acquaintance, among those in the courtyard.

Even in late April it was still cold in Erzerum. Ominous things that they heard and observed depressed the prisoners further.

> One afternoon we noticed a wretched-looking Armenian, emaciated and half-dead, being led and almost carried towards

the Town Commandant's office by several gendarmes. Our guard told Kemal the prisoner had tried to escape, and had been caught in the hills.

We wondered what would happen to him, and we kept quiet, for the sound of voices began to reach our ears from the building next door. We heard sharp words; questioning words, but no answer. The voice became louder and sharper. There was a whimper in reply. A blow . . . A scream . . . An outburst of curses. Then two or three high-pitched yells and the whimpering continued and great sobs told their story.

We three condemned prisoners looked at each other. We had not much colour in our cheeks, for imagination is quicker than sight. I think the poor fellow was bayoneted. At any rate they carried him out with a sack over his body and he was quite still.[20]

Soon afterwards, Maksout and Kemal had a fierce argument about a spider and a fly. The former, with Oliver, was watching the spider secure its prey, when Kemal came along and knocked the fly out of the spider's grasp. Maksout hit Kemal, and immediately they were at one another's throats, hitting and cursing; the sentry had to break them up. Oliver kept a sensible distance. The two did not speak to one another for a fortnight.

Oliver wrote another verse at about this time, on the subjects of freedom, return home, green fields. The language is sub-Georgian and stilted, and there are some ugly assonances, but the four stanzas are well structured, with the prisoner seeking to return in the course of each of the English seasons. In the final stanza he accepts the possibility of no return at all. The final two stanzas read thus:[21]

Not then? Have mercy on me Lord.
Perchance I shall return
When russet leaves from golden trees
Give colour forth midst fern
And moss; and all my little birds have flown
And Nature, wild and bleak, is all alone.

If it be, this poor shrunk body
Must find a lonely grave
In this wild land. My spirit, fly
Away, away and crave,
When, blended into one, come death and birth,
Sweet peace for one who knew it not on earth.

At this time, in a mood of deadly prison gloom, Oliver observed the effects of hunger. There was no real effect in the first week, he noted. The second was characterized by an interest in the arrival time of food. Hunger developed significantly in the third week, and by the fourth the prisoner was ravenous. By the fifth week the system had dropped, and hunger had lessened. In the following week, he found that he became used to it. In the seventh week, the system dropped again; this was followed by what he called low internal vitality. In the ninth week and beyond he found that he longed, in a dull lifeless way, for a piece of white bread, which seemed to be the height of edible luxury. The experience of the fourth week was the worst: Oliver and his fellow-prisoners would crawl with wet finger tips across the prison floor to pick up the crumbs – and dust – which had fallen. From this, and from what the cracks between the floorboards yielded up, they made a compote of crumbs and dirt, and obtained further relief by sucking on pieces of wood from the doorpost.[22]

He gained some spiritual peace from a dream, which he was able to embellish in his imagination in the weeks which followed. In this dream, Oliver and three of his wartime comrades had landed on a beautiful wild island. From the north, a high range of hills could be made out to the south; these appeared to divide the island into two. The friends walked to these hills, and camped at their base; there, they saw a long tropically green valley, which they named 'Avalon', where they decided to found a new country. Here the dream ended. But imagination began. In the following days, Oliver mapped out the island, and planned its future with his absent companions.

They divided it into three parts, and brought in more friends, who were settled on farms. Towns were built, and governors appointed. Precious metals were discovered. They grew crops, and reared livestock. Every man (there is no reference to women in Oliver's fantasy) had to join a trade union, based not on militancy, strikes and violence, but on the old spirit of the craftsmen's guilds. Large industries and factories were forbidden, though electricity – and presumably power stations – were permitted. Mining was nationalized, and all other work was done by the guilds. Masonic and other lodges made class distinctions impossible. There was a national dress, and equal education for all. A gendarmerie was established, and the worst punishment was deportation. Immigration 'was strictly limited', and art and religion were the main occupations of the people. The state funded the opera and theatre, which were given a competent director whom Oliver knew.

There were cooperative stores and dairies. Ownership of wealth was regulated to no more than £2000 a year and no less than £100. (It is a little unclear whether he meant owning or earning.) Motor cars were banned; transport was by rail, with horses much used. Birds could not be shot, though it was permitted to shoot lions and leopards in the hills.

On one occasion neighbouring islanders invaded, and Oliver spent a whole day conducting the operations which led to their defeat. The dream island became in many respects more real than the prison.

Oliver recommended such fantasies for all prisoners. Conservatives could imagine an island 'bristling with guns, public schools, tariff reform, wealth and poverty.' Liberals could consider 'a teetotal island, based on Free Trade, taxation of land values and nonconformity'. Socialists could improve on Oliver's island, but he warned them that raiders would have to be repelled by force, if such invaders failed to understand conferences and red flags.[23]

Nevertheless, despite this – and other fantasies, derived from the pleasurable and imaginative observation of cloud formations – the misery and crushing monotony of prison existence dragged itself out. Maksout devised an unrealistic plan of escape. Oliver says that partly through cowardice, and partly through indolence, and acceptance of the fact that they were going to die anyway, there was no point in attempting to flee. It was Ramadan. As a bonus, they received a bowl of soup at sundown. But it gave Oliver little pleasure; he bitterly contrasted the warmth, liberty and food of Ramadan in 1920, which he had spent in Algeria, with the cold imprisoned ghastliness of Erzerum.

In early June Maksout offered Oliver a Turkish pound for the silver Caucasian belt, which he had originally bought from Kemal. With the proceeds he bought yoghurt, which they all shared. It was a unique belt, and Oliver was to regret the transaction.[24]

One Sunday in mid June Oliver woke very early to find Maksout and Kemal in earnest conversation. A group of about 20 gendarmes were in the square; people were coming and going. What was it about? Deserters? A mutiny? Oliver thought they had been called in to keep the peace. His fellow prisoners disagreed. An hour later a sergeant came in and asked for Maksout. He rose. The sergeant said: 'The Town Commandant wishes to see you.' 'Shall I bring my bundle?', asked Maksout. 'No.' He followed him out. Oliver saw him pass through the main gateway of the barracks, where he lost sight of him. Some ten minutes later he heard a faint volley. Kemal heard nothing. Thus died, as Oliver noted, 'our little kindly friend of many months', a deserter and paid Bolshevik spy. Some hours later a mullah came in to collect Maksout's belongings, including the silver belt.[25]

Oliver sensed that the end was now near for him. At least he would not be killed today. Kemal for his part almost went to pieces in panic during the following days. Both prisoners were terrified every time they heard a step on the stair. They expected to hear uttered the fateful words: 'The Town Commandant wishes to see you.' But it was not to happen yet.

At about this time Oliver wrote a message, in indelible pencil, on a flimsy scrap of paper, addressed to the Town Commandant. This was in effect his will. In his published account of his time in Armenia and Turkey, Baldwin made no mention of this document, perhaps because it was so personal. The full text was as follows:[26]

Au Commandant de la ville d'Erzeroum.

Si je meurs et si les derniers voeux des condamnés ont aucun réponse dans le coeur de mes condamneurs, je vous prie M. le Commandant pour l'amour de notre Dieu commun de bien vouloir faire la suivante:- 1. Donner ma bague, ma pipe, ma montre, mon carnet, mon collier d'opal et mon crayon d'or a M. le Colonel RAWLINSON, en le priant de mon part, de le rendre a mon père, The Right Honourable Stanley Baldwin, P.C., 93 EATON SQUARE, LONDON, quand il sera libre. De lui dire que je n'avais pas peur; que notre séparation n'est pas pour toujours; et que, si je puis, je viendrai voir ma mere adorée en ésprit. Que ma famille et mes amis étaient ma dernière pensée, et que j'étais le victime de la misfortune. Je crois fortement en Dieu et en notre rencontre au ciel. Je viellerai de l'autre monde sur ma famille et je les attenderai.

O.R.Baldwin.

[Translation. To the Town Commandant, Erzerum. If I die and if the last wishes of the condemned elicit no response in the heart of those who have condemned me, I beg you, Sir Commandant, for the love of our common God, to be so good as to do the following: 1. Give my ring, my pipe, my watch, my note-book, my opal collar-stone and my gold pencil to Colonel Rawlinson, asking him on my behalf to give them to my father, the Rt. Hon. Stanley Baldwin, P.C., 93 Eaton Square, London, when he obtains his freedom. To tell him that I had no fear; that our separation is not for ever; and that, if I can, I shall come to see my beloved mother in spirit. That my family and my friends were my last thought, and that I was the victim of misfortune. I strongly believe in God and in our meeting in the sky. I shall watch over my family from the other world and I shall wait for them. O.R.Baldwin]

This surely is a moving testament, showing warm humanity in the concern for family and friends.

About four days after Maksout's death, on a mild afternoon, there was much activity in the courtyard. The sergeant appeared at the door. 'The Englishman?' 'Yes, sir.' 'The Town Commandant wishes to see you.' Baldwin followed, and was soon in the presence of the commandant and his bejewelled adjutant. The latter spoke. 'You are going to Trebizond.' Silence. 'You need not be frightened. You are being sent home to England.' Silence. 'Don't you believe it?' 'No.' '*Wallahi*, it's true. You are leaving this evening.' Oliver mentioned the fate of Colonel Alfred (Toby) Rawlinson, who had left for Trebizond, only to be brought back to Erzerum as a hostage. This, Baldwin was told, was different, and all was arranged. He must prepare to leave; another Englishman would be accompanying him.[27]

Oliver was not offered a cigarette, so he felt inclined to believe the adjutant. On his return to the cell, Kemal fell into a paroxysm of panic. 'They will kill you away in the hills, where no one will know. Poor Maksout, poor Baldwin! And what will they do to me?' Oliver felt that it might be true, but he was past caring.

Soon a tall man in khaki was in their presence; he was the Army Service Corps driver from Alexandropol, who had been taken by the Turks; his name was Mahoney. He was now implicitly trusted by the Turks; indeed Colonel Rawlinson, Baldwin's predecessor in captivity in Erzerum, was convinced that Mahoney had joined the Turks and had been responsible for his own terrible treatment in prison.[28] Baldwin was unaware of his companion's allegiance; all he says is that he enjoyed conversing in proper English for the first time since leaving Alexandropol. A Turkish sergeant-major joined them, and told them to follow him. They were soon on the way out of Erzerum, travelling in a horse-drawn carriage with no brakes.

They stopped at a khan some twelve miles outside Erzerum; Oliver found the coffee and real Turkish bread wonderful after the ghastly prison fare. After it they slept in the khan.

Oliver awoke the next day to the half-dreamlike sensation of being secure in the hands of a deity; an apt metaphor for his deliverance from prison. Now freedom was real; the day dawned fresh and new, after the foul enclosed horror of the prisons. He rose to watch a brilliant Eastern morning under the open sky. There were camels on the road, their distant bells tinkling clearly in the still crisp air. He stretched. It seemed too good to be true.

On they sped, in their alarming brakeless vehicle, as far as Khojapunar. They looked weird, Oliver noted. He himself was bearded, his hair was down to his shoulders, and he was wearing a Caucasian hat, a khaki over-coat, Guards plus-fours and Russian boots. The Turks here appeared to take him for a holy man of great devoutness, because they were most polite and humble.

Next morning, after a delicious swim in the river and fifteen minutes of serious clothes de-lousing, they continued to Trebizond. Past a batch of Armenian prisoners, wretchedly begging for food – Oliver felt like the marquis in *A Tale of Two Cities*, driving by in his coach heedless of his starving tenants – they reached the first important town, Baiburt. Beyond Baiburt the mountains reared up unceasingly, one chain after another, until the Pontic Alps themselves appeared, 'terribly high'. The air grew cold. At every stage Oliver relished his freedom – his ability to gather the wild flowers which bedeck this landscape, and to bathe in the waterfalls. As they travelled through the heart of Pontus, the villages and individual houses were noticeably Greek in style. (Only a year later almost all the Pontic Greeks were to be deported or killed.) Finally, Baldwin was granted Xenophon's vision – the Black Sea – and he could not forbear to exclaim the words uttered by his Athenian predecessor, *Thalassa, thalassa*. (Not being sure of the pronunciation, he also called out *Thalatta, thalatta*, just in case.) Trebizond itself reminded him of Mytilene, with its small white villas with red roofs.[29] A visit to the barber and the baths were urgent priorities, soon accomplished.

Baldwin ran into Charles Peers again, and caught up with news of Yerevan and of Dr Ussher.

On 29 June 1921 Baldwin and Mahoney sailed out of Trebizond harbour aboard the Lloyd-Triestino steamer *Avantino*. At every stage Oliver, unaware that his companion was a Turkish agent, thought he might meet a Turkish soldier, who would order him back to Erzerum and to prison. The vessel sailed west to Constantinople, stopping at Kerasond, Ordu and Samsun, which afforded the weakened former captive a chance to swim.[30]

In Constantinople (which was still under Allied control) he stayed at a small Greek hotel, and ran into Shakhkhatuni, who had now finished with politics and was longing to get back into the cinema. Baldwin had to wait some time in the city before money arrived, and after obtaining a temporary British passport he set off aboard the Orient Express for Paris. At the Serbian frontier he was arrested as a suspected Bolshevik, but allowed to pass with an armed guard in his compartment: he managed to convince the authorities in Belgrade that he was not a Communist. From Paris he travelled directly to London, arriving on the day of the unveiling of the statue of Edward VII at the Duke of York's steps.

In Oliver's words, 'There is no more to tell.' His astonishing Armenian adventure, comprising warfare, revolutions, long lonely journeys in the bitter cold, arbitrary nightmarish imprisonments, near-starvation, and impending dread of execution, was now over.

If his travels were over, the political conclusions that he drew from his experiences were of significance for him for much of his life, and so merit a glance.[31]

Baldwin took as his starting point the Treaty of Sèvres of 10 August 1920, which recognized an independent state of Armenia, with frontiers to be determined by President

Wilson. He recalled Lloyd George's glowing statements on behalf of Armenia in the closing months of the war. But nothing said or done by the Allied powers had had any practical effect in the region. As the Transcaucasian republics hastened to the end of their brief first independence, a number of factors were responsible, but the chief was 'the lack of foresight and knowledge displayed by Mr Lloyd George's foreign secretary', i.e. Lord Curzon.

Baldwin also blamed the British Labour Party, which had consistently urged withdrawal of British troops from Georgia, at a time when their presence would have saved both Armenia and Georgia from communism, though he admitted that part of the problem lay with the Georgian Menshevik government, which had seen the presence of British troops as an infringement of its sovereignty.

Curzon, Baldwin surmised, would have realized the outcome of a British troop withdrawal. He should have resigned rather than been party to the surrender of free countries.

As for Bolshevism, Baldwin saw it as a psychological disease rather than a form of society. It was a reaction – a form of twisted tsardom, of anti-religious mania resulting from too much religion. This is a helpful and insightful way of looking at totalitarian ideology, and one which Baldwin was to repeat when in 1939 he pointed out the 'suicidal mania' of Nazism. Few commentators today like to look too closely at the elements of psychopathology within totalitarianism. It is easier just to say it was (or is) wicked. At the same time Baldwin noted how 'step, by step, without any apparent effort, the powers played into Lenin's hands'.

Baldwin made a comparison between Bolshevism and nationalism: the latter was a fine creed to draw a nation together, he believed, but later on, intolerance often sets in, leading to arrogance towards strangers and even fellow-countrymen, resulting, in Armenia, in 'the tactless, alienating treatment of the Erivan Tartar population by the Armenians'. In other words, the Armenian government's high-handed behaviour towards its minority Muslim population had been foolish and wrong.

Allied treatment of Turkey after the Ottoman defeat in 1918 Baldwin summed up wryly: 'Turkey acted as a man who is being taken to prison by guards who pay no attention to him – he escapes and bands himself with others against the forces of law and order. Luckily for him, the guards gave up and returned home and told the newspapers how brave their prisoner was and how polite. The fact of his having murdered thousands of Christians did not matter – there was no oil in Armenia.'

Some rather unwise comments – but typical of the time – on 'national characteristics' follow Baldwin's political reflections. He returned to the attack on Lord Curzon; and concluded that foreign policy should not be in the hands of one man, but in the hands of a committee – a remarkably impractical idea. However his premiss was sound: there was a need for fresh minds as permanent secretaries, to avoid the syndrome of 'Ah yes, I know all about it, I was in Zenda in '87.'

Baldwin also put in a word for the Assyro-Chaldaeans, the Christians of the East sometimes known as Nestorians. They had fought valiantly in 1917–18, but had been completely forgotten in the settlement. Their leader, General Agha Petros, became a good friend of Baldwin's, visiting him in Oxfordshire after the war.

Showing – for once – an accurate Macdonald foresight, Baldwin predicted in the last chapter of his memoir that 'one day independence may come again to Trans-Caucasia,' something that almost every other commentator, before 1991, had considered impossible. His forecast was however based less on Celtic fantasy than on empirical evidence. He had seen that Leninism was not rock solid, as others held it to be, and would continue to hold it to be. The experience of seeing communism crumble in Armenia on 18 February 1921 had indicated to him the possibility of its final demise.

CHAPTER 6

Recovery and Disillusion;
East Africa and Lausanne

Oliver Baldwin returned to England dressed in the same jumble of clothes that had elicited devout respect after his release. His shabby, *outré* appearance was an accurate representation of his fragmented self, worn down and disorientated by the eastern experiences.

It had been an adventure, and he had sought adventure. But it had developed a momentum of its own, which had nearly destroyed him. Infantry instruction in Armenia had been a natural consequence of the competence he had shown as an officer on the Western front. However, he had not bargained for the remoteness of his destination, amid the treeless cold of Asia; and he had made a misjudgement in seeking to escape the return of the Communists via Turkey rather than Georgia or Iran. He had overstretched himself. At the same time he had gained a moment of political inspiration in witnessing the overthrow of Bolshevism on 18 February; and the mere fact of having survived the rigours of flight and prison had strengthened his capacity for survival.

Astley was not a good environment to return to, and he became convinced that he would have to leave home. The family reduced him to childhood dependency again. Their generosity, expressed in acts like taking him to France for a holiday, induced feelings of claustrophobia, depression and the desire to escape. He needed distance from his parents and sisters, and other surroundings in which to explore his selfhood and come to terms with what he had been through. Images of prison guards were often with him; there were recurrent nightmares; and not all the family were sympathetic. One of his sisters (probably Margot) was the severest. She casually declared to him that she didn't believe a word of what he told her of his experiences; he had never been to prison, but had invented the whole story, with the aim of drawing attention to himself. Such baseless and narrow-minded harshness was more than Oliver could bear (especially in that there was a grain of psychological truth in it, since attention mattered to him). He pulled out a pistol and threatened her with it. According to his sister Lorna, he was only restrained by the intervention of his aunt, Lily Whittington. One evening – it may have been the same day – he was on the point of shooting himself in the garden.[1]

He had to get away, and he went where he had in the past found peace and tranquillity: the Kiplings' house at Burwash. Even there he felt ill at ease, and escaped again. He borrowed a car from Elsie Kipling, and made off to the west country. After some weeks of peace and recovery he returned to Astley.

In the following winter Oliver saw much of a young woman, Dorothea Helen Mary Arbuthnot, known as Doreen, to whom he became engaged on 22 January 1922. Her father, Gerald Arbuthnot, had been a political ally of SB, having been vice-chancellor of the Primrose League in 1912; he had been killed in action in 1916. Her mother, Dulce Oppenheim, had been a lively social butterfly before her marriage. Doreen had taken part in some of the theatrical frolics held at Astley, and Oliver had flirted innocently with her. Now he thought that marriage would enable him to escape from home. Ten years later Oliver accepted that this had been his main motive for the engagement. Love for Doreen played no part in it.[2]

Conveniently, early in February he was offered the post of special correspondent for the *Morning Post*, and was told to go at once to Kenya, via South Africa, to cover the Indian question, which was then the main issue in East African politics. Shortly afterwards he left from Southampton. George Bambridge was to accompany him as far as Madeira. Doreen came to the quayside to see him off. George, with a sense of realism, said to Oliver, 'You'll never marry her.' The engagement was eventually broken off, and five years later Doreen married a certain Hubert Woodward.

Oliver was glad to get away from the English winter to the longed-for south, but he had not escaped the English. He found that he was allowed no peace to read, as his shipmates played non-stop games or charged about the ship while whistling tunes with mouths filled with biscuits. He felt a stranger here, as he had in the grey chill of England. Thereafter he preferred to take a German or Dutch steamer.

South Africa was in the grip of the Rand rebellion at the time, a bitter industrial dispute which had started at the Kimberley diamond mines. Oliver did not linger at Cape Town. He sailed on to East London and Port Elizabeth, and finally Durban, where he stayed with an old comrade from the Bushey days, Lewis Reynolds. Reynolds introduced him to surfing: Oliver was given a surf-board, and told to wait for the wave, then dive under it. Unfortunately the board reared up and hit him on the head, and despite an attempt to retrieve it, it made off on its own to the beach. Oliver, having turned a couple of somersaults in the raging brine, was covered in bruises and confusion, and tried to look composed as he left the water. It was the end of his surfing. But he loved Durban.[3]

Slowly he made his way up the coast, finally disembarking at Mombasa for Nairobi. Here too there were riots (against a recently introduced poll tax, and Kenya's change of status from protectorate to colony). There was a dispute too about the status of the Indian community, who made up the merchant and foreman class: should they be classed as whites and be allowed to live in white areas, or be classed with the blacks? The question remained unsolved for some time. Oliver met the Indians, and found them good company. The paper at home did not like the articles that he wrote for it, and after printing one of them spiked the rest.[4]

From Nairobi he travelled to Nakuru to see the salt lakes, and he passed through glorious country. He went on to Molo, staying with Mr Powys-Cobb, one of the first settlers. He travelled on to Koru, to stay with 'CA' (possibly Ambrose Coghill), to whom he had been given a letter of introduction by Harold Nicolson. The scenery here he described as a veritable Vale of Avalon, and he half-expected to see King Arthur's white sarcophagus. He took a train inland, to stay for a week or so with a friend running a school for children of settlers, at which he briefly taught.

Restlessness seems to have stayed with him, and it was not long before he felt a need to see England again. En route he paid a visit to Djibouti, which seemed to him the hottest place on earth.

The autumn of 1922 found Oliver in better shape, but still feeling the effects of his experiences in the east. He worked on a novel at Astley, and lived in extreme peace, breathing in the healing air of the English countryside, exploring the woods, gently observing the insects and wild animals, and talking with local farmers. These were times of deep relaxation and serious consideration of the future; of working out his allegiances, and of studying political and economic matters in a radical way. Apart from visiting London to appear in a fringe comedy (Harold Chapin's *The Marriage of Columbine*), he spent the time at Astley. He read a number of serious texts on politics, society and economics, by Thomas Gisborne (whose writings on social ethics were back-lit by the rich natural scenery of the then unenclosed Needwood Forest), P. J. Dunning, Henry George, Karl Marx and Lord Hugh Cecil. Two authors especially attracted him: Disraeli, whose novels depicted the English class system as he saw it; and William Morris, whose *News from Nowhere* he read with excitement. Here was a picture of life as he would like to live it, and one which he thought would be attractive to the thousands of people living in factory towns.[5]

His curiosity led him to read the biography of Morris written by Professor J. W. Mackail, husband of Stanley Baldwin's first cousin Margaret, nee Burne-Jones. This made a deep impression, and he made a special note of part of Morris's speech at the grave of a certain Alfred Linnell, killed in the Trafalgar Square riots of 1887:[6]

'Our friend who lies here has had a hard life, and met with a hard death; and if society had been differently constituted his life might have been a delightful, a beautiful and a happy one. It is our business to organize for the purpose of seeing that such things shall not happen; to try and make this earth a beautiful and happy place.'

But Morris and his socialism did not solve the problem of what Oliver should do. He was no nearer finding a job. He thought over the possibilities: 'soldiering, war, travel, the lonely places, exploring.' No conclusion. 'Business, office work – no, the thought was intolerable.' Politics? But which side? He thought of Toryism, maybe even as one of those maverick Tories who are thorns in the side of the party machine, but the critique of existing society that he was developing seemed to put allegiance to the Tories out of the question. There was only one thing to do: wait.

While waiting he received a telegram; could he join the Armenian Delegation at the forthcoming Lausanne Conference, which had been called to work out and regularize the matters outstanding between Britain and the new Turkey of Mustafa Kemal (Atatürk)?

He agreed, and set out for Lausanne in late November 1922. He was to be attached to the delegation of the Armenian Revolutionary Federation (Dashnaktsutiun), of which he had indeed been a member since 1921 – he was the only non-Armenian member. Always in his mind was the party's brave decision which had led to the ousting of the Bolsheviks from Yerevan on 18 February.[7]

Relations between himself and the British delegation at the Lausanne Conference (led by Lord Curzon, whom he disliked) were characterized by disharmony. Oliver noted that British diplomats do not like to find, at conferences on foreign affairs, British subjects attached to foreign delegations. They are classed as 'unhelpful'. Oliver was seen as such. He recalled the example of Lawrence of Arabia, someone with whom Baldwin shared certain characteristics, though Lawrence was more inclined to self-dramatization. The situation was undoubtedly made more complex by the fact that Harold Nicolson was a member of the British delegation, and he was a friend of Oliver. Here Nicolson was a servant of the crown, in close attendance on Lord Curzon.

Turkey won all the diplomatic sets at Lausanne; the Armenian delegation was not even allowed a hearing in the main conference hall. By any standards, except those of weak compliance with sheer power, that constituted a grave injustice. It slammed shut the furnace door of oblivion on the Armenian genocide of 1915, and invalidated the brave efforts that Armenians had made in the months following the defection of Russia towards the Allied victory of 1918. It reinforced the notion that parts of the political and social experience of nations are expendable, and can be ignored or overruled for reasons of diplomatic convenience.

Although the Armenians were not admitted to the full sessions of the conference – the Turks threatened to walk out if they were allowed to participate, on the technical grounds that the Soviet state represented Armenia – they did gain access to a meeting of the conference sub-commission, at its meeting of 26 December 1922. Alexander Khatisian records the intense anxiety and strain on the entire Armenian delegation, poised at last to be heard in an official capacity. The Turks were absent. The day was bitterly wet and cold. Five individuals travelled in the same car to the conference sub-commission: Avetis Aharonian, Gabriel Noradunkian, Leon Pashalian, Khatisian and Oliver Baldwin. As the Armenian leaders entered the conference chamber, Khatisian records: 'Baldwin was moved. He waited three whole hours before the conference door, saying that, at a moment like this, it was impossible for him to be apart from us.'[8]

But the Armenians gained no benefit from the Lausanne Conference. Curzon, by not seriously challenging Kemalist Turkey on the Armenian question and by indirectly colluding with Soviet Russia, allowed a diplomatic error and consequent injustice to take place, which from the early 1990s has begun to be put right, with, following the collapse of the Soviet Union, the re-emergence of Armenia with an independent and authentic voice of its own. Hitherto its status had been that of an adjunct of Soviet Russia, which is what Curzon's diplomacy permitted.

In 1922–3 this matter was of consuming importance for Baldwin. He had identified with the Armenian cause to a great extent, with the idealism and hatred of injustice typical of youth. It was moreover part of his experience, and no mere intellectual or emotional exercise. The Armenians' response to him was positive: we can see this by the fact that he had travelled to the meeting of 26 December with leading Armenian national figures. But now the struggle was seen to have been in vain. European diplomats had destroyed Armenia juridically, as surely as Turkish general Kiazim Karabekir had destroyed the independent state militarily. The significance for Oliver was that it constituted the diplomatic equivalent of his sister saying to him 'You made it all up.' It made him feel even more alienated from the English upper classes (who had often indeed been keener to identify with the ruling Turks – who after all too ruled an empire – than with their subject nationalities, whose Byronic romantic nationalism was ridiculed by the icy impassive whimsy of imperial superiority). It fuelled a sense of injustice.

Oliver Baldwin returned from Lausanne disheartened and disillusioned. Political changes were taking place at home – changes would occur too in his own life. On 19 May 1923

Bonar Law resigned the premiership owing to illness. He was a good friend of the Baldwins, and they were saddened. Three days later Stanley Baldwin became Prime Minister, and the family moved from 11 to 10 Downing Street. Oliver had stayed at no. 11, but he was destined never to stay at no. 10. The changes in the family fortunes were a symbol and a mirror to changes which were taking place in his own life. Oliver was emerging from the indecisive, weakened state brought on by prison and uncertainty. The time was approaching when he would claim his life for himself.[9]

CHAPTER 7

The Break with Astley

Baldwin had to make decisions about the future – indeed about his own essential being and identity. These decisions were of two kinds, political and personal. They were hard to make, so it is not surprising that they were accompanied by pain and hurt. Oliver's decisions taken in 1923 affected the rest of his life.

Despite the friendship with the Law family, he had viewed the government headed by Bonar Law (in which his father had served as Chancellor of the Exchequer) as ineffective, and, as he put it, tolerant of flagrant injustices.[1] He felt indignant. A note of real anger colours his political reflections of this time. There is no doubt that much of this indignation was genuine and appropriate. All Oliver's public and political experience so far – in the war, in Armenia, and at Lausanne – reflected badly upon conservatism and the old order; and his radical Macdonald and Ridsdale heritages were persuasive enough to indicate to him that alternatives were possible. Yet however strong the intellectual and theoretical bases for his anti-conservative stance, there is at the same time a half-hidden element of defiance of his father, and an unconscious edging of wild anger. On the conscious personal level father and son stayed on close terms all their lives. His father was at his most gentle, humane, tolerant and forgiving when writing to Oliver, and Oliver responded with sentiments of great fondness, even if they lacked the instinctive affection of his father. But at the same time the son rejected the world-view and politics of the father. Personal fondness could not co-exist at close quarters with theoretical rejection, and in 1923 a fundamental break occurred, which brought resolution.

Oliver expressed his anti-Tory scorn in newspaper articles. One does not have to be a dedicated follower of anthropological or psychoanalytical theory to see this as a way of – probably unconsciously – confronting his father, in the fierce struggle (originating in early life, yet often acted out well into adolescence and beyond) to challenge and supplant father. This can be seen in Frazerian terms of destroying the old ascendancy so that a new age might be born: in the standard myth, the supplanter hunts to death the incumbent king, pursuing him with his sword through the wood. It can also be seen in Freudian terms, of the child struggling with father in order to prize mother away so that he can win her for himself. There were classically Freudian elements to the relationship between Cissie and her son; she idealized him, and invested in him more emotion than mere mother love. He for his part basked in this affection. In the context of the Freudian struggle, he had virtually won mother, and seen off father, although sometimes the power of taboo emerged in him, and the love turned to rancorous hate and anger. Oliver had strong rational reasons for the clear break with his father's conservatism, but he also seems to have been working through primitive conflicts which relate as much to the King of the Wood, the Fisher King or to Oedipus as to poverty and unemployment.

If we look at the anger which Oliver expressed at this time, it is perhaps appropriate to ask: how much of it was mature anger and indignation at public events in the real world, and how much was unresolved infantile narcissistic rage, that is, a hang-over from a child's fury either at not being the centre of attention, or at not having the total attention of the mother all the time, a private anger which can become inappropriately projected on to public events in adult years? At this distance, there is probably no certain answer; what one can say is that sometimes Oliver's anger showed an emotional content which indicated a link to his own life history. It was not a dominant issue in his outlook – indeed, for the most part his temperament was placid, and he hated noise and fuss – but sometimes we catch a glimpse of this anger, and it could be fierce.

In the conscious world of public affairs things were moving towards an open break. In May 1923 the *Westminster Gazette* published an interview with Oliver.[2] Its opening paragraph read, 'Mr Stanley Baldwin must be the first Prime Minister with a son who is a proved Socialist.' The interviewer learnt, 'in the quiet seclusion of the drawing room at 11 Downing Street', of Oliver's adventures and privations in Armenia. Much of what followed concerned his loathing of the Bolsheviks, who had (he said) showed themselves 'completely regardless of the welfare of Socialists and the lovers of liberty'. Baldwin also said how honoured he felt to be a member of the Armenian social-democratic party Dashnaktsutiun. But his public stance was somewhat undermined by an adolescent colouring of semi-nihilistic disillusion, in which private self-obsession was interwoven with, and masked by, concern for the public good: 'There is nothing for me to do here now . . . The British Labour Party have broken my heart because, whilst ostensibly belonging to the Second International, they back up at every turn the Third International of Moscow, which is every day crushing liberty and murdering anyone who raises his voice in defence of public right.' He concluded by saying that he was planning to go to East Africa in September.

However, political salvation came in terms of an open letter printed the following month in *Justice*, the organ of the Social-Democratic Federation (SDF). This letter, written by Fred H. Gorle, invited Oliver Baldwin to join the Federation, on the strength of the interview published in the *Westminster Gazette*. The SDF (founded in 1884 by H. M. Hyndman, a wealthy, business-orientated radical, who also had a talent for cricket) was a genuinely socialist, anti-capitalist organization. It was non-dogmatically Marxist, and was the furthest left constituent of the Labour Party, being a member of the Second International. It opposed Leninist Communism. (Social-Democracy should not be confused with the British Social Democrats of the 1980s. The two were quite unalike. The SDF's political equivalent in our time would be something between the Socialist Labour Party and Old Labour, or perhaps a less in-your-face version of the Socialist Workers' Party.)

The letter in *Justice* informed Baldwin that he had the chance to 'render inestimable service to Socialism'. Indeed he had. The Tory prime minister's son would be a great catch for the SDF. Gorle ended his letter by saying: 'In all humility I urge you to throw in your lot, if not as a member, at least as a co-worker for a common object, into the Social-Democratic Federation. We would welcome you greatly as a fellow member.'[3]

The letter gave Oliver pause for thought. He was convinced that conservatism was moribund, and would never cure unemployment and the likelihood of future war. Socialism was the only possibility for the future. (The brotherhood of socialism might also become a replacement family for him.) Yet – for his father had just been raised to the premiership – how could he become a committed socialist, and still remain in the house of the Conservative prime minister?

There appeared to be two options. One was to stay silent. To shut up and stay at home. To do nothing about injustice, unemployment, the destruction of small nations such as the Armenians, but instead to become a political eunuch at Astley and mouth pleasantries about happy family life to the popular press. That way he would entirely suppress his allegiance and his identity in the service of his father's career and of the politics of his father's generation. This course of action would have been commensurate with a Victorian idea of duty.

The other way was to get out; to go and live somewhere else, and to achieve the painful and complex matter of separation from the family home; thereby to become a full individual in his own right, Oliver, no longer son-of-Stanley (though still son of Stanley), able to make up his own mind and write and do what his experience and his conscience told him was right to do. This is the course of action he chose. Gorle's letter offered him a way out of the stifling dependent passively dutiful inertia of the drawing-rooms of 11 and 10 Downing Street. It also showed him a way forward, so that he could emerge from the deadened negativity of adolescence into positive action and the quest for maturity.

Undoubtedly too the decision to get out was spurred on by sexual matters. After the fiasco with Doreen, he realized that she was quite wrong for him, and that, really, sex with women was just not his thing. His emotional life centred much more on men. He had shown devotion beyond duty to his men in wartime (especially to his pal Jim Brady), he had become entangled with Joseph Markossian in Yerevan, his dream in captivity in Erzerum had only included men; the whole gist of his emotional life was homosexual, and indicated the need for a male rather than a female partner. Needless to say, for all the broadmindedness of the Baldwin family, it would not have been possible to have a live-in male lover at the parental home in Worcestershire, let alone at 10 Downing Street.

At some date in the first half of 1923 he met John Parke Boyle, perhaps in a hotel. (Oliver's sister Margot, not an impartial witness, held that they met in a gents' lavatory.) John – Johnnie as he was almost always known – was to be his companion for the rest of his life. He was almost six years older than Oliver, having been born on 30 July 1893. He was the third son of Major Charles John Boyle and Lilian Kennedy Boyle (née Pochin), of The Priory, Great Milton, Oxon, today a most distinguished restaurant. Major Boyle's father, Johnnie's grandfather, was the Revd Richard

Cavendish Boyle, the fifth son of the 8th Earl of Cork and Orrery. John was educated at Bradfield, and seems to have done surprisingly little thereafter, apart from dispensing his great charm and wit to all his friends – though during the Great War he worked in some capacity at the Ministry of Labour. At one time he ran a teashop in Oxford, a stone's throw from Carfax – perhaps something like the Moorish Tea Lounge of 44 Queen St; here the chief innovation was that the customers, most of whom would have been young, romantic-looking undergraduates, were required to lounge aesthetically on cushions on the floor rather than to sit upright at table. (Another Oxford teashop of the time had the appealing name of The Candid Friend.) In his passport he described his occupation as 'gentleman'.[4]

John Boyle's sister Lilian Joanna had married the 7th Earl of Macclesfield in 1909; the Macclesfields, like the Boyles, were an Oxfordshire family, with their seat at Shirburn Castle, Watlington. John did not get on easily with his sister; nevertheless the Macclesfields (who owned extensive lands) rented to him one of their properties, Farm House in Shirburn. He was living there by 1923.

Oliver did not instantly go to Oxfordshire to live with Johnnie and start making a home together. In the spring of 1923 he went back to France, to re-visit the battlefields for the second time (he had been with his father a couple of years earlier); from there he went on to Madrid to stay with George Bambridge, who was with the British Embassy there. He found Spain deeply feudal – the outlook of the nobility was 'at least 200 years behind the time', and visited Toledo and Aranjuez; he also went walking in the Guadarramas for a couple of days with a young Russian. Oliver was somewhat bemused by driving habits in Spain, especially by the regulation that in town one drove on the left, but out of town on the right. He noted the pile of cars on the edge of town.[5]

Family relations seem to have been fraught with tension and misunderstanding at this time. SB wrote from

10 Downing Street to his elder son on 25 August:

'You have vanished into thin air and I don't know where you are or what you are doing, but my love is with you and I follow in spirit! I am just at the end of my tether and am off to Aix to try and get a short rest. Don't you ever try my job: it doesn't stop night or day.'

Stanley wondered whether Oliver was off back to Kenya; clearly the elder son had somewhat defiantly not told the family of his plans. Father would tell his banker to send a contribution, since steamer journeys were expensive. He added that he could not send as much as he would like, since he was rather heavily overdrawn. (SB had made over vast sums to the British treasury as his own contribution towards the war effort – a gesture of unequalled generosity and gratitude to the country.) Oliver was encouraged to seek fortune abroad. His father thought that he would be far happier in a new country; there was much to trouble and discourage in the old world. Stanley reminded him that he was never far from his thoughts. He signed off: 'Your loving old Father'.[6]

Oliver took his time before deciding to move in with Johnnie Boyle. The earliest letters to survive from him to Johnnie date from the summer of 1923, and are about plans for the weekend. They are couched in straightforward, business-like language, almost curt; the second, dated 1 August 1923, is as follows: 'Friday I shall, *deo volente atque spiritu volente* [God and the spirit willing], take the 4.40 to Watlington, arriving at 6.10, where I shall see you. *Que les connaissances d'un hotel deviennent les amis de la ferme.*'[7] [May hotel acquaintances become farm friends.]

There were still some doubts about their shared menage. These are indicated by a letter from Alex Carlsen, the Baldwins' housekeeper in both Astley and London. She claimed to have been an illegitimate descendant of the Danish royal family, and a photograph of her portrait does show a strong resemblance to Queen Alexandra. She later married an American Rhodes scholar named Oscar Fulton Davisson Jr. Alex Carlsen was clearly a woman of great directness and humanity, who spoke her mind unreservedly. Writing from Astley to Johnnie Boyle on 31 August, she said:[8]

> My dear you must not trouble your mind about Oliver, his mind is quite made up to go to you & make his home there, and he could not go to any one better than you. There is nothing he dislikes about you that I do know, he would not go if there were anything; but what about you John I have told him he must give as much as he takes, for I am afraid you will give him all & receive so little in return, to a nature like your[s], I am so afraid for you. John tell me how it is you love Oliver as you do? to me you are like a lover to some wonderful woman instead of it being a man. I am going to London with him next Thursday to look through his things & to have packed up what he wants to be sent down to you. We shall go up by the early train[,] arrive at Paddington about 11 & go straight to 10 Downing Street. I expect you could not manage to come up for the day in your car, it would be nice. I am so glad John you feel so happy about your visit here last weekend, it was really lovely to have you here, but these beautiful dreams alas so often have a very short life so many of us are apt to forget, & turn our backs on things that are beautiful & thereby often live in a sea of regrets in after years . . . I wish you all the best of luck in your undertakings I know what it will mean to you in many ways, you will always find me on your side in what ever way destiny will point out for you.

The letter is remarkable for its openness, and for its spirit of acceptance, and of seeking happiness above all, and not even considering what conventional moralists and prudes (or the law) might think. Its message is simply, be happy. It also indicates that Alex Carlsen was very devoted to him – more so, it seems, than to Oliver.

By the late summer Oliver was living at Shirburn, and had joined the Social-Democratic Federation. At the same time he was finishing his novel, which he entitled *Konyetz* (Russian for 'The End'). It was written under the nom-de-plume of Martin Hussingtree, the name of a village just outside Worcester. He says he used a pseudonym because he anticipated sniping on the grounds that his work had only been published because he was the son of his father. However, the author liked disguises and pseudonyms, and the false name probably generated a gratifyingly theatrical thrill.

Oliver still travelled, despite the apparent decision to live with Johnnie Boyle. In the autumn he went to Holland to meet a socialist leader. At home, the issue of Protection vs. Free Trade had in November forced Stanley Baldwin to call a general election. In the following weeks, Oliver campaigned for the first time for socialism, giving assistance to a fellow SDF member, E. J. Pay, in his North Buckinghamshire constituency. *Justice* expressed its appreciation of his work, and noted that he 'would have done more had he not had an attack of malaria at the weekend preceding the polls'.[9] The London *Evening Standard* gave a rather more sceptical account of his support for the left: 'Mr Ostwald [sic] Baldwin, who had so far contented himself with emitting startling interviews of an advanced nature from his father's address at 10 Downing Street, last night appeared on a Labour platform . . . The government, he declared, had been in office a whole year and have done nothing but twiddle their fingers . . . "The only Protection I desire is protection from a government like this Conservative government"'.[10]

He also, more significantly, spoke on behalf of the Islington candidates Fred Montague and Will Cluse. Oliver's speech of 30 November 1923 was seen by a section of the popular press as a confrontation with his father – the external dramatization of a family feud, amounting almost to treachery. But what did Oliver say? The following day the *Evening Standard* reported his appearance and speech beneath a quadruple headline: 'Comrade Oliver Baldwin /

Impression of Premier's Socialist Son / As a Labour Lion / Expounding His Creed to London Audience'.[11]

'Amid plaudits of delight, a rather tall young man with tawny hair parted in the middle, a little upcurled moustache, and a short pointed beard stood on stage of the Caledonian Road baths last night . . . A young Russian of the aristocratic type . . . or again an art student, exceptionally well groomed, from the Quartier Latin . . . perhaps you are reminded of John Tanner in *Man and Superman* – or in other words, Mr Bernard Shaw when he was young . . . He has the arty appearance of the William Morris days because mentally he is living in them . . . This young man, with the arresting blue eyes of a visionary, is Mr Oliver Baldwin.'

The *Evening Standard* gave its readers some of the speech: 'As regards my father, I am not opposing him. I am opposing principles that are not going to lead anywhere.' The young socialist then attacked Curzon for making peace with Turkey at the expense of the Armenians. 'Then [the *Standard* continued] we had some William Morris phrases about replacing the class-made distinctions with a solid fraternity of love and the joy of work.' Oliver ended by saying one should live up to the ideal 'in spite of the shunning of one's so-called friends'. This was hardly the stuff of family treachery.

The father-son theme was repeated in another interview with the *Westminster Gazette*.[12]

'People all over the country have been demanding to know why I am opposing my father. I do not oppose my father. But I do oppose principles which I can see are leading nowhere, and I do oppose any government which has failed to carry out even in part the post-war promises that were made to the men who went out to the trenches.

'I told my father once that he ought to come over to the Labour cause. He would make the finest Labour leader in the country.' (Maybe, in this confident irony, the psychoanalytically minded can hear a suggestion of Oedipus not slaying his father but offering him a night with Jocasta.)

The Prime Minister's son stressed the importance of courage and idealism in politics, qualities that the Tories had lacked. He had received many requests to speak on Labour platforms; but since he was ill with malaria, he would have to return home immediately. The paper also remarked that, at the Islington meeting, Baldwin had been introduced to a sandy-haired youth wearing a Communist badge, to whom he had said, 'I don't like to see that you know,' adding:

'I will never stand on the same platform as an avowed Communist. I have suffered from the Communists, been imprisoned by them for standing by a down-trodden people, and seen unspeakable massacres perpetrated by them before my eyes.'

Oliver's malaria, contracted in East Africa, led him and Johnnie to take a recuperating holiday in North Wales. Relations between elder son and the rest of the Baldwin family appear to have continued to be turbulent. Lucy (Cissie) Baldwin gave vent to her downcast feelings in a letter to Johnnie of 7 December, written when Oliver was in the middle of his bout of sickness:[13]

Dear Mr Boyle,
    Thank you so much for writing to me about Oliver. – It is only those who really love him who know how ill he really is, mentally & physically – & who understand the mental suffering that he endures sometimes since his dreadful experiences in the East. I can assure you that the surface Oliver is completely changed it is as though a devil sometimes got possession & raised an Ego of which one knows nothing. an Ego that tramples on those who love him best & [?takes] a devilish delight in saying & doing things that hurt. It is especially painful to me personally because I feel so much responsible. In early life Oliver & I were so much to each other. – I tried to teach him the Love of his Fellowmen & that Love is everything in this life which leads to the sacrifice of self. But I have failed & nobody realizes their failure more than I do. I don't speak of it, it cuts too deep, but you who are his friend may realize the high ideals

that I have always wanted him to have – I may be wrong but now I only see idols with clay feet which have [illeg: ? reached] a high level on which ideals started & the Ego reigns over all. Darling Oliver told me sometime ago that the rise of the Ego was a disease which got possession of people & I think that possibly he may have felt it rising & therefore wanted to prepare me. In such illnesses one can just keep on loving & praying for him. He knows that he has my love always & that when he wants me I am always ready & so is his Father who grieves with me. I do wish that you and he would go abroad to light & sunshine I feel that that would help the cure enormously. Either Algeria or Kenya. Forgive this long letter but when one aches it just helps a bit to write. I hope we shall meet someday & in the meantime thank you for loving my Oliver

>   Yours sincerely
>   Lucy Baldwin

This remarkable letter, with an analysis partly in terms of a strange theology of devils yet partly with a modern perception of mental illness, expresses the distress and incomprehension present in the family at this time. Cissie also appears to have been trying to rationalize away Oliver's black moods of hate, by making them appear physiological and medical, and therefore beyond blame. It must have been very hard for her, after Oliver's childhood in which they were 'so much to each other', to see his devilish delight in saying and doing things that hurt. It was obviously easier for her to deal with the pain and guilt by taking refuge in her weird explanation – which was all the more potent since it had been given to her by her adored godlike son. Grief at the collapse of a too-great intimacy in the mother-son relationship was being brought home to her, and pain too at the conclusive act of an ending: Oliver's achieved adult separation from her. No wonder she found her son's kind, sympathetic and loving friend an appropriate person to whom to unburden herself.

Apart from campaigning in North Bucks and Islington, Oliver did not contribute to the 1923 election campaign. He was recovering. Following the election, held on 6 December, the Tories found themselves without an overall majority, and after a few weeks Stanley Baldwin resigned; in January Ramsay MacDonald became prime minister.

Oliver and Johnnie returned to Shirburn soon after the election, and started living together as a couple. Money was tight. Oliver had declared that he would not accept any further cash from his father, after the political break with him, apart from gifts for birthdays and Christmas. He sought to make a living as a writer. The proofs of *Konyetz* were being corrected, and work was beginning on a book about his time in Armenia. This memoir – *Six Prisons and Two Revolutions* – is a lucid and factual account of his eastern adventures, which also shows great sensitivity to mood and place. It is written with passion, and ends in disillusion. The narrative is clear and uncluttered, and it is easily his best book. Maybe its lucidity and clarity were the result of the clarity in his own life: that, now that he was living with Johnnie, he had left the tense and often stormy atmosphere of family, and had avoided the need to bolt to East Africa. He was being true to his own nature in his own country.

Oliver Baldwin returned to the rostrum at the Caledonian Baths, Islington, for a post-election rally on 27 January 1924: 'the finest SDF meeting held in London', *Justice* proclaimed. Other speakers were the SDF Labour MPs Will Cluse and Fred Montague. Baldwin spoke 'with wit, sally and parody, making scathing criticisms of the late Tory government, and attacking the dilatoriness of the Foreign Office on important issues regarding the Near East and Britain's relationship with it'; that would almost certainly have been an attack on the Treaty of Lausanne. Others at the meeting asked for more details about these matters, since the speaker had had first-hand experience of them.[14]

At home, life in Farm House seemed remote from the world of Social-Democracy. Indeed, there was always a contrast, which was also a complementarity, between Oliver's public, political stance, and his private, country life with Johnnie. Maybe there was a small element of hypocrisy; but Oliver could not have re-invigorated himself for his socialist work bringing a sense of hope to depressed industrial regions in the Midlands and North, without the healing balm of the Oxfordshire retreat. Although the house was staffed with servants, it was not grand, and Oliver was always willing to hear all sides to any dispute which arose. In their home the two lovers worked as poultry farmers, keeping hens, turkeys and geese. (Chicken farming had quite a vogue between the wars; Lady Redesdale kept chickens, so did Robert Byron's parents. Matthew Ponsonby, one of the archetypal Bright Young Things, farmed chickens with unusual seriousness.) Johnnie was good with the hens, and they did well. The couple also took in lodgers, some of whom disappeared without paying. Later too they tried to breed Alsatians, but this was a failure, since Oliver had no affinity with big dogs. The time was one of hard work. Oliver was trying to be a politician, writer, housemaid and poultry-farmer all at once.[15]

The atmosphere was to a great extent one of gentle, amicable, animal-loving primitive homosexual socialism. Maybe it was this originality which made Farm House something of a magnet for young men who stood rather outside the system, and were not quite sure about their feelings towards society and their own future. One of these was Lionel Fielden, author of a lively and idiosyncratic auto-biography, given a wittily paradoxical title, *The Natural Bent* (1960). Fielden was a couple of years older than Oliver, a complex, half-lost individual, bright (he had worked as an interpreter), difficult, and with a sizeable streak of masochism. He enjoyed servility, and revelled in performing menial, grubby tasks, while others were in charge.[16] Gaily he pumped up bathwater, and cleaned out the geese, a job which consciously he came to hate, yet which his inner, abased self found fulfilling. When he fell in love with someone unsuit-able, Oliver declared that his time was up.

The anguished, adolescent, servile nature of the relationship forged in the 1920s was re-emphasized in a couple of
sentences in a letter which Fielden, who had forgotten
nothing, wrote to Johnnie after Oliver's death in 1958. He
seems to have craved more service. 'It seems so strange to
look back on those Watlington days, when my whole heart
was given to you and Noll – but you didnt want it! Such is
life.'[17] Oliver and Johnnie could have reasonably countered
that they were happy with each other, and did not require a
third party. And it is arguable that, from its very nature, the
dependency shown by Fielden's mentality required closure.
To continue to indulge his whims would have been to
prolong his pathology.

One of their weekend guests, who sent them rather a
gushing thank-you letter, was Beverley Nichols. Nichols was
at this time an original and even radical journalist, if one
discounts the 'look-at-me' aspect of his writing; he was quite
a different figure from the familiar cat-calendar man of his
later life. Oliver had originally met him in August 1923, and
confided to Johnnie 'I have met Beverley . . . Adonis is quite
out of the running.' Beverley wrote about Oliver in his book
Twenty-Five, 'a young man's candid recollections'. The
author was recovering from a minor operation when Oliver
visited him. Beverley saw, standing in the doorway 'a youth
with fair hair, agreeable features, quizzical smile and
appalling clothes.' He luridly painted Oliver as 'the most
violent revolutionary' with a loathing for his father's party,
who filled the bookshelves of 11 Downing St with treatises on
the best way to blow up cabinet ministers. The convalescent
hesitantly asked whether it was right to attack one's father in
public. Oliver made the point, which he was often to repeat,
that he was not attacking his father but the programme he
stood for. The sick man, like others, by projecting a personal
hatred into the Baldwin father-and-son relationship, appears
to have been exploring fantasies of violence towards his own
father The friendship between Beverley Nichols and the

Shirburn couple does not seem to have lasted, although Oliver reviewed Beverley's novel *Crazy Pavements* for the *Daily Herald* in 1927.[18]

At about this time *Konyetz* was published. If Oliver's new social life was beginning to draw out the stable, in-control side of his nature, this novel harked back to the chaos and confusion that he was in the process of leaving behind.

Konyetz is a pretentious and over-blown work, a candidate for the worst novel ever published. Its plot is about war in Europe, in a time of revolution and chaos, and it ends with the end of the world. Some passages are expressed in the language of the biblical book of the Revelation or Apocalypse, and the image of the four beasts is frequently invoked. Just as the final book of the bible is full of psycho-wrecked paranoia, so the tone of *Konyetz* is for the most part one of bleak nihilistic scornful half-mad rage. Portions of the text too had to be excised by the publishers on the grounds of possible libel. In its favour, there is a chapter, based on his own experience, in which Baldwin describes the imprison-ment of the hero, which has truth and pain in it; and the author's idea of a compact between Russia and Germany had a certain prophetic quality. His reflection on the dangerous purposelessness in central Europe after 1918 was also valid. But *Konyetz* remains depressing and virtually unreadable. Its chapters have grandiose and empty titles such as Before, During, Desperation, Fading. The overwhelming impres-sion is of the frantically preserved stage machinery of a near-collapsed mentality.

Its characters (who are denied characterization) include, as a partial self-portrait, a magical prophet-like Russian called A. G. Bobrishev, known as Ogone, 'And Ogone means fire . . . '. There is an agreeable English diplomat called David Tryton (who at the same time manifests the unresolved per-manently dissonant quality of the musical tritone, the 'devil in music'), a kindly clergyman named the Revd Septimus Ridsdell, who has a daughter called Lorna – the last two have obvious family echoes. Perhaps the main character is a seething revolutionary crowd of humanity in Hyde Park – a symbol of the haunted confusion in Oliver's mental life before the two events of 1923 which brought him inner peace: meeting Johnnie Boyle, and joining the Social-Democratic Federation.

Another point in the novel's favour, a passage of simple clarity and communication, as opposed to the dense mêlée of the rest, is the dedication: 'To the Dashnakzutun of the Second International, in great admiration and thanks for February 18, 1921'. These words show again how the moment of political heroism which Baldwin had witnessed in Armenia reverberated within him. A challenge to dictatorship had become a defining matter for his personality. The events of February 1921 had been much more than a political decision made in a foreign state: the dedication in *Konyetz* showed that the political had become personal for him. The Dashnaks' political courage in the face of murder by the communists gave him a sense of inner hope; the decision they had made not to give up had become an elemental inner symbol of liberty, and he paid homage to their terrible choice in words of deep conviction.

Despite the work's muddle and unreadability, *Konyetz* was given an astonishing and brilliant review by one of Oliver's disciples, Robert Byron, who was later to become – partly under Oliver's influence – one of the great travel writers of his generation, the author of *The Road to Oxiana*, a modern classic. Byron was then aged 19, and had been introduced to Baldwin earlier in 1924 by the byzantinist David Talbot Rice. Oliver was immediately perceived by the younger man, by reason of the breadth of his experience, and his rejection of the narrow 'family values' of the time, to be someone of great importance in mapping out the new world of social and sexual dissidence.[19]

Byron saw in Baldwin's work elements which the author may have been only dimly aware of. '"Konyetz" means end:

in this case the end of the world. Mr Hussingtree has adopted the methods of a film producer and swept before us a panorama of bewilderingly disastrous historical prophecy – parts of which are already fulfilled – until with the final spread of Bolshevism comes the disruption of Western civilization – and almost as a natural consequence the sounding of the last trump.' Here the reviewer disentangled several obtuse, repetitive and self-reflexive parts of the novel.

Byron continued with an arresting account of the artistic response to the First World War, contrasting it with the actual experience of our author, who had been 'the victim of vicissitudes described in this book, beside which the exaggerated significance of the unexaggerateable horrors of the Western Front paled into their historical perspective. As his mental stereoscope receded, the root, the evolution and the overwhelming forces behind the blood-stained embryo of the New Era gradually emerged into high relief. And in the excitement of his prematurely adjusted vision, impelled by unique experience of the horrors of communism, yet inspired by its organic force, stirred to satire by a commonplace discontent with English conventions, yet consumed by a burning patriotism, he has poured his political emotions into an allegorical novel . . .

> The purpose of the book is to shew the menace of a Soviet Russia organized by a Soviet Germany, to foretell the heroism of France and the apathy of England and to illustrate how all the objects for which the last war was fought will be eventually disregarded by the insane pacificism of the proletariat government. The author definitely believes, he says, that the virulent communism of Slav and Hun will eventually overwhelm Western civilization, as Goth and Visigoth did Roman. But his faith in that very civilization is such, that he makes the world end, rather than exist without it, thus vindicating its durability to any of his readers who are convinced that the day of judgment will not coincide with the next war. So anxious however is he that his purpose shall not

be lost in the 'human interest' that he says in the foreword:
'The characters in this book are of little importance in the rapid
sequence of fateful events.' And so successfully has he
attempted to minimize the attention due to them, that he has
robbed his work of almost all pretensions to literary merit
whatever. It consists for the most part of a rapid succession of
short sentences which hurry us with dazing celerity all over
Europe and the Near East, in the attempt to parallel the
different advances of the wave of destruction . . .

We are treated to a series of atmospheres, entirely devoid of
literary construction or balance, though in their comprehensive
presentation of international war conditions something of an
achievement. But in the personal passages lies the real talent
and it is in these, despite the author's fears to the contrary, that
his moral is most forcibly pointed. What can be more
historically realistic than the man who foregoes marriage with
the girl he loves, because he foresees the impending
dissolution of the social fabric of which they both form part?
. . . The whole is an inspired confusion, but let those who feel
they cannot at first disentangle it turn to chapter five and
behold the soul of the prisoner laid bare over memories of
freedom and travel and other prisons . . .

Robert Byron's review, much more lucid and direct than
the novel itself, was a true act of homage, and showed that
Oliver, even with his confusion and stylistic emptiness (the
lack of 'almost all pretensions to literary merit') had the
capacity to inspire others, at a time when the old world and
old values were perceived to be compromised, misleading
and inadequate.

Oliver indicated that *Konyetz* had been written in
'Keringet, Molo – Red Sea – Astley', that is, in 1922, while he
was still very disturbed after his Armenian and Turkish experiences. It is an interesting document in the pathology of
human suffering and deprivation. Despite Byron's advocacy,
reading a couple of pages of the novel leads one to the conclusion that it would probably have been better kept in
medical archives.

One aspect which is present in *Konyetz*, but which is not mentioned by Robert Byron, is the author's attitude to Jews. Like that of a number of people who have hovered on the edge of paranoia, it was unfavourable. Baldwin can hardly be called anti-semitic, but there were some pretty nasty things said about Jews in *Konyetz*, and occasionally elsewhere in his writings; though it is noticeable that in 1933, when he was fully in control of his life, he said of the situation in Germany that 'this persecution of the Jews will kill half the literature in Germany and push the country back into that barbarism from which it has only lately emerged'. In the same year too he introduced radio audiences to the Shakespearian actor Alexander Moissi. Six years later he was to publish a short story in the *Strand* magazine entitled 'The Watcher, the Stranger, the Listener and the Witness', which was a serious meditation on Jewish suffering in a Christian world. But in *Konyetz* we read that 'Hebrew Ministers longed for titles, and had visions of becoming old Scot families'[20] – standard crude (but not vicious) English sentiments of the shires, which one might have thought Oliver with his Labour allegiance would have seen through. The situation was complicated by the fact that some of the more enthusiastic Bolsheviks he had encountered in Armenia in 1920 had been Jewish; so a mind used to thinking in Platonic generalities rather than in Aristotelian particulars could easily say to itself, 'Ah yes, I see, the plot . . . ' (a line which might have come from *Konyetz*). Belief in the machinations of Jews seems to have been part of his semi-paranoia at this stage; it was not something that lasted. But it was disagreeable while it was around.

Konyetz, and the attitudes that it contains, belong to the old world of Oliver's life. The book encapsulates the pain and irresolution felt by someone who has not made a vital decision. Now that the decision had been made, Oliver could afford to feel more centred and whole, and less a slave to illimitable pessimism.

CHAPTER 8

Dudley and Koot Farm

Konyetz did not have much sale. But in his new mood its author was moving seriously into the political arena. In the summer of 1924 he approached the Labour Party's national organizer for a constituency. He was initially offered the choice of either East Aberdeenshire or Southern Norfolk, both of which he declined on the grounds of distance. Then the choice of Dudley came up. This was the home territory of the Baldwin family, not far from his father's seat of West Worcestershire. In a somewhat defiant spirit he agreed to fight it. The seat did not look promising. In the 1922 election the Tory, Cyril Lloyd, had polled 60% to the Labour candidate's 40%. The following year, in a three-cornered fight, Lloyd had again won, with over 49% of the vote. The Liberal came second, with 41%, and Labour trailed with just over 9%.

Oliver liked the fact that it looked hard: that he had set himself a difficult task. Again we find a desire, or perhaps need, within him to test himself by tough standards. He also admits that he was obstinate. He would take on those who had abused him for his Labour allegiance, and for being (as they saw it, but as his father did not) a traitor to the family.[1]

Dudley was then a constituency in two parts: Tory Dudley to the east, and Labour Netherton in the west. Baldwin began work as soon as he had been selected. Even in July the atmosphere seems to have been tense with election prospects. A brief line to Johnnie on 15 July noted that 'I am working hard here & things are very favourable', and the following day he wrote simply: 'Full of work, but surrounded by friends'.[2] Local Tories grew worried. A Mrs Remfery, of the Dudley Primrose League, expressed her disquiet at the presence of 'this young boy, Oliver Baldwin'. She was concerned that the voters might be confused by his surname. Her shock was almost palpable, that the son of her party's leader should be standing for Labour.[3]

Oliver gave a major campaign speech on 20 July. Its main themes were, according to the *Dudley Chronicle*, the nature of patriotism, the evil of class divisions, and the housing shortage. After attacking the 'influence' (i.e. bribery) of the Tory campaign, he contrasted the outlooks of the parties. The Tories, he noted, called themselves the party of patriots and empire. Yet after the war they had sent shell-shocked men into pauper lunatic asylums. The Labour government had paid the first debt to those afflicted men who had helped save the country.

The Tories, he continued, had bemoaned the shortage of housing, especially in London. But what of all properties with For Sale or To Let notices on them? No working man would be allowed access to them 'because of the system of class distinction which the two parties which represented the capitalist class had thrown in the face of the working class as a challenge'. The government should place in those vacant properties some of the poor people who were now without homes of their own. Baldwin seemed to have been arguing for something like a mass-squat. It would not matter to him if the Duchess of X or the Countess of Y was annoyed because Mrs Smith did her washing on the doorstep.

He attacked the Tories for rushing through legislation to prevent the imprisonment of their own home secretary, who had got into an absurd self-incriminatory position over the Irish Question. Baldwin then spoke about Armenia. Perhaps his audience knew that he had fought alongside the Armenians. This people believed that Turkey had been beaten, and that they, the British, had pacified that very dangerous part of the globe. But through the incompetence of the foreign secretary (Curzon), the Tory party had ignored every sacrifice, and gave back to the Turks even more than they had had before, so that the name of Britain stank in the nostrils of the peoples of the Near East. A change only came with the assumption of office by Ramsay MacDonald, whose brains and intelligence were recognized abroad, and who represented the awakening consciousness of the people of Great Britain. (This was not a view which Baldwin was to hold for very long.)

Walking the streets of Dudley, he said he saw that some of the worst houses were plastered with Tory posters and Union Jacks. Indeed, the worse the housing, the larger the Union Jack. (Baldwin had no answer for this paradox.) The houses seemed to say 'This is our system.' Well, it was not his system. Toryism kept people, in their struggle for existence, from developing their intelligence or their soul. Tories were proud of a system which kept people beaten down, and left them with little higher hope than that they would eventually have to face the workhouse. 'The people had never had a chance, and never would have a chance so long as they kept a Tory system in operation.' Baldwin seems to have been edging towards a theory of 'false – or at least undeveloped – consciousness', which was arguably responsible for Tory support amid crumbling housing.

He wanted to see land nationalized and in the hands of the people again, 'so that houses could be built, communities set up, and something of the old village life be brought back again.'

He returned to the subject of class divisions and the wartime spirit. At that time there had been a mood of service and sacrifice. The classes – by which he meant the upper classes – had begun to understand that they were human, and not artificial. People worked together, 'and great consid- eration was shown by even titled people for the welfare of wounded soldiers'. They threw open their palatial houses to them, and on their departure it was possible to hear a lady say, 'I hope you have enjoyed your stay with me. Probably when the war is over you will call on me.' But if any ex-serviceman were to do that now, he would have to be very careful to knock at the back door, where if he was lucky he would eat his bit of cake in the kitchen. At the end of the war there was a chance for a better system, but when he came back he was, along with thousands of others, completely disillusioned. He asked his audience to think about these things, and he was confident that they would conclude that Labour's policies were the only ones based on justice and right.

Private enterprise in electrical power generation meant filthy factories belching forth foul smoke. Things would be brighter and cleaner with a centralized system of power distribution, he asserted. This was just one of the things that the Labour Party stood for. They also stood for the brotherhood of man, for workers having a share in management, for people to be real craftsmen, not mere cogs in machinery. Labour's message, he concluded, was one of brotherhood, service and sacrifice; otherwise all would be heading for chaos and collapse.[4]

Two days later he sent a brief note to Johnnie about its reception: 'Wonderful meeting – handkerchiefs waved, 3000 people in the Opera House & 800 in a cinema – packed. Tiring work going round the wards though.'[5]

The campaign paused during August, but continued energetically thereafter. Oliver was soon describing himself as 'full of work, thinking in the intervals of our K. Farm'.[6] (K., or Koot, was Oliver and Johnnie's word for homosexual or gay. It was presumably derived from 'Queer as a coot'.) Oliver sometimes addressed more than one meeting a day. On 29 September he spoke to Dudley Women Socialists on the dumping of Belgian iron ores in Britain, and its damaging effect on the steel industry in Dudley.[7] The day before he took a moment off to write home:[8]

Only one week more my B.K. [beloved koot]. Speaking at Wolverhampton to-night. Counting the days

Monday – when you get this
Tuesday – only the day after
Wednesday – half a week gone
Thursday – spare day
Friday – week-end begins
Saturday – enjoy yourself
Sunday – get ready for me
&
then the 2 Ks will meet, D.V.
Yr O.D.K. [own devoted koot]

The following day he jotted:[9]

My B.B.K.

No lett-lett this morning, but I expect you wrote at Chequers on Monday night, so I shall get it 2nd post. I go to B'ham for a meeting to-night. On Sunday next I have a meeting at Tipton at 10.30 a.m. One at West Bromwich at 6.30 p.m. And my two here at 7.30 & 8.30. You'll get this on Wednesday & then

Thursday is a quiet day
Friday you go shopping
Saturday you prepare
& Sunday you get ready for the arrival of 1 who is longing to get home, & is always
Y.O.D.B.K. [your own devoted beloved koot]

The campaign began in earnest with the fall of the Labour government on 9 October 1924, following a successful vote of censure over the prosecution and withdrawal of charges against a communist named J. R. Campbell. The election was marked by hysteria over the Zinoviev Letter, something Baldwin could not understand, since he saw it as the job of communism and the Communist Party to foment revolution. There was (he says) a wild popular expectation that the Russians might arrive on polling day. A lady in Brecon found a trench outside her front door surmounted with red flags 'and it took the combined efforts of the Tory canvassers and the gas inspector to persuade her that the revolution had not begun.'[10]

In his memoirs Oliver wrote rather sullenly about the campaign: he said he had faced a personal campaign of 'beer [that is, a pint for a vote], lies and bitterness such as I never wish to experience again'. He borrowed the £150 for the deposit, and the campaign itself cost him about £200, of which he paid £10, and received the rest from constituents. His letters home are more positive and animated, if brief. In the middle of October he snatched a break to write:[11]

My O P K K [own precious kootie-koot]
    All love. Full of work.
    We're winning
        Y.O.B.K. [your own beloved koot]

At about the same time:

My O.B.K.,
    No Liberal is to come in, & we're having a close fight. It will be within 2,000 either way.
    All my love, my B.
        Your O.B.K.W.L.Y.Alone

There was a hint of excitement on meeting his Tory opponent: 'Yesterday we were nominated & I met Cyril Lloyd for the first time. Very nice looking, about 45 years old.'[12]

In Oliver's election address he returned to the high style of his speeches, in contrast to the humorous intimacy of the letters to Johnnie. Here, he again delineated the past achievements and future policies of Labour in government. Labour (he wrote) had in its short term in office sought to lay the foundations of peace in Europe, and to improve education and service for the people. Unemployment had been reduced by 121,000: however, he believed, no real cure could be found for it without the socialization (i.e. nationalization) of land, mines and large industries. The effect of the Labour budget had been nullified by 'the big capitalistic food combines'. In foreign policy, Baldwin noted the atmosphere of peace that MacDonald had created, something that had been impossible under 'the regime of Lord Curzon'. He attacked the Treaty of Lausanne as anti-British and scandalous. In education, Baldwin reminded the voters that Labour had abolished many school fees, reduced the size of classes and restored state scholarships. In housing, the 1924 act laid down that the courts had no powers to grant landlords possession, unless alternative accommodation was provided. The Tory 1923 act had permitted almost 10,000 ejectments of tenants, many with no alternative but the street. On Russia, he rather tamely – as if seeking to avoid controversy – mentioned fishing rights, and satisfaction of those who had invested in bonds under the old regime, but no other issues. The peroration to his address had a certain inspirational quality to it:

> We own no class distinction. We simply see a dread future for England if this present system of monopoly, jealousy and materialism continues. We offer you in its place cooperation and harmony. Give the people education. Give them a chance to know beauty rather than everlasting drudgery. With that ideal before us, I ask your help, believing with me, that God gave the earth and its abundance for all men and not for a few.[13]

Policy matters were not always addressed at meetings, and the campaign grew personal. In a speech of 20 October he had to issue a denial that he had been turned out by his family. In true Oliver style, he ridiculed the idea. The *Dudley Chronicle* reported him thus: 'Much reference, he said, had been made to the fact that the policy he was advocating was different from that which his father was advocating, but he failed to see why there should be any surprise in that. He wanted to tell them that his father was the only member of the Baldwin family who had spent all his life as a Tory. All the other members for years back had been either Radicals or Liberals. Therefore they could hardly blame him (Mr Oliver Baldwin) if the germs of his ancestors were in him, and if he were out for progress and not for reaction.' He went on to talk about the proposed treaty with Russia, protectionism, and unemployment, the cure for which he saw as socialism and nationalization.[14]

As election day approached, enthusiasm for Labour grew. On 21 October he wrote home to Johnnie:[15]

My O.B.K.
　　You don't send "Justice" along as I asked. Vests arrived this morning. Last night, my K.[,] I held my first meeting in the Tory Ward. Packed out. Wonderful & then I addressed double the number in the street. Then they carried your K shoulder high round Dudley for over an hour. The Tories have the wind up. Betting 4–1.
　　Yr O.B.K.

How Johnnie Boyle received that news is not recorded. Johnnie was basically a life-long Tory – a typical sociable, charming, unserious, slightly feather-brained shires' Tory. (It is not hard to imagine him being a welcome guest of Oliver's parents for a weekend at Chequers, creating a warm atmosphere wherever he went. His natural Boyle charm could always uncoil the cold steel of inhibited English convention.) Oliver's public moral ardour was alien to him. Nevertheless his deep devotion to his partner led him to accept Oliver's enthusiasm for socialism as one of the compromises that people have to make when they decide to live together.

Polling day was 29 October 1924. Three days beforehand Oliver sounded a note of tempered optimism:[16]

Sunday
My O.B.K.
　　Just got up 12.45 p.m. Five meetings yesterday. Everyone seems very confident, but one never knows. It will be a close fight anyway.
　　All love
　　M B K from
　　　　Y.O.B.K.

The Dudley result was as follows:

| C. E. Lloyd | C | 11,199 | 52.1% |
| O. R. Baldwin | Lab | 10,314 | 47.9% |

Conservative majority, 885   Turnout, 80.2%

Back at Labour campaign headquarters, the *Dudley Chronicle* recorded, 'hearty cheers were given for "Good Old Oliver"' after the declaration. He for his part hoped that his supporters would 'set to work from that night onwards'.[17]

Taking as a basis the 1923 results, it was a good result for Labour and its candidate. Comparing it to the 1922 result (which, like 1924, was a straight fight) it was also good, but not outstanding; a swing of just over 7% to Labour. Labour lost the election overall, and Stanley Baldwin returned to 10 Downing Street.

Oliver seems not to have been unduly upset about losing Dudley. The margin was narrow enough to satisfy his honour. The effect of Dudley was to increase his dedication to socialism: he got moving, and finally shook off the ennui that had been plaguing him since returning from the east. The fact that he was living apart from his parents, and had ceased to be dependent, living now as a mature adult in a relationship, added an indefinable calm, poise and purpose to his life. He found the capacity to work hard at spreading his political ideas, to write seriously (the text of *Six Prisons* was finished a month after the election), and above all to be fulfillingly intimate with Johnnie at Koot Farm.

In the spring of 1925 Baldwin was invited back to Cologne by a friend in the Military Intelligence Department, Captain Guy A. Fenton, R.A. The reception he was given was warm. He travelled via Brussels, where he met Shura Khansorian, the companion of his harrowing time in Armenia and Turkey. He was now living none too prosperously, but living, which for an Armenian was an achievement. Baldwin also met George and Elsie Bambridge (née Kipling). They had got married the year before: in June Oliver had received an excited letter from Elsie:

Oliver my dear,

I do hope you'll be pleased with my news; George & I are engaged & most gloriously happy! but also most sensible & nice!

George himself wrote to Oliver the following month saying how happy he was about the whole affair, noting: 'You certainly were instrumental in bringing us together and I am ever so thankful for it.' Writing again in August, Elsie begged Oliver to meet them both in London; 'Somehow I feel you would bring John's special blessing with you.'[18]

They were married in October, and soon left for Brussels, where they lived in some style in a large house, attended by 'two very handsome footmen and a more handsome chauffeur'. They asked kindly after Johnnie, so it would appear they had no difficulty in accepting the relationship.

Oliver made some interesting political observations on his continental visit which he penned for *The Social-Democrat* (as *Justice* had been re-named). What struck him most was a paradox: that France and Belgium seemed like defeated nations, whereas Germany was the land of 'the real conquering people'.

'In the occupied territory the towns seem alive with virile manhood; the German pride is in their faces; their destiny in their carriage; and you know the moment that the Rhineland is free these men in their thousands will parade the streets and sing Deutschland über Alles with a greater fervour than ever, for they will have a real object – revenge . . .

'Anyhow, if you don't like that, let's say all is well and that there will never be another war, because Lord Robert Cecil says that the League . . .'[19]

However, it was home politics, social life and domesticity which absorbed his energies in the years that followed. Farm House became of central importance to him; it was an oasis of rural peace amid the confrontations and din elsewhere;

after the exhaustion of travelling around the country, and the stress of making political speeches in urban waste-lands, it was a place of deep and almost holy peace and calm. The house was a big enough to entertain at weekends: there were three stories, and six bedrooms, if only one bathroom. It was staffed by a cook, a housekeeper, and a chauffeur and general handyman called Ernest Didcock, who remained with Oliver and Johnnie all their lives. The garden was a place of deep relaxation; Johnnie planned it and shaped it, and Oliver drew much pleasure from it. Here was Oliver's own Arcadia, a magic garden of timelessness, and a solvent for cares. Inner peace was still what Oliver needed most of all after his experiences in the east. A two-stanza verse he wrote to Johnnie ('For Kootie') in December 1925, maybe after a domestic incident, shows Oliver's yearning for calm:[20]

> Winds of the night bring pardon
> Breath of the morn brings pain
> But the light of the sun of Heaven
> Brings peace to my heart again
>
> Lips of my loved one burning
> Give calm to my troubled brain
> Touch of the hand of friendship
> Brings peace to my heart again.

The two 'koots' worked together in their small estate. Johnnie could be difficult, and complain a bit – at least, so one learns from Oliver's letters to him; almost none of Johnnie's appear to have survived. But it is interesting that Oliver seems largely to have been able to confront such problems, while never losing the sense of intimacy which was important to both of them. A letter written by Oliver on 24 April 1926 shows him facing up to Johnnie's tendency to querulousness, and making a joke of it; it also shows how the deep peace of the garden at Koot Farm linked in with his political beliefs – how the two apparently disparate worlds of public politics and private life were in fact connected.[21]

My O.B.B.K.

This lett will wake you in the morning & make you hap for the time I'm away. You must not fuss or worry because very few things are worth bothering about & there are so many millions of peeps who are poor and miserable that U mustn't be selfish.

C?

When I go to the black coal pits of S. Wales, I shall think of the sun in our gard & wish everyone in Aberavon could see it too! Don't forget that Your K.L.U., & wants U to be hap & strong & sensible, because U R much more worth than anyone that used to worry U. So keep our little house hap & then you will be helping me to do that which we both know is right, fighting for happier lives for everyone who has never even seen a flower . . .

You've got so much around you that is luv & so have I, so just get up and sing a sing in the bath-room & laugh all day till I come back.

I shall D.V., arrive by the 4 whatever it is on Wednesday.

Always Y O B K

P.K.K.

Another letter, also from April 1926, pencilled from the Dudley Labour Club and dated Fry-Fri, went thus:[22]

My B.B.K.

I don't feel I told you enough how 7. 7. [= 'at sevens and sevens', as opposed to 'at sixes and sevens'] the house & garden were & what joy it gave me to see F/4 [=our] little home again. Here in this miserable Black Hole I am always thinking of it. The destitution up here is really getting serious & the feeling is running strong. But I mustn't bother you with it though there is so much of it. Take care of yourself. I will let you know about Eton later. Be hap because you ought to be & so am I except when I see poor devils starving owing to Conservative restrictions of benefit.

Bless U., B.K.

Yr O.P.K.K.

As part of his political tour of depressed industrial regions, Baldwin went to Burnley in late 1926, under the auspices of the Social-Democratic Federation, to rally the faithful, and to raise spirits in areas beaten down by the failure of the General Strike and punitive Toryism. He pencilled to Johnnie, 'Four meetings yesterday & 2 to-night. Quite strenuous but all packed out & enthusiastic.' The meeting was excitedly reported in *The Social-Democrat* by the local SDF secretary, J. Tomlinson:

Not since the formation of the Burnley Branch nearly 40 years ago have we had such meetings as those addressed by our National Organiser [E. J. Pay] and Oliver Baldwin. It was necessary to have an 'overflow' and both halls were packed to the utmost capacity. Both Oliver and Teddy were in splendid form and they soon had their audiences tremendously enthusiastic. Capitalist press criticism previous to the meeting only made things better and hundreds of the opposition were present. New members have rolled in ever since, and it has been almost epoch-making so far as the creation of a new spirit is concerned. It was a real revival for Social-Democracy . . . Dormant members have been roused and young comrades inspired. Oliver Baldwin's tour proves the need for more national speakers' visits to branches.[23]

Other towns of the North and Midlands were visited in the course of this tour. He also travelled widely seeing friends and relatives. He still saw a lot of his Aunt Lily, married to a doctor, Richard Whittington, and living in Hove. From there Oliver wrote to Johnnie in 1925:[24]

I had a great time watching the sheep trials & I walked over the moors with young Trevelyan (18 years old) & bathed in a lake. Yesterday Beverley [Nichols] lunched with me & I met D. for a minute or two before I caught the train down here. What do you think was by my bed? Two oranges & a glass & they won't tell me how they knew but I guessed . . .

The significance of 'two oranges and a glass' was left for Johnnie to determine.

Baldwin received another journalistic commission in June 1926. J. W. Drawbell, the editor of the Manchester-based *Sunday Chronicle*, had read *Six Prisons*, which had evidently impressed him, and he suggested a weekly article from Oliver on current affairs, of about 1100 words. The *Sunday Chronicle* was a popular paper which nevertheless contained serious and radical articles; Baldwin's fellow columnists included Rose Macaulay, Bertrand Russell and Julian Huxley. Oliver worked out an agreement with his agent, A. P. Watt, and he wrote eight articles for the *Chronicle*; the fee was £10.10s [£10.50p] per article. The pieces were not an entire success; one was returned by Drawbell as 'altogether too platitudinous and not sufficiently down to earth for my readers'. However, in August Drawbell indicated that he would continue to request an occasional article from Baldwin.[25]

Here he had a platform for his radicalism, broader than that of *The Social-Democrat*. He wrote on the possibility that Britain might become a really Christian society (which would bring about 'a shattering of materialism, a hope for unborn generations' – and what of the Stock Exchange, and the Law Courts?). He mixed challenge with mild irony in a piece on narrow social values, discoursing with a hint of waspishness on the futile feuds carried on between Aspidistra Avenue and Geranium Villas.

On 18 July 1926 he wrote on the ever-popular topic of the generation gap. Today (he wrote) respect was no longer automatically shown by children to their elders. Why? Largely because of the war, into which the older generation had led their offspring headlong. Nowadays 'happy homes can only be made by sympathetic friendships between parents and children.'

Oliver looked further at general attitudes of the young, of particular but unspoken significance to himself. 'There is a tendency today for youth to keep to its own sex; the sexes are not so interested in each other as formerly. This is probably due to the freedom of youth, both sexes having lost much of their mystery in each others' eyes, with girls possessing more masculinity and boys becoming less boorish.' (Not 'more feminine', a reflection of the taboo on feminized boys.) Oliver naturally assented to the development, feeling grateful for 'these signs in modern youth which tend to kinder hearts, finer feelings and nobler minds.'[26]

Topics in the following weeks were 'The good old days: why we should forget them and have faith in a better future', and country versus town living. After writing on cricket, he turned his attention to the law. In a piece headed 'Less justice and more mercy: is the "eye-for-an-eye" law still right?' he criticized certain police and court procedures. One paragraph was especially noteworthy:[27]

'The police habit of looking for crime is a detestable idea. Let them "look to prevent" crime by warning individuals whom they see, or know are, about to do wrong. It is time enough to act when a thing happens since the question is probably a man's existence as a respected citizen. This can be done, for instance, to prevent the constant cases that occur in the parks.' In other words, the police should not act as agents-provocateurs for acts of 'gross indecency' committed between consenting males in the bushes and in public lavatories.[27]

Oliver was naturally circumspect in supporting gay issues. But he seldom ducked them. One homosexual case which famously came to court in November 1928 was the prosecution for obscenity of Radclyffe Hall's lesbian novel *The Well of Loneliness*. The author was an acquaintance of Baldwin, and the two corresponded: she told him of her determination to tell 'the truth and the truth and the truth whenever opportunity offers!'[28] Oliver put his name forward to appear as a defence witness if needed, but the defence seems to have decided that his services were not required.

As far as his political journalism was concerned, his most pungent offerings – scornful of Tory tactics, which he had

observed from the inside, but tempting fate by making predictions – were reserved for *The Social-Democrat*. He wrote
for its special anniversary issue of May 1927, on the topics of
China and the forthcoming Trade Union Bill. China was of
importance in view of the recent successes of the Nationalist
revolution, which had weakened the economic privileges of
the Europeans. Baldwin did not foresee the rise of the grass-
roots nationalist party, the Kuomintang, in China. His perspective was rather of the alternatives for the British in
China: to get out, or to protect their economic concessions by
force. He continued:[29]

'This latter will be undoubtedly adopted, and every
incentive given to draw fire on our people, whereupon all our
newspapers will scream for revenge, the Primrose League
will play "Land of Hope and Glory", the Constitutional Club
will wave Union Jacks and before we know where we are we
shall be adding further property to the glory of the British
Empire . . . We have always behaved like that; our diplomatic
moves have always been similar: all you do is get one British
subject killed, and then our "Christianity" can show the
Chinese who is the better killer.'

*

In Shirburn, Oliver and Johnnie lived a fairly private life,
except for weekend parties with friends. Although they kept
open house, they were not part of 'society', with its vanity and
competitiveness. They were to a great extent self-sufficient.
This was in part the cause of a splenetic outburst by 'Janitor',
the joint pseudonym of J. G. Lockhart, a political journalist,
and Mary Lyttelton (Lady Craik). Their book *The Feet of the
Young Men* (Duckworth, 1928) was widely read at the time. It
was an example of publishers' cyclical niche-marketing: a
gossippy (preferably bitchy) look at the up-and-coming
generation, especially at toff-ish sprogs. A passage on Oliver
Baldwin followed one on Malcolm MacDonald, son of the
Labour leader, who had been praised for his judgment and

ability, and for his freedom from vanity or egotism. The text continued:[30]

> Of that other product of Number 10, Downing Street, Oliver Baldwin, little need be said. At elections he emerges from the obscurity of his chicken farm to belittle his father's policy and achievements. He is curiously unaware that were he not his father's son no one would pay the slightest attention to him; and that the favour which is shown him by the Labour Party is an unintended compliment to the Prime Minister and not a recognition of any special virtue in Oliver Baldwin. In extenuation of his extraordinary conduct we must remember that during the War he was severely wounded, was imprisoned by the Bolsheviks, and suffered misadventures sufficient to unbalance a stronger mind than his.

It is clear that Lockhart and Lyttelton had done no more than a minimum of background research. The aim seems to have been just to smear their subject, by implying that he was a war-damaged crackpot unfit for public life. Baldwin had not of course been severely wounded during the war. (This assertion was deleted in the book's second edition, and a reference was coaxed out of the authors that Oliver had a sense of humour.) Lockhart and Lyttelton apparently knew nothing of their subject's speech-making visits to Burnley, Clitheroe, Oldham, Grimsby, South Wales or even to the constituency he was nursing at Dudley. They had not checked up on his motivation for joining the Social-Democratic Federation, or for standing for the Labour Party. Instead, believing that there was no need to go out and find the truth, they held that they knew it all in advance, by some kind of instinctive journalistic osmosis. Why then did they hold this distorted and angry view of Oliver Baldwin? Why did they apparently find him so threatening, that any fair and factual estimate of his life and work was lost in their sea of prejudice? The story of Baldwin father-son hostility was repeated within living memory in Martin Green's curious and wrongheaded book *Children of the Sun* (Constable, 1977).

In an age which was still in many ways conventional, Oliver was being unconventional. By adopting socialism, in direct conflict to his father's politics, and by leaving the family home at Astley, he was living by the light of his nature and of his social conscience, and not by the canons of society. (At the time, to be the cause of a dispute within the family, and to leave the family home, were greater social sins than to live with another man, since the idea of two men sharing a house did not, as it would now, immediately lead to gossip of sex; but one seldom deserted the family home entirely unless one married.)

However, acting by the light of nature and conscience was, for a scion of the Ridsdale family, and with their discursive heritage, nothing out of the ordinary. In a letter to his mother, roughly contemporary with these events, Oliver writes 'Aunt Lily and Uncle R[ichard] send their love, they are on their way from West Malvern where they discover that Esther is a Ridsdale, having NO respect for authority!'.[31] Stepping outside the norm is often threatening to those not brought up in an atmosphere of discussion. Oliver Baldwin may have been, at some unconscious level, getting at some paternal image, or sloughing off the past and asserting the present, by espousing socialism. But there were sound rational reasons for his political stance, and father and son remained the best of friends, with no hint of strain in their correspondence; indeed, it seems that the political difference, by becoming open and articulated, allowed a real father-and-son friendship to be navigated between the rocks of generation difference – the hazards of Oedipal jealousy and anger, for the psychoanalytically minded. Oliver always stressed that it was policies which counted; he sought to attack the destitution and starvation which resulted from Toryism, rather than petulantly to attack his father. There were large areas of disagreement on public affairs. But no record exists of an attack on his father. But Lockhart and Lyttelton, conventional to the core, and devotees of the empire/ public school/ hierarchical family values of the day, found Oliver's determination to do as his conscience told him intolerable. So judgment came to them more quickly than informed fact.

One episode shows how personal friendship between father and son coexisted with political difference. A fine new town hall had just been built in Dudley, and the opening ceremony was due in the autumn of 1928. The Town Council asked Stanley Baldwin to honour them with his presence. With his customary magnanimity he wrote back declining, on the grounds that Dudley was the constituency that his son was nursing for Labour. But then Oliver wrote to his father pointing out that the ceremony would be a non-party affair: the sitting Tory member (Cyril Lloyd) would be present, as would the mayor of Dudley (a Liberal), besides the Labour contestant. Oliver asked his father to reconsider.[32]

In reply SB wrote to his son (3 September):[33]

Dearest Son,

This is only a line to say that I had turned Dudley down but when I got your letter I told 'em to try and fit it in when I go to Kidder. to receive the Freedom . . .

I shall like to feel we have shared a platform once . . .

Your loving

F.

In its glowing account of the ceremony, the *Dudley Herald* noted in its issue of 20 October: 'In the vestibule of the Hall the Prime Minister met his son Mr Oliver Baldwin, who is prospective Labour candidate for Dudley, and whom he clasped heartily by the hand.'[34]

The substance of this incident is foreshadowed in a comment of the previous year made by Beatrice Webb. Oliver Baldwin had been to stay with the Webbs at their house in Liphook in the summer of 1927. In her diary she described her guest: 'An attractive figure: tall and upright, square shouldered, delicate aquiline features and clear skin; fair hair and blue eyes. He might be an artist except that he is unexceptionally tailored and peculiarly direct and sedate in manner and speech. His hands are well formed and carefully manicured.' She noted his 'combination of fastidiousness and unconventional simplicity (a small attaché case his sole baggage).'[35] Oliver, she went on, was reported to be 'acidly contemptuous about his parents', but she did not endorse these 'reports'. Rather, as she noted in a letter to a friend, following the visit of this 'attractive youth', 'I should have thought he and his father would have a good deal in common. I imagine that he is really sympathetic to Mr Baldwin's general outlook, if only that could be disentangled from the Diehard section of the Conservative Party.'[36]

The Dudley incident, and Beatrice Webb's comment, challenge the story of poor relations between father and son during the inter-war years. Why the harmonious relationship has had apparently to be characterized by commentators as hostile is an interesting question. Perhaps it relates to the unconscious hostility felt by them towards their own fathers, which would lead them to fantasize on such possibilities in the lives of others; or perhaps to the need of party politicians and of ideologically committed writers to subordinate family relationships to political convictions.

Not all the journalism about Oliver was negatively biased. An intelligent and unprejudiced interview with him at Farm House appeared, complete with a photograph, in the *Daily Express*, in November 1926. It was headed 'Socialism on £400 a Year: Premier's Son and a Chicken Farm'. Oliver was allowed to speak first:[37]

'This is an attempt at practical socialism. I have £400 a year from shares which were given to me some years years ago by my father. My partner is a Tory and has about £50 a year. He manages the farm and when I am not speaking publicly I help. Our revenue from eggs, after feeding ourselves and our guests completely, is about £20 a year.'

The (unnamed) *Daily Express* representative described Oliver's clothes, and continued: 'His light blue eyes are almost humorous. His soft, flaxen moustache turns up, revealing a mouth that is not quite sensuous, not quite idealistic and not quite determined. His gaze and manner are frank. When he dislikes what is said to him, he does not answer back sharply. He draws deeply on his pipe.'

Together in the garden they talked of the summer-house where he worked, and of the fact that the house had a wireless and a telephone; then up strolled his partner, 'a typical public school man', with a bag, 'out of which he deposited five minute ducklings on the ground. "They're three days old", said Mr Baldwin . . . "The nearer a living thing is to God, the more beautiful it is. A baby's eyes, or a baby's hand."' It was a confident Oliver who asserted the relationship between beauty and the nearness of a creature to God.

Talk of babies seems to have activated a circuit in the brain of the *Daily Express* representative. 'Are you married?' he asked, somewhat imperiously. Oliver fielded this one with a 'No, I shall not have time.' (Perhaps the odd use of the future tense indicated that he was, well, tense.) This was standard evasiveness in the 1920s; at least he did not invent a phoney fiancée. Oliver could hardly say we're a couple of koots; the Thames Valley constabulary would have come knocking on the door of Farm House. The issue was not pursued and the conversation passed to politics.

'I never attack my father publicly . . . I disagree with him and deplore his policies and his lack of policies, but I am an obscure Socialist candidate and he is the Prime Minister of Great Britain. I never attack a man who obviously can't answer back.'

'But you think he is –'

'All wrong,' said the Socialist.

Lunch was ready, and they walked towards the house, 'a most attractive country establishment of some ten rooms or so. Various cats and good-humoured dogs converged on us as we went.' Oliver was asked if he regretted the life that he had left. No, he replied, adding somewhat testily, 'the whole business of titles and flunkeyism and money-grubbing makes me ill.'

The young socialist said he was nursing Dudley. Would he win it at the next election? 'Yes.' Would he then attack his father in the House? 'They would throw me out of the House in no time.' He indicated that he might give up the seat and go and fight a by-election – an odd fantasy, which never became reality. He saw himself as essentially a propagandist, and reeled off the names of the places he was to visit in the course of the next few weeks. He charged two guineas (£2.10) for a speaking engagement, but he refunded half the fee in strike areas where there was poverty.

It was time to go to the piano, rummage among some dog-eared music, and sing a socialist song of his own composition. 'In the writing and in the rendition there was a simple kindliness which was admirable,' commented the *Daily Express* man, clearly won over. But a doubt remained. 'Is this lovely country place in keeping with your socialist ideas?'

'Absolutely . . . We do it on £450 a year. This is the way everyone should live. We work, we produce, we feed ourselves, and we entertain our friends when we have any spare time. Can you sing?'

The *Daily Express* man admitted he could, and was induced to join in, not a socialistic song, but a familiar passage from Gilbert and Sullivan's opera *Patience*, which included the words:

A most intense young man,
A soulful-eyed young man,
An ultra-poetical, super-aesthetical,
Out-of-the-way young man.

Was Oliver tempting his journalist visitor to come to a conclusion? If the interviewer made the connection between Oliver Baldwin and Oscar Wilde, about whose followers Gilbert was writing, he did not let on. It was nearly time to go. The intense young man, puffing away at his pipe, 'strangely lovable, strangely nebulous', gave the visitor some autumn leaves to take home. As he was leaving, the Tory partner, attending a sick fowl, waved good-bye to him. Not many political interviews, then or now, can have been conducted in this manner, by turns off-beat, engaging, direct, and allusive.

One further element in Oliver's life at this time was Algeria. Ever since he had visited it in 1920 with George Bambridge, he had been enchanted by the country. His uncle, Arthur Ridsdale – known as Uncle Bhai (pronounced Bye) – owned a villa there. The Villa Aurelian was about 17 miles east of Algiers, and over-looked Cape Matifou, the harbour from which in 1541 the Emperor Charles V had set sail after a disastrous attempt to seize the Barbary coast. To Oliver the Mediterranean landscape was alive with quivering light and sentient with a compass of intermingled scents. His return, in January 1926, awoke the earlier enthusiasm. To Johnnie he wrote:[38]

My O.B.K.

Here I am at 6.30 in our verandah writing to you. This place is wonderful & this morning the sun was so hot I had a sun bath after my ordinary one. The food is excellent & the house like a new pin. We can see the ships come in from the roof & I am longing to see yours. There is a spare bed for Geordie if he wants to come & the house is like a dream. Oranges on the trees in the garden & a glorious sky.

I am longing for you to come so I can show it you all.

As I walk & see all this beauty I think of my K. & how he will love it. There is red salvia in the garden & bougainvillea on the house. The woman who cooks adores cats & has 5 (1 Angora). There are 2 canaries in a cage & the woman is longing to show you her cats. I've told her all about you.

Everyone here loves Uncle Bhai & he is also looking forward to your coming. Hurry up & come along, the sun is warm but not too hot & Arab music & smells are all around.

I long for your ship to come round the bay.

We will have such a lovely time & no worries.

Always Y.O.B.K.

A further letter, dated 'Sunday, on the terrace in a bright bright sun', elaborated on the garden and the villa:

> Well we have orange trees & tangerine trees in full fruit & a glorious smell, a vine, roses, salvia, bougainvillea, two palms & a lot of stuff I don't know. It is only a baby garden. There is a wireless (new & at the moment out of work), the whole roof terrace, another outside the bathroom & one (where I am sitting) at the end of the garden which is only about 30 ft long! The rooms are about the size of ours at home, except the long salon which is an Arab room with cushions. I have bought you a picture here which awaits you. Uncle Bhai says he is leaving the villa to us & is going to make a special French will about it.
>
> Our bedroom has a view over Algiers & the sea, gets the full morning sun & looks on Cape Matafou.
>
> I hope you leave before the 20th so that you will be here as soon as possible because the weather is now superb & February often is rainy. Uncle Bhai is buying a Fiat for us, so that we can pop off into the desert if it rains too much . . . Hurry & come. The sun is calling & the sea is blue & sparkling. The bell from the English church is ringing & I wish you were there instead of Shirburn.

Soon Johnnie had joined him at the villa, and thus began their first winter holiday to Algeria. For the next five years they spent between two and three months there annually, using the villa as a base to explore the country. The holidays, translucent with warmth and light, were for Oliver an essential re-charging of energy expended in travelling around cold industrial Britain on political work. Also, on a practical level, the time spent in North Africa enabled him to escape the malaria which had been plaguing him each winter since the visit to East Africa.

With the inauguration of winter holidays in Algeria, Oliver Baldwin had achieved some sort of a balance in his life. He was not rich, and though his career was lived in public, he was not an MP; but he shared a beautiful house and garden in Oxfordshire with a man he really loved, and he was doing work which satisfied a need within him to improve the society he lived in, and to give hope to those who had hit hard times. This he did by going directly into the heart of industrial Britain and inspiring the working people and the unemployed with hope and enthusiasm for change. He was writing as well as speaking, and for creative relaxation he played the piano and painted. Now too, to provide the complete change of scene which Farm House could never give, while England was shivering and slipping on dank pavements in the fog and dark of a northern winter, he would travel with his lover to a peaceful holiday villa in the balmy south.

CHAPTER 9

Oliver Baldwin, MP and ex-MP

Oliver Baldwin found the campaign of 1929 more invigorating than that of 1924. There was less Tory beer-bribery now, and policies played a larger part than personalities. Five years on no one questioned the Labour allegiance of the prime minister's elder son. The economic conditions of the country and of the constituency were the main issue. But there were still some doubts. Baldwin refers to 'the strain of being continually alone without encouragement' – probably a reference to all those who ignored or hated him for opposing his father's politics.[1] Perhaps too it refers to the in-fighting among members of the Dudley Constituency Labour Party, which he disliked. It is also just possible that it is an oblique – even unconscious – reference to the fact that Johnnie, while providing so much at home, was not actually a political comrade.

Baldwin fought the campaign on basic socialist lines, without going into detail about the implementation of his programme. His election address for 1929 was austere and pared down compared with that of five years earlier. It dealt with unemployment, declaring that the party stood for public-sector jobs in slum clearance, land reclamation, transport improvements, and afforestation. It proposed an increase in unemployment benefit. The school age was to be increased to 15, and as regards housing, Labour would build houses for letting, and continue rent controls. Nationalization of the mines was a prime element in the industrial programme, and the Health Insurance act would be extended to include dependants of the insured. Improvements would be made to pensions, and working hours in factories would be limited. Internationally, Baldwin urged support for the League of Nations, disarmament, and restoring commercial diplomatic relations with Russia. He summed up the contest as one 'of the forces of vested interests, land and money-power against the ideals of the cooperative commonwealth'. A vote for Labour would be a vote for 'a state in which service of the community for the community would take the place of the present system of private greed and gain which has brought such sorrow to so many'.[2]

His speeches, at least as they appeared in the *Dudley Chronicle*, were more demotic in tone, almost verging on the simplistic. In its issue of 9 May, the paper reported him speaking of the people's disillusion with the Tory government, which worked only for the interests of the rich. The Tory solution for unemployment was to take men out of benefit and put them in the workhouse. They had no other solution, because one class owned all the property and were rich, while another much larger class made all the money for them to live on. Suppose, he suggested, someone in the audience was the member of a family of six. Would they like it if two of the family said, 'You four can sleep in one room, and we will have the other two rooms. We will have a car and luxury and you must give us all the money you get to enable us to go to the pictures.' If they would not permit such conditions in their own families, they should not permit them at all. England was one big family. One class should not be allowed to do what it liked with the money.

People had said in the past that they should vote for the party with money; a vote for Labour was a vote for a party without money. But his party had no money because the small class of the bosses had taken all the land from others.

Baldwin then attacked the contribution paid to the mine-owners for each ton of coal produced. It was his view that the raw material was in the ground for the good of all. The life of workers consisted in work, food and more work. 'A continual round of work.'

He did not just stress the issue of re-distributing the national cake more fairly. Part of Labour policy on unemployment (he told his audience) was to create more opportunities, by raising the school-leaving age. The party would also introduce maternity allowances. Pensions were proposed at the age of 60. Businessmen would not be subsidized to employ labour, but the government would run enterprises as state concerns, thereby guaranteeing all a state pension.

In conclusion, he called on all to vote Labour. The polling booths would be open till 9.00 p.m. this year, so everyone could vote. The other side would be providing beer, tea and corned-beef suppers, but people should vote with their heads, not with their stomachs. Labour made no rash promises, but he gave them his word that if the Labour Party did not stick to socialist principles, then he was finished with them. If the electorate of Dudley planned to support Labour, he did not want them to do so thinking that they were going to get ninepence for fourpence, because they were not. They were going to get a new system, and not one which would enrich the few.[3]

Two days later, at an open-air meeting in Dudley, he continued the main socialist theme: that it was entirely wrong that 42.5 million people should be working so that 2.5 million could live in comfort. He renewed his criticism of the mine-owners for demanding high rents for the operation of coal-mining, at a time when miners themselves were near starvation.[4]

Polling day was 30 May. At the declaration Oliver could feel satisfaction in the culmination of a long campaign.

O.R. Baldwin	Lab	13551	47.6%
C.E. Lloyd	C	10508	36.9%
T.E. Clough	L	4399	15.5%

Labour majority, 3043   Turnout, 81.6%

It was a Labour triumph, echoed countrywide. Oliver received 62 telegrams of congratulation. Labour, led by Ramsay MacDonald, formed the government.

Once in the House of Commons, the Labour member for Dudley played a fairly low-key role. Within the Baldwin family his election victory created complex and difficult feelings. Lucy Baldwin had been used to visiting the Strangers' Gallery during debates; but now, with her husband on one side and her son on the other, the confusion became too great and she gave up attending. SB himself was leader of the Opposition, and later said to his daughter Lorna, 'I nearly died when I saw Oliver on the benches opposite.' Oliver for his part sent a hesitant and diffident letter to his father, approaching him as if with great discretion. He wrote thus on 3 June:[5]

My dear Father,

Now that the agony is over, & you can get a little rest before the House meets, I thought I would tell you what I have meant to for some time past: but now, it seems a more opportune moment & I hope it will soothe the mosquito bite of defeat.

Wherever I have gone on my political rounds during the past six years I have never heard any of our supporters speak other than in a kindly way of your personal self. Our only regret is that you have not been able to put what you have said into practice. That is all. To you, who have generally been victorious, the results may disappoint you, but take it from one who, until the other day, has always been on the losing side, always in the minority & generally alone, that victory or defeat are both flatterers & as such are of no serious consequence. You may be judged by History by your political actions, but you will be judged by God for the Spirit that is in your heart. On re-reading, this seems unsatisfactory, & somewhat presumptious [sic], but it is meant to tell you that I have every admiration for you – (does that amaze?) –, & that you must not get depressed. I am afraid I am one of those to whom Matthew 10 v. 35–38 apply [the verses relate to Jesus' saying that he came to set a man at variance with his father and family, and that the cause was more important than the family]: & it has been the hell of a fight both outwardly and inwardly to remember it. I don't think I could have gone on much longer: but as God sustained you in the old days, so He has sustained me: but what fools find difficult to understand is that He cannot support all Parties. Bless you, & don't bother to answer. I am off to Paris for this week-end, & to Dudley for the next. We go up to London to-morrow to find a room somewhere for me.

　　Oliver

SB replied nevertheless: 'Dearest Son, Your letter gave me real pleasure . . . I was glad in my heart . . .'. Six months later, writing from Astley on New Year's Day 1930, and enclosing a belated Christmas present, the father's benevolence was echoed: 'I saw you in the House on Thursday but got no word with you and on Friday you had gone. . I see [Arthur] Ponsonby is a peer. I had a nervous qualm lest you become one: I can stand a good deal but I couldn't bear seeing you go in to dinner before me . . . Your loving Father'.[6]

Oliver's work in the Commons was not one of making grand revolutionary speeches, or seeking the overthrow of capitalism. A big speech which he promised never materialized. He restricted himself largely to putting down questions for written answers, often on constituency matters. One of these, on 9 July 1929, put forward the idea of 'making use of the government's national projectile factory in Dudley by transferring it into workmen's flats on the Viennese model, or using it in some other way under his [the minister's] scheme for the unemployed'.[7] The minister, J. H. (Jimmy) Thomas, gave a cautious reply.

Other PQs were about diverse matters: a criticism of the use of a military guard to protect the Bank of England, which was a private institution (and one which Oliver hated for its secrecy, self-protection and self-enrichment, and its imperviousness to the national good); another was about the cleaning, levelling and utilization of the unsightly and uneven ground in the Black Country area – Oliver Baldwin showed an early interest in the environment, almost certainly derived from the central significance of his own environment, the magic and ideal garden in Oxfordshire. An interesting question came up on 23 July: he asked the Home Secretary 'to remove censorship on Russian films which deal with incidents of Russian history, such as the cruiser Potemkin, etc.' In answer, he was told that this would be considered; the ban had been imposed because of the films' propagandist nature.[8] Again on constituency matters, on 24 July he questioned the minister on two cases of denial of unemployment benefit in Dudley.

In the autumn parliamentary session he put forward the idea of a tax on advertisements; and on 9 November he asked the Foreign Secretary 'whether he would consider the advisability of making alterations in the method of selecting candidates for the diplomatic service, in view of the increasingly democratic nature of foreign governments.'[9] At the time the Foreign Office was of course laughably old-fashioned and out of touch. He also asked a question about the government's apparent endorsement of *mui tsai*, or child labour, in Hong Kong. He called for the abolition of corporal punishment for midshipmen administered by senior sub-lieutenants, to be told that this practice had already been discontinued. He asked for legislation to provide proper accommodation for hop-pickers during their season of work; and for free postage for MPs within the precincts of the House. Returning to the environmental theme, he expressed a wish for legislation for oil-burning ships to use separators, in order to reduce the incidence of sea-bird slaughter.

Baldwin was also in favour of the principle of what we now call the ombudsman. On 5 December he called for the establishment of a tribunal composed of MPs to deal with cases of injustice suffered by British and foreign nationals in their past dealings with British officials or government departments. He was evidently keen on this idea, for he returned to it three months later, on 12 March 1930.[10] He saw it as a way 'to defend people from alleged injustices against government departments'. To this the minister, Philip Snowden, a man imbued with a stern and narrow Treasury mentality, gave an emphatically negative response.

In a rare speaking appearance he participated in a debate held on 24 January 1930 on the blasphemy laws, which was an attempt, initiated by Ernest Thurtle (Labour MP for Shoreditch), to modify and modernize them, and to limit police powers, something Baldwin was altogether in favour of. 'We all remember what happened only a few days ago, when D. H. Lawrence's pictures were raided by the police, and the police not only carried off the pictures, but also some of the works of William Blake, which they thought were immoral also.'[11] The novelist-painter himself wrote a witty poem about the incident, regretting that figs did not grow in the land of the free.

A number of the things Baldwin fought for have been adopted by later legislation in the natural course of parliamentary events. But he found his spirit severely tested by experience in the House: 'The House of Commons is a heartbreaking place. The wasted hours; the old-fashioned machinery of government; the opposition for the sake of opposition; the interminable talking that has not the slightest effect, and the pile of legislation that need never come to us for decision throws a pall on all and sundry.'[12] At the same time, he wrote of the presence in the House in 1929, 'on all sides, of some of the finest characters this country has produced; men capable of sacrifice; men capable of great love and men whom the bitterness of life has made far gentler than ever it could have been supposed . . . In the smoking-room alone you can hear little groups, of mixed political faiths, discussing every conceivable subject under the sun, from finance to poetry, from etymology to old furniture, from science to histrionics; and my two years there have found me many new friends.'[13]

Life became gentler to Baldwin, he found, after his election. The attacks (such as that by Lockhart and Lyttelton) diminished, and a career of sorts seemed to be developing.

But Britain, and the Labour Party, were moving into crisis. Although the country was prosperous at the time of the election, the background had grown sombre, with the world slump following the Wall Street crash of October 1929. W. J. Brown, one of Baldwin's fellow Labour MPs, has said that the tragedy of the 1929 Labour government was that it had a choice: either to go all out and implement socialism, or to join in an alliance with the Liberals to try to defeat unemployment. It did neither. The impression grew of an administration with little grasp of reality and barely in control. Moreover the Labour leader, Ramsay MacDonald, grew increasingly vague, morose and out of touch. Political stances at this time were indeed confusing. A puzzled foreign observer remarked on the curious situation of Britain having a Tory leader who was a liberal, a Liberal leader who was a socialist, and a Labour leader who was a conservative.[14]

The Labour Party was largely at a loss over how to deal with the Depression. Many members just blamed the capitalist system, but had no idea how to run things better. Oswald Mosley, Labour member for Smethwick since 1926, was the exception. He first put forward a memorandum in January/February 1930, calling for government intervention in industry and foreign trade. The Labour cabinet, still imbued with a strong element of *laissez-faire* economics, rejected his ideas three months later. The Labour conference rejected them too in the autumn of 1930. But the proposals took shape in a new document. In December they were published in a third and final document. W. J. Brown has pointed out that this third memo was the work of several hands – John Strachey and Aneurin Bevan were among them.[15] It was hoped that when a final text was published, many Labour MPs would put their signatures to it, signifying commitment to planning, socialism, and administrative change. But this was not to be. On publication only 17 Labour MPs signed it, plus the miners' leader, A. J. Cook. Oliver Baldwin was one of the signatories. From the copy of a draft which exists in his papers, it would appear that the changes he made to the drafting of it were limited to small matters of wording only.

The preamble to the Mosley Manifesto highlighted the serious nature of the crisis, which threatened the industrial life of the nation. The current situation was one of emergency. The proposals sought to streamline the machinery of government: parliament should remain sovereign, but the government should be given increased powers. An Emergency Cabinet of not more than five ministers should be given the power to carry out policy for the duration of the emergency. A section followed on the need for economic planning, pointing out the changed industrial nature of the world. To cope with this, industry needed to be modernized and re-equipped, and rationalized. The manifesto noted the importance of the markct: the home market was to remain the basis of British trade; a home market depended on popular purchasing power, which in turn indicated high wages. Some form of protection was necessary if industries were not to fall victim to price fluctuation, organized dumping and the competition of sweated labour. In agriculture, there should be a regulatory body, ensuring the farmer received a guaranteed price. To protect manufacturing industry, there should be an import control board. For export trade, the Commonwealth and the Dominions were seen as key elements, which should be built up, since they were endowed both with raw materials and markets for finished goods.

The manifesto also recognized the need for an impetus in house building by direct labour; and taxation should be reformed to stimulate production. The document again stressed the need for major reorganization and reconstruction. It ended by saying that the signatories were not surrendering any of their socialist faith. The issue was not the ownership of British industry but its survival. Later on the debate on the ownership of industry would continue. At the moment the country faced a national emergency. In place of slow drift to disaster, the manifesto proposed 'a programme both more advanced and realistic than anything attempted or proposed by government'. The proposals should secure a measure of agreement.[16]

Despite what was at the time perceived as dangerous radicalism, there were no punitive policies in the measures. It was not so much the Lubyanka and the Gulag which were round the corner, as Roosevelt's New Deal, or Harold Wilson's industrial planning of the 1960s. It opened up, rather than closed off, the options for humankind. There is also, in the idea of involving the state with industrial decisions, an approximate parallel with some Japanese economic practice, where members of the national industrial committee are present in the boards of important private companies. Despite Mosley's later career, there was nothing totalitarian in the spirit of the document.

According to Baldwin, the manifesto frightened the Labour Party. It was seen as an attack on the leadership, verging on the traitorous. There remained the option for its supporters of popularizing its ideas by a campaign of speeches. In this Oliver assisted, speaking in Newcastle, Manchester and Birmingham.

As a result he was soon in deep trouble with his constituency party. It repudiated him. He did not care. On 27 February 1931 he resigned the Labour whip, and would henceforward sit in the House as an independent. Despite breaking with his CLP, he decided not to fight Dudley again as an independent socialist, against an official Labour candidate. That would let the Tory in. He had no further contact with the Dudley party.[17]

But what prospects did he have as a supporter of Mosley and his ideas for curing unemployment? In April 1931, one of Mosley's supporters, Allan Young, stood as a candidate of the 'New Party' (as the Mosleyite group became known) in a by-election in Ashton-under-Lyme. This seemed to give a chance for the kind of situation which Baldwin had determined to avoid at Dudley, a splitting of the progressive forces; and this was just what Young's candidature at Ashton achieved. The Tory got in with a slim majority. After that, Oliver Baldwin had nothing more to do politically with Mosley. He had been one of the earliest followers, believing that planning was the way out of the slump. He was also among the first to be disillusioned – some months, for example, before C. E. M. Joad, who left in July 1931 on detecting 'the cloven hoof of fascism' in Mosley's movement.

By mid 1931 Oliver realized that something was up with Ramsay MacDonald. In the summer of that year Britain was, as ever at that time, enjoying its annual shut-down, when despite slump or unemployment crisis, life comes to a standstill. In August MacDonald was in his beloved Lossiemouth, and Baldwin was in Inverness, umpiring a cricket-match. On returning south in the train he found himself in the carriage next to that of the Prime Minister.[18]

MacDonald invited him into his carriage. The Prime Minister talked gloomily of the prospects: there was a financial crisis, the Stock Exchange would crash; Britain would be forced off the Gold Standard, which was be disastrous. Baldwin disagreed on the significance of all these points. It would be admirable to leave the Gold Standard. The Stock Exchange was not sacred; the money barons, who controlled the Bank of England (private at this time) wanted to bring down the Labour government. Let them suffer. But he did not win MacDonald to his point of view.

Baldwin elaborated his understanding of the 1931 crisis in a letter to the *Manchester Guardian* of 20 August 1931. The reason for the situation he said, was simple, 'and is merely the result of English banks investing in foreign countries instead of helping British industry, and the failure of the foreign banks to pay the high interest that was the original attraction. The result is that the nation has to bear the brunt of bad investment, since the medium of exchange is not nationally controlled and we are at the mercy of the monop- olists.[19]

> Money [he continued], intended mathematically and logically as the medium of exchange, has become a commodity to be speculated with, and there will be no prosperity for the world until this state of affairs is altered. As long as there is production, actual or potential, and consumers desiring to consume, there can be no crisis. There is only a complete collapse of the means of distribution and consumption owing to the lack of purchasing power caused by monopoly control of the medium of exchange.
>
> For a state to allow a private company to issue a nation's currency and then borrow that money back at interest is sheer lunacy, and is further enhanced by permitting speculation and investment without control. Will no one bother to save the nation's currency for the nation?'

This letter is, one can say, an attempt to grapple with economic issues at a time when little was understood about them, but it is so dense, and refers to so many different points, none of which is properly worked out or related to any other issue, that is cannot really be said to have been a useful contribution. And it is arguable that a nation's money has to be in part speculative, otherwise there would be no interest on savings, and no buying and selling of govern- ment bonds (or gilts). Baldwin, in his discussions of economics and monetary theory, remained literalistic and unintellectual, and failed to show anything of Keynes's imag- inative understanding of the subject.

MacDonald, after several cabinet meetings, failed to resolve the crisis; so he asked for a dissolution, resigned, and returned to head a National government. As ever in a crisis, when there are desperate actions which lead to charges of

betrayal, motives are searched for evidence of either cock-up
or conspiracy. Oliver Baldwin believed there had been a conspiracy – that MacDonald had been 'intriguing with the
Tories, behind the backs of his cabinet colleagues', and the
Tories had offered him the job of deputy prime minister
under Stanley Baldwin, though MacDonald had insisted on
keeping the job for himself, otherwise (he believed) he would
not bring the party with him. (In the end he did not take all
the party with him, and the real Labour supporters lived to
fight another day.) But A. J. P. Taylor believes that the charge
of betrayal is false: that MacDonald was just seeking a
temporary solution to a situation similar to a war-time crisis.
Oliver Baldwin again showed a penchant for conspiracy
theories.

There was now a curious constitutional problem. It is
widely held that, on the resignation of a prime minister, the
monarch should send for the leader of the largest party, who
in this case was Arthur Henderson, the Labour leader who
wanted to have nothing to do with the coalition. But he was
not sent for. So MacDonald called an election, to clarify the
situation.

Baldwin sensed that the Labour Party had ditched its
major liabilities, and was better, if temporarily weaker,
without MacDonald, Snowden, Jimmy Thomas, and others.
Despite its smaller size, it had now returned to roots, and
would not now sell out to the bankers. So he went, perhaps
somewhat meekly, to Arthur Henderson to say that he was
prepared, if the party would have him, to fight the general
election for Labour anywhere.[20] He was offered Rochester
and Chatham, accepted, and set about the task with determined professionalism. He was officially selected as
candidate on 10 October. In his acceptance speech he spoke
of his opposition to cuts in social services and unemployment benefit. In questions following his speech, he was
asked about the New Party. He said that when he had signed
the Mosley Manifesto he had not foreseen the formation of a

separate party. He had believed that the scheme could be operated within the existing framework of the Labour Party. 'Afterwards the Mosley party went to the Right, and that, of course, finished everything so far as I was concerned with them.'[21]

Two days later, on 12 October, he spoke for almost an hour at Chatham Town Hall: a major speech, even gargantuan, covering mammoth slabs of economic history, starting with the enclosures, and detailing the rise of industrialization. The topics were mostly familiar. Two issues were new, one of which was pretty weird, and the other progressive and forward looking. The half-barmy notion was that America was, through international banking contacts, behind the Bank of England's unwillingness to raise unemployment benefit, and indeed wanted the UK to scrap it altogether, since there were 8 million unemployed in the US, and to pay them benefit, on the precedent of UK unemployment benefit, would be to bankrupt the US Treasury. The forward-looking notion that he sought was one of the measures outlined in the Mosley Manifesto: that British wages had to be increased, in order to bring about more buying power and so stimulate the circulation of goods, which would create wealth at a much greater rate than that occasioned by individual increments.[22] From the perspective of the twenty-first century it is arguable that the high-wage economies of some Continental countries have brought about higher standards of post-war living, and a more substantial reduction of the under-class, than has occurred in relatively low-wage Britain. British parsimoniousness, the greed of British bosses, as well as government deference to negative, class-based, Treasury and civil-servant sentiment, effectively scotched a high-wage economy, and the chance of the British economy lifting off in the manner of comparable economies on the Continent.

Despite the rapidity of the campaign, he managed to poll over ten thousand votes. The results were:

Sir P. Goff	C	19991	62.3%
O.R. Baldwin	Lab	10837	33.9%
M.F. Woodroff	NP	1135	3.6%

Conservative majority, 9154.   Turnout, 75.5%

The result was not disheartening, given – within one turbulent year – Labour's crisis, and Baldwin's own resignation from and return to the party.

*

Oliver also had a busy social life. Although this centred largely on Farm House and Johnnie, at this time too he took the lease of a London house, 11 Graham Street (today Graham Terrace), SW1, and paid frequent visits across the channel to both France and Algeria. Paris was the home of several of his friends, including the painter Roger Duval, whom he had known since his first visit to Algeria in 1920, and some Armenian exiles, notably Alexander Khatisian, who lived at 134 avenue Wagram. Clark Martin and Martin Brown, nicknamed Clarkie and Brownie, the two NER field-workers Oliver had met in Alexandropol in March 1921, appear to have been sharing an apartment at 7 rue Daubeton. Although Oliver always put Britain first, despite its fogs, gloom and class system, he responded to the freshness and vigour of French society; it had an ease and a lack of social bossiness which he found attractive. Oliver was not a wildly sophisticated man, and was too busy and socialist to be chic and fashionable, but he relished the charm and brilliance of French society. Moreover sex between men was not a criminal offence across the channel.

Domestic life was settled and trusting, still not always harmonious, but Oliver showed tact and insight in dealing with difficulties. Many of the letters he wrote to Johnnie are witty and affectionate, and if they show criticism, it is tempered by good humour. Oliver found it hard to tolerate fuss and bother, and tried to treat lightly Johnnie's tendency to find problems where none existed. For one of their sea-crossings, Oliver wrote a short verse, typical of his manner of dealing as much with his own aversion to fuss as Johnnie's penchant for the same. Above it he wrote the instruction: 'To Be Repeated Night and Morning':[23]

When I am sailing on the sea
And all my world is well afloat
Nice and gentle I will be
I won't cantaker on the boat.

I may have pain; I may be ill;
I may have quinsy in the throat
But I will not pass my illness on -
I won't cantanker on the boat.

However late old C. comes in -
Or if he walks without his coat -
I will be nice and smile at him
And won't cantanker on the boat.
              Signed J. Koot

(The reference to 'old C.' is presumably to Oliver himself; maybe another spelling of 'coot'.)

Oliver's ability to express feelings about anger and the darker side of life was also shown by an 'ang lett' (angry letter) that he sent to Johnnie, which consisted of a sheet of House of Commons notepaper whose sole message was an array of exclamation marks and ink-blots. But, as evidence of the balance which he achieved (somewhat precariously) in his life, at about the same time he also sent Johnnie a 'Not Ang Lett', also on Commons stationery: 'I'm coming to have dinn. with Mr Koot at 8 p.m. at 11 Graham St, unless Mr K would prefer to go out with me-me to a nice restaurant. So just expect me & behap . . . 8 o'clock & a luvely dinn & if you'd like to go to a play get ticks & we'll dine at 7 only you must telephone here & say Dinn at 7.
A & A & A.Y.O.L.K.
W.L.U

Anger, or Angra-Pangra in their private language, featured elsewhere in the Member for Dudley's letters. In one of them he drew an amusing sketch of the two of them at the funeral – over-hasty? – of Angra-Pangra; another (of 1929) said simply: 'Just heard from the solicitors Messrs Quarrel & Rage that Angra-Pangra left no money having spent it all on Tempers – whatever that is, but I suppose they are steel shares about some new process of tempering steel.'[24]

Good-humoured, and sometimes ironic, references to friends abound. 'Stayed with J[ohnny] Dodge last night. Lionel F, I hear, has been to Italy with "Dreams Fade"!! Silly fellow.'[25] Lionel F was of course Lionel Fielden, Oliver's submissive friend, the complaisant drudge of Farm House. (Later he got a job with the BBC in the Talks department.) One can only speculate about the identity of 'Dreams Fade' – presumably the inappropriate love object, some fey young man diligently absorbed in his own beauty.

A letter written from Paris in April 1930, when Oliver was making a semi-official visit to the Chambre des Députés, gives a flavour of his social life there:[26]

Lunched with Noel [?Coward], Clarkie, Brownie & Mace who asked very nicely after you. Went to see a film with Parker Steward in afternoon. Dined with charming 3rd attache of our embassy – Robin Hankey & then went on to Boeuf sur le Toit where the same black woman who sang at Dinard was singing. Ralph Radcliffe was there with young German friend. Lunching to-day with George [Bambridge]. Weather keeps warm – little rain yesterday

Behap – one really ought to have an appartement in Paris – Hotels are no good!
Y.O.K.W.L.U.

Oliver travelled much more than Johnnie, who seems to have preferred the comforts and reassurances of home to adventures abroad. Johnnie was kept well informed of the travels; thus, in October 1930 Oliver took a villa – the Villa Claude Vignon Rouvier – with some friends in St-Jean de Cap Ferrat, where he went to do some 'reading and writing and bathing'. He wrote home daily. The first letter enclosed a sprig of honeysuckle – 'There's a walk by the sea with this growing all the length.' St-Jean was the kind of place Oliver liked: 'This little fishing village is certainly a "queer" place: mostly Italian parentage but very friendly'. He also asked Johnny to keep copies of the *Daily Herald*, so that on his return he could keep up with what had happened at the Labour Party Conference. Cap Ferrat and its diversions were obviously more fun than composite resolutions put from the floor at conference.[27]

When they were both at home, there seems to have been a party most weekends. Names recur in the visitors' book: principally Miss H. A. Bold, a friend of Johnnie's from a time when they were both living in King's Bench Walk. She was a solicitor's clerk, and was always known as Boldie. She had originally met Johnnie when he knocked on her door to tell her about a stray kitten, which she then took in. Thereafter, she always called him Fluff – her own personal nickname for him. She was very much a *femme seule*, eccentric, fairly ignorant of the ways of the world, but devoted to them both. She retired to Bexhill-on-Sea, and named her house after Oliver and Johnnie's second Oxfordshire home.

John Drinkwater, the late-Georgian poet and playwright, and his wife Daisy Kennedy, a violinist of some distinction, were neighbours in Shirburn. They too enjoyed the hospitality of Farm House – so much so that on one occasion in 1927 Drinkwater sent a sonnet to Johnnie and Oliver, by way of a thank-you letter. Entitled 'J.B. and O.B. Entertain', it is printed in Drinkwater's 1933 collection of poems entitled *Summer Harvest*. It is a delightful (if minor) poem in its own right, with a glance back to Horace and Ben Jonson; but what gives it special significance is that it was a positive acknowledgement of the hospitality of a male couple:[28]

Wars have been made, as we again may make,
We being cursed by envy as of old,
And heretics have chanted to the stake,
And princes bought dishonour with their gold,
Poets have sung, and orators have pleaded,
Stars have been charted on a patient sky,
And prophets gone to paradise unheeded, -
Thus have the labouring ages been – and why?

Why, but that closing here a summer's day
We friends, since friends may on a moment be,
Should meet, and gossip, idly of the way
The world has gone, still goes, and pause to see
The dusky carters bring, as sire by sire
They brought the wagons home in Oxfordshire.

Maybe the phrase 'sire by sire' carries a reference to more than oxen.

Another visitor, enigmatic and charged with magic and mystery, was Michael Redgrave. Oliver and Johnnie had originally met him in about 1924 in Veule-les-Roses, Normandy. Redgrave was then probably aged sixteen. He describes Oliver: 'Tall, with straight, reddish-gold silky hair, a trim officer's moustache, and pale but piercing eyes, he had an air of distinction and indeed, beauty which would not have disgraced a pre-Raphaelite hero.'[29] A passionate friendship developed between the two; Redgrave says that Oliver was his first hero.[30] The circumstances of their meeting (as described by Michael Redgrave) were curious. The hotel at the resort had a piano, and it was here that the future actor met an enigmatic youth with cropped hair who was playing Chopin waltzes with an exaggerated rubato, while wearing a long silk scarf. He claimed that Oliver and Johnnie were his 'two jailers'.

However, it seems that the young man (named Sidney in Redgrave's narrative) was a fairly fluent fantasist. His mother had had no idea what to do with him, so she had handed him over to Oliver and Johnnie for a holiday which she had paid for. They had agreed to take him, on condition that he cut off his long, dramatically highlighted hair, and promise not to wear make-up. (He was known as 'The Painted Lady of Sidmouth'.) Through Sidney, Redgrave got to know Baldwin, and having dismissed Sidney's strictures on the couple as fantasy, grew very attached to both Oliver and Johnnie. Redgrave gives Oliver credit for being the first person to suggest to him that he should take up acting seriously, and for persuading him that socialism was the only morally tenable political philosophy. Indeed, it seems certain that the kindling of the socialist blaze which was and is so much a feature of the Redgrave family can be traced to the twigs set smouldering by Oliver in 1924. Baldwin also – seeking to help him widen his experience, or in a moment of irony, manifesting his own sense of self-control? – suggested that the young Redgrave should try heterosexuality.

Redgrave's subsequent letters (including one written from Cranleigh School, where he was a master), while saying little, show a profound almost unearthly calm, and inner peace, and a great affection for Johnnie. In his memoirs Redgrave noted: 'John Boyle, when he set out to charm, seldom had a failure.'[31] Of later visits to Oliver and Johnnie, Lady Redgrave has recalled: 'The sun always seemed to be shining with those two happy friends.'[32]

Other friends of the Farm House couple included Oliver's childhood friends Buster (A. J. C.) Browne and Renée de Vaux (now renowned as a 'dramatic actress'), and local Oxfordshire people, such as Dunstan and Oswald Skilbeck, of Bledlow. These two brothers were typical of the weekend guests: original and artistic people, whose careers were only incidentally connected with making money. Dunstan eventually became principal of Wye Agricultural College; and Oswald, who married a singer, became much involved in the theatre. Oswald Skilbeck recalled lengthy talks with Johnnie in the garden, while Oliver accompanied his wife on the piano.[33]

One acquaintance Oliver made in 1928 was Roly Gwynne, otherwise Lieutenant-Colonel Sir Roland Gwynne, DSO, High Sheriff of Sussex, Mayor of Eastbourne, and owner at the time of Folkington Manor, Polegate, Sussex. His brother Rupert had been Tory MP for Eastbourne, and had gained a minor post in Stanley Baldwin's government before his early death in 1924. He left a widow and four daughters, one of whom was the highly distinguished culinary writer Elizabeth David; another was the much-admired Felicité, who worked for many years in John Sandoe Books of Chelsea. The sisters referred to Roly as 'the wicked uncle', partly because he was fairly undisguisedly homosexual (which was wicked but alluringly glamorous) and partly because, after their father's death and their mother's re-marriage, he had rather unceremoniously evicted the family from the house (which was wicked but unglamorous).

Oliver met Roly through his uncle Arthur Ridsdale. A letter of 10 August 1928 says that 'Uncle has been staying in Sussex with Roly Gwynne & was much impressed by his new secretary who was head of Lancing College last year. He was surprised he hadn't a woman secretary.'[34] A month later Oliver wrote to Colonel Gwynne, asking to be put up for a couple of nights in October, 'to fulfil a long-standing invitation on your part & an interested desire on mine.' The letter had been sent indirectly, because 'except that you have a Rolls-Royce & a charming secretary my uncle has not provided me with your address.'[35]

As well as enjoying a varied social life, the serious side to Oliver's existence continued. He had to work hard for a living. This meant principally writing. He was, somewhat precociously, writing his autobiography, which he finished in late 1931; he wrote a three-act stage play which was put on at a London theatre club on successive Sunday nights in October 1931, and articles poured from his pen on a wide range of subjects, for any paper which would print them.

Oliver had a backlog of short dramatic works dating from Astley days, one-acters which showed a taste for crime, horror and the supernatural, a genre which he continued to write. Some of these are effective. *The Wrong Bus* and *The Fog* were both performed by the BBC during the 1920s, *The Fog* apparently in 1926. They show an inclination towards the bizarre, the sinister and the violent, and often manifest an underlying spiritual bleakness. There is no redemption, and little compassion, in Oliver's crime dramas.

The Wrong Bus (written under the pseudonym Martin Hussingtree) is a vivid radio script: the writing is economical, and the dialogue shows real bite. A weary couple is waiting somewhere in the country for a late-night bus to take them home after the theatre. Their names are Elsie and John Williams – Christian names derived directly from those of the author's Kipling cousins. Eventually the bus arrives. No sooner have they got on it than John is aware that his wife is not with him. He looks frantically for her on the top of the bus and begs the conductor to tell the driver to stop. Horror strikes him when he sees that the face of the conductor, who refuses to try to stop the vehicle, is covered in blood. John tries to stop it himself but is equally shocked to find that there is no one in the driving seat. The conductor seems to speak in riddles, though John does learn the name of the non-existent driver, Bill Jenkins. The bus careers along on its own. The conductor's language becomes ambiguous and sinister, eventually indicating that the vehicle will crash. Just as it is about to hurtle over a precipice he is told to look into the mirror himself, and receives a terrible shock: his own face is covered in blood. As the bus crashes, and the passengers scream, the conductor calls out the Williams' destination, and Elsie, materializing beside her husband, calls to him to wake up: 'You are all hot . . . you must have been dreaming'. Leaving, he asks the conductor if he knew a driver called Bill Jenkins. 'That was 'im wot went over Redrock Cliff some years ago. We're more careful now though . . . Good night, sir.'[36]

The blend of an ordinary setting, with ordinary people, and violent fantasy, together with additional ingredients of prescience and remote knowledge, were typical elements of Baldwin's literary life. He liked the ordinariness of life, and believed that unremarkable people were almost by definition remarkable; but at the same time he believed in ghosts and the other side. There is a real ambiguity here. He had attended seances in the 1920s, in one of which John Kipling had 'come through', and he believed that he had been able to identify the manner in which his cousin had been killed at Loos, and to know where his body lay in the ground. The ghostly realm of esoteric knowledge was not foreign to Oliver. But at the same time his rewritten life of Jesus was to be bracingly rationalist and devoid of mysteries. Puzzlingly, he let the world of mystical Neoplatonism and gnosticism coexist with rational modernism. In some strange way, he did on occasion appear to have an insight into matters for which he could have had no *prima facie* information: for instance, W. J. Brown relates that when an MP had collapsed at the far end from Baldwin of the Harcourt Room, a parliamentary dining room, other members rushed round to help and to try to resuscitate him, but Oliver said simply 'Don't move; the man is already dead', which happened to be true (though it might have been a guess). The claim of being party to esoteric knowledge is arguably the corollary of narcissism and grandiosity. The belief that one has a privileged access to a certain kind of knowledge denied to others is an exclusivity that echoes the experience of childhood, when it was briefly a condition of existence that oneself and no other had access to the unqualified love of mother. Belief in rational, Aristotelian, Socinian, equality and modernism allows a person to break the emotional chains of the past, and to live as a free and creative present-day person. Like many people, Baldwin veered from a Platonic mystical elitism to a shared Aristotelian common sense, which never fully supplanted the magical but sterile and regressive beliefs of childhood.

Another of Oliver's radio plays which received a broadcast was *The Fog* ('by Hanley Child'). This had been written in his teenage years, and it is one of the dramas whose production Oliver had planned while imprisoned by the Bolsheviks in Yerevan. It is a competent one-act crime play, making the point that places and things, even more than people, may cause death. Here humanity is almost out of rational control. We are in the private house of A. E. Rancott, a private detective. He is discussing with his assistant, a man called Maydon, an unsolved murder, the Archbourne case. Archbourne, a wealthy businessman, had been killed on Beverley Moor, a bleak stretch of Yorkshire, but nothing had been taken from him; there had been no attempt at robbery. Which of the suspects was guilty? Williams, his former partner; his brother; the gardener; or Hanwell, the well-educated secretary of the deceased?

The blows had been dealt with extreme force. Williams, Maydon tells us, was a man of great strength, and so he inclines to the hypothesis that he was the killer. Rancott believes it was Hanwell – who might have been physically incapable, but was not psychically incapable. Maydon declares he has no idea what that means. Rancott explains by pointing out that Beverley Moor is a lonely and desolate stretch of land, part of an ancient forest and swamp. It was the site of druidical ceremonies. In the past a number of murders and violent deaths had occurred on the same site. The moor had drawn deadly deeds to itself.

Rancott elaborates to the sceptical Maydon about the potent unease of place, telling of locations where we naturally imagine footsteps and sounds, and which draw us as well as repel us. Even in the London parks there are places where tramps will not rest after dark. The reason, he insists, is that the places have an influence attached to them which is antagonistic to man – something supernatural, something pre-human and frightful. Anyone who witnesses it goes off his head, or dies of a heart attack.

Rancott says that he intends to prove his thesis, and to this end has invited to his house Hanwell, who duly appears.

Maydon observes the scene from a corner of the room. The detective and his visitor discuss the killing of Archbourne, Rancott initially indicating that he believes that Williams was the culprit; but he goes on to put forward the hypothesis that the victim might have been killed both by a human and a natural agency: the fog. Hanwell becomes hysterical with guilt, and relates his walk with Archbourne across Beverley Moor: suddenly the fog sprang up, and within the fog, a presence which cried 'Kill him, kill him', a presence which possessed Hanwell so that he felt compelled to murder Archbourne. As they speak, Hanwell senses this same presence to be close, coming in through the curtains, and as his screams of guilt and panic reach a pitch of terror, he rushes to the curtains, the window flies open, and he falls dead. 'It came in the fog, Maydon, it came in the fog', says Rancott.[37]

The originals of such a drama would appear to be O. Henry, E. W. Hornung and perhaps Sir Arthur Conan Doyle, but the drama has a tension of its own which would have built considerable excitement for the radiophonic audience. Its enclosed gloom and pessimism reflect the bleak, troubled dark-Oliver side of the playwright's personality, in contrast to the witty, sociable light-Oliver, recalled, along with Johnnie's effortlessly gracious persona, by Lady Redgrave.

Oliver's career as a playwright received some sort of recognition was the production, at the Embassy Theatre Club, Swiss Cottage, of his full-length three-act play, *From the Four Winds*. This was performed on successive Sunday evenings in October 1931, just at the time he was being selected to stand as Labour candidate for Rochester. Despite the need to campaign in Kent at the same time, he seems to have managed the division of work without difficulty.

From the Four Winds is a curious drama, part realistic, and part symbolist. Unlike the one-act shockers, it takes on major issues of human change and spiritual insight, and it challenges the audience as well as entertaining it. It is at once a society play, a consciousness-raising socialist drama, and an enactment of spiritual transformation. It is undoubtedly ambitious, and it is unlikely that it would work on the stage today.

The opening is conventional. We are in the drawing room of a country house, with a door, centre back, giving on to a garden. It is early evening. The clock seems to be behaving oddly, but otherwise there is nothing to distinguish the beginning from that of a score of society plays of the time. One by one, a cast of twelve disparate characters assemble. First to arrive is a financier, George Morys, looking for a client. (Morys was played by Francis L. Sullivan, a distinguished stage and film actor, perhaps best known as Mr Bumble in David Lean's 1948 *Oliver Twist*.) He is followed by a working man, Eli Rudge, and a married woman, Mrs Moor, both of whom have come to the house in the hope of meeting different individuals. All are a bit perplexed by seeing unexpected people there, and seem to have arrived as a result of indistinct messages.

The dialogue in the first act reflects the puzzlement. We learn something of their backgrounds and preoccupations. George Morys, the financier, presents a confident, businessman-like exterior to the world, but at one moment he speaks confidingly of recurrent bad dreams. This disclosure may derive from Baldwin's own experience of nightmares, following his return from Armenia and Turkey; also, in a wider sense, he believed in the power and significance of dreaming, though he never harnessed that belief to psychoanalytic theory. In a newspaper interview he said that the first two acts of his play came to him in a dream, adding that he tried unsuccessfully to dream the third act, and that as a result the ending gave him difficulty.

A trade union official, Cusdon, is the next to enter; he is under the impression that he has come to a union meeting. He has a sour exchange with the non-unionized Rudge. A 'modern young society woman' appears (played by Leonora Corbett); her name, Elsie Kirtling, is very close to that of the playwright's cousin and its obvious original. She is followed by a young man about town, Cedric Fetherway, who is vainly hoping to find his girl-friend. He engages in a mild flirtation with Elsie by way of compensation. A poor travelling (gipsy) woman, Mrs Perry, is the next arrival, selling boot-laces, and offering to tell fortunes. All the different types, especially the poor ones, are observed human beings. There is nothing condescending about the manner in which their characters are drawn. It is as though Oliver knew the poor people he was writing about, as he knew the well-off, and to him they were as real as each other.

A lawyer, Ernest Feltham, of Monks, Liver and Feltham enters (played by Charles Lefeaux), looking for a client. He is followed by Private Daniel O'Hare, clearly of the Irish Guards, who has something of the stage Irishman about him, but whose energetic dialogue is largely unstereotypical. A servant girl (Edith Barker; played by Joan Harben) enters, hoping to find a whist drive. Last of the women to arrive is a peer's daughter, Lady Angela Crowle, entering with gushing gratitude to express thanks to the person reported to have found her lost bracelet; however neither bracelet nor finder is present. The company is made complete when a journalist, Matthew Sparks (played by John Boxer) turns up; he is looking for a story he'd been tipped off to find in the house. They seem an odd bunch to him.

The bell is rung, with no result, so they wander off into other parts of the house. They come back none the wiser. Trees are in blossom outside, even though it is autumn – some fruit trees, and a Judas tree. Tempers become a bit frayed. It grows dark, and the fortune-teller senses that something is going to happen.

Suddenly the main door shuts and locks itself, the curtains close, and the lights switch themselves on of their own accord. The mood becomes edgy and fearful.

Music sounds, and a voice is heard, from high in the room, inviting the characters to dinner in the grey room. To get there they will have to go through the little door, downstage on the right. They grow anxious and embarrassed at this unseen invitation – is it safe, and who has precedence? – but finally they accept. The fortune-teller alone seems pleased. As they leave to dine, a slow curtain brings act one to an end.

Act two finds the cast at dinner, at a long table with a large chair empty in the middle at the back for the absent host. Banter calms anxieties. Lady Angela is reminded of a Primrose League gathering – Oliver getting a dig both at respectable conformism and at his former fiancée. They are puzzled by the voice. Was it the wireless; or did it come from the window, or the chimney? To O'Hare it was like a voice heard once in the thick of battle.

They discuss the manner in which electrical gadgetry might simplify their lives, and Lady Angela expresses advanced views for someone of her grand background: 'I always think so much could be done that way to simplify having children. It's so terribly tedious as it's worked today. If it were done properly there would be no need to bother with husbands.'[38]

Class and income become the main topics. Lady Angela, a devotee of 'trickle down' economic theory, says 'Look at the employment I give to poor unfortunate girls when I have a new dress.' The poor characters, especially Mrs Perry and Cusdon, the trade union official, are unimpressed. Cusdon says emphatically to Lady Angela: 'Our outlook on life has never entered your head . . . To us there are only two things that matter – enough money to feed the children and ourselves, and a roof over our heads. To you it matters where you eat your food, how your wants are looked after, what impression you make on others, how you spend your leisure, who your grandfather was, and how you can keep things as they are so that your pleasures are not interfered with. You see, there's a great difference. It's like two different races.' Here is an undisguised echo of Disraeli's 'two nations'.[39]

Elsie Kirtling tries to placate both sides – maybe reflecting a calming role played by Elsie Kipling between Oliver and her father when relations were ruptured following Oliver's espousal of socialism.

The discussion between Morys, the businessman, and Cusdon becomes more heated. The argument is a standard right-left one, Morys (and Fetherway) arguing for things to stay as they are, the latter claiming that the overwhelming majority of the people want things to continue unchanged. Cusdon argues that the system is geared towards the rich, and that lack of education for the poor is keeping them down. They had (he says) fought for a country of which they do not own a square inch; they had been wounded in a quarrel which was not of their making. Are they content to spend week after week in a workhouse, so that their family, away in a neighbouring town, might receive a paltry issue of grocery tickets to keep them from starving?[40]

George Morys dismisses him as a discontented stirrer.

Anxieties surface; Morys grumbles about wanting to leave. Most of the characters seem to be a bit drunk, or slightly crazy. Someone hears a cock crow outside. Edith Barker feels strange, and takes a piece of bread from the plate; the businessman does the same. Another hand seems present on the plate. Matthew Sparks the journalist remarks on the fact that there are twelve of them.

Here the drama undergoes a scenic metamorphosis. The directions indicate that the stage grows dim, and slowly the dining room changes into a smaller grey room of whitewashed mud. We are transformed to the upper room where Christ and his disciples partook of the Last Supper. The twelve guests are the disciples re-incarnated.

The dialogue takes on a heightened quality, which is effective and unembarrassing. They were fishermen; Matthew Sparks was the tax-collector and evangelist. (In *Konyetz* Baldwin had referred to Matthew, Mark, Luke and John as the 'four great journalists'.)

Morys's anxiety enters a new dimension: 'Don't go on talking like this. If anyone did anything they shouldn't have

done, it was to fulfil things . . . He was causing discontent.
He was stirring up the people. He was against the Church. I
did God's service. I . . .'

Sparks: One, two, three – they all go by with the waggons
and the donkeys. Here a rich man, here a poor man; all must
pay at the gate.
Cusdon: It comes back to me – the clinging of the garment
round my ankles and the rain that made it wet, and the hard,
round pebbles on the soles of my feet.
Cedric: The heat, the great heat and the smell of burning
wood, a sweet smell; and the meat and the flies upon it, and the
gleaming teeth of the endless multitude.
Elsie: How the boat rocks. A man stood on the waters and all
around him was glory . . .
Mrs Perry: He loved me.
Cusdon: They wouldn't hear him, the rich and the priests.
They tried to trap him and they mocked him for living with the
poor.
Mrs Perry: The rich have not changed, nor have the priests.[41]

Morys is partly in and partly outside this trance-like
evocation of the life of Christ. He now condemns it as pure
devilry, and demands that the light be turned up. But the
scene grows dimmer. He is tormented by a sense of guilt,
and demands: 'Speak, you in the corner; why are you
torturing me?' Rudge, the working man, says, 'There is no
one but us.' All hear a knock at the door, except Morys. It is
repeated. Still Morys denies hearing it. They must open the
door, but who shall do it? It must be Morys. In desperation
he says that he dare not; he cannot move. He begs the others
for mercy. 'I have not seen him since Gethsemane.' But they
insist that he open the door. 'We have a guest.' Morys's hand
is on the door as the curtain falls.

In the final act, the setting is the same as for act one. Elsie
and Cedric are puzzling over what happened. Cedric thinks
it was all a trick; but Elsie feels different, 'as if a whole new

world has opened up before me'. Cedric tries to take her hand, but she asks him not to. She is still coming to terms with the transforming experience. But he returns to his subject: 'I want to say something . . . you and I might get engaged.' Don't be silly, she retorts. He replies that he is quite serious, and regrets that the whole episode at dinner had happened. She seems colder as a result.

> Elsie: Colder? No. I'm becoming human, that's all. I have a new outlook. I seem to have left my body somewhere away . . . You see really there's no such thing as sex; no such thing as man or woman. We're just, oh, it's so difficult to explain if you can't see. The purely man and purely woman are useless. The ideal is half and half. The perfect balance.[42]

Cedric interposes that she seems to be wanting men to be soft and spineless. She replies:

> Soft, yes. Not spineless. Why shouldn't men be soft and gentle. What good has the hard man ever done to make the world kinder, gentler, more understanding? That's what's wrong. Our values are wrong. We expect men to be hard and domineering and women to be soft and feeble, when the perfect man or perfect woman is obviously none of these things, but just perfectly balanced like the Christ.[43]

Cedric replies that that would not wash these days. Elsie says we must make it 'wash'; only thus can wars and hatreds and unkindness be ended, when we have adjusted our values. To this Cedric replies with the standard response of the right-winger: you can't change human nature. Elsie's reply is interesting:

> Have you ever tried? Have you ever made yourself not do something because it was cruel or unspiritual? Of course you have. We can all change our actions, even if we can't change our thoughts. And yet thoughts are so strong . . . But we can change. I know we can.[44]

Cedric notices that she had changed. Looking around the room, he finds photographs of the guests as they had been in childhood. This was presumably an evocation of Jesus' saying, 'Except ye turn, and become as little children, ye shall in no wise enter into the kingdom of heaven' (Matthew xviii, 3).

Elsie and Cedric pause to think. She feels different, and regrets that he's still as he was. He takes that as a hint to leave. But she calls him back. They have been thrown together. So they must make a go of it, as a kind of 'brotherhood'. Not marriage? he asks. There's no point, she replies, adding:

> You're tired of it all before you are thirty. The appeal has always been body to us moderns, and if there's anything else, well, we just don't notice it till the craving dies, and then it is often just comradeship, and that's its enduring part. We find each other a habit. We don't bother much about each other when we're there, but we sort of miss each other when we're apart, like you miss a dog or a cat or a piece of furniture.[45]

Cusdon enters. Cedric tries to downplay the experience to him too, to see if he will agree that it was all trickery and nonsense. But Cusdon insists on its validity. The servant, Edith Barker, enters, and has a lengthy dialogue with Elsie, about her life. Baldwin used the exchange to explore the hardness of servanthood and disability, since Edith had a sister who was blind from birth. Their father had been compelled to end his life in the workhouse, since the Board of Guardians had said that his cost on the rates was shameful.

Morys enters, and emphatically says that the events at dinner were a trick. Nothing happened. But he senses the threat to his values from the revelation of which he was part. He is furious when the servant girl calls him 'brother'. We cannot allow all we hold most dear to be upset. Survival of the fittest was a law of nature; strife and war are essential to thin out the population. He derides meekness, gentleness and humility. He proclaims himself proud to be a materialist. Each man for himself. Free and unfettered competition. Edith calls that a cruel way of living, and insists that it could be different. Rubbish, Morys retorts, and says that the heart of opposition to his views is discontent and envy. The Have-nots have no right to take away from the Haves. Footsteps are heard, and Morys departs.

Cusdon and Sparks enter, in conversation on class and accent. The trade unionist is looking for a broader education syllabus to end the waste of class distinctions, and to teach other viewpoints and other religions.

A number of the characters assemble, and the mood is one of contentment and comradely friendship; the reverse of the earlier snobbish bitchery and social disquiet. The harmony continues for all except the absent Morys. Mrs Perry says it's time to go. From her purse she offers Mrs Moor some cash. Cusdon has to be off too. As he leaves he takes some notes from his wallet, and hands them too to Mrs Moor. Feltham too leaves, convinced that now life is really worth living: 'To have so many chances.' He too digs into his wallet.

Elsie ponders life and its new chances, thinking of the emptiness and insincerity of what had gone before. Mrs Moor comments that 'ambition and power, greed and materialism can make a desert of the soul', and Elsie recalls that 'we were always told to admire ambition and the strife for gain. It seems so petty to think of that now.' Lady Angela remarks that she always thought things were all right, before. For us?, asks Mrs Moor. 'Yes, I didn't think of the others.' Elsie and Cedric leave, Elsie giving Mrs Moor her necklace, and Cedric parting with his note-case. O'Hare has to go, too. He does not hand anything over. Edith Barker hands Mrs Moor her ring on leaving, and Mrs Moor responds by giving her money for her mother in hospital. She replies 'Thank you, brother,' a linguistic use which today seems laughably male-centred, but at the time 'sister' might not have carried the right weight of comradely equality. Or perhaps, since

Oliver had problems with his sisters, the word 'sister' was a difficult one for him.

Sparks leaves too, handing over money; he seems embarrassed as he goes, and the stage direction indicates that the experience had left him mystified.

Rudge is perplexed by the giving of money to Mrs Moor. She replies with a New Testament verse about holding things in common, and selling possessions so as to give to each person according to need.[46] He is persuaded to give her a shilling.

Lady Angela is left with Mrs Moor. She is disheartened that, while some have understood, others have not. Mrs Moor tells her to give them time. The symbolism of the trees – there are eleven – and one Judas tree is brought very directly into their dialogue. Is there hope for the withered Judas tree? It had received more sun and more rain than the others. Mrs Moor seems optimistic, though she thinks that the tree might be dead. They hear Morys coming, and she leaves.

Morys is adamant to Lady Angela. The experience had been a practical joke. She speaks kindly to him, talking of the good qualities in him. He considers this patronizing, and says he needs to think it all out when he gets clear of the house. She asks, 'You will think it out then? You will . . . . pray?' Pray?, he retorts, adding, 'You sound like one of those Come to Jesus fanatics.' He came to us, she replies.

She looks at the Judas tree, still hoping it will bloom. He feels unwell and insists that the person behind this trick will be punished, if ever he finds out. She rounds on him angrily, and calls him an insolent devil, recalling that he too once had qualities of kindness and gentleness. She was once prepared to give her life for him, and loved him; Morys is amazed, until she recalls the details of the past. He remembers: 'Long ago.' She says: 'You were gentle then. Be gentle now. You were loving then. Be loving now. You were young then; come back to your lost youth and start afresh.' 'What must I do?' he asks. She tells him that he knows, but he responds in the negative: What is done is done. He is a sinner, and will go on being one; it pays best. He accuses her of trading on his illness, which is presumably a heart condition. He won't listen any more. 'I am myself again.'

Lady Angela admits failure. He tells her to go away; it's all rubbish, weak-kneed rubbish. She leaves, handing her necklace to Mrs Moor, who has entered to ask Morys for a gift. He has nothing. As she goes she reminds him that he has thirty pieces of silver.

Morys, alone, admits haltingly that he has thirty pieces, but she cannot get them. He has invested them at 6.5%. He feels in his pocket and takes out some coins, which he drops as though they had burnt his hand. The door slams and locks. Let me out, he shouts. He listens. Again, not again, he calls out, in desperation. He falls headlong. The clock ticks on. 'He is alone with time and eternity.' The stage fills with a mist, lit faintly, as the curtain falls.[47]

From the Four Winds rides several of the author's hobby-horses. There is the idea that the people of the nation are one community; that rich and poor are the same people, who happen to be artificially divided by economic circumstances. They can all partake of the same meal together, though some cannot see this, blinded by snobbery and bitterness and mean-mindedness. Only some sort of deep change of heart (symbolized in the play by the religious experience) can restore their sight. What is the main element which crushes the creative unity and shared progress of the nation? The hard-hearted meanness of the bankers and financiers, killing their own souls and stunting the lives of others.

It is of course a cliché for those on the left to attack bankers and speculators, ignoring the part that they play in creating wealth and employment. But in 1931 bankers were more likely to cause unemployment than employment. The impassive narrow-mindedness of Montagu Norman at the Bank of England was a symbol of the economic condition of

Oliver aged 5

At Eton aged 12

Feeding the turkeys Oliver (l) and Johnnie Shirburn, Oxfordshire, 1927

Oliver (l) and Johnnie, probably in Paris, circa 1930

Oliver Baldwin, 1933

Lord Baldwin arrives in Antigua, March 1948

His Excellency and Ross Hutchinson, Antigua 1948

His Excellency bathing, c. 1948

At Clarence House, Antigua

Gerald Bryant, the cook at Government House,
Antigua 1948–50

A relaxing moment, Ross Hutchinson and friends

One of the houses built in Antigua on Lord Baldwin's
suggestion, 1949–50

His Excellency taking an interest

2nd Earl Baldwin in his Coronation robes, 1953

the age, where unemployment was created is order to protect pointless and unexamined economic fetishes; Norman himself was probably Baldwin's most hated person, although most self-enriching bankers were equally loathed. Bankers and class divisions were the aspects of British life which kept the nation separated and disunited. A spiritual revelation might break down the divisions which history and economics had created in society; with it, people would redis-cover their essential classlessness, and they would experi-ence a common sense of unity and inner purpose.

Oliver Baldwin believed that human harmony and spiritual growth would develop, once the hard partitions of greed and class had been discarded. He saw this as the essence of the Christian message. For that he went back to the gospels, and ignored the accretions added by the church after their composition. Creeds and doctrines and sacra-ments were invented and meaningless. The story of Christ was a common one in the Middle East, and an inspiring one, he believed. Baldwin himself was to write it as such, giving it an Algerian atmosphere – a kind of Christ Came to Algiers. This work appeared in 1936 with the title *The Coming of Aissa* ('Aissa' being a transcription of the Arabic name for Jesus; see below). In both *Aissa* and *From the Four Winds* Oliver wrestled with the Christian theme and message, despite his emphatic rejection of conventional Christianity. In the stage work he explored through it ideas of class, economics, and spiritual renewal. *From the Four Winds* represented a sincere look at the society he knew, and an idealistic vision of the way in which it might change.

CHAPTER 10

Creatively Adrift in the Thirties

An American Tour

Oliver was short of money, and in mid 1931, while he was still
an MP, he decided to undertake a lecture tour of America. W.
Colston Leigh of 521 Fifth Avenue, New York, chief puller-in
of European celebrity lecturers, worked out a vast transconti-
nental programme for him. All the travelling was of course to
be done by rail. Oliver took two main speeches, both with
suitably vague titles, which acted as vehicles for his socialist
views. One was on 'Europe and the future of nations', and the
other (delivered mostly in East Coast locations) concerned
'the future of British politics'.[1] He set sail in a second-class
cabin on the German liner, the SS *Europa*, on 30 December
1931. The crossing was reasonable – Dutch gin proved to be
a good antidote to seasickness – and a Fabian author, S. K.
Ratcliffe, who wrote occasional articles for the *New Statesman*, was on board. He also found time to do some writing.[2]

Arriving at New York, the liner berthed at Brooklyn, so
Oliver missed the Statue of Liberty and the famous skyline.
His fame (or notoriety) had preceded him, and he was interviewed and photographed at the quayside. He went to the
New Weston Hotel, where a mystery telephone call offered
him whisky, which he declined, wisely in view of Prohibition.
Some of his time was spent seeing American leftists,
including Willard of *The Nation*, H. W. Laidler, later to write
a major work on socialism in the US, and the defense

attorney Morris Ernst, author of *The Best is Yet*.[3] For at least part of the time he appears to have stayed with a gay friend in the city called Robert E. Turner – 'his friend very nice'. Oliver described Robert's house as being 'full of amusing people but very rough and full of backward ideas'.[4]

Oliver spoke first at a girls' school, Beaver College, Jenkintown, Mass., on 9 January 1932, where the audience was agreeably attentive. Travelling on to Columbus, Ohio, he found mid-westerners surprisingly interested in socialism. On the 11th he spoke on Europe to the Women's City Club of Kansas City; then, striking north to Des Moines, Iowa, he addressed an audience at the Jewish Community Center, where the questions were animated and challenging. Two days later the pattern was repeated at Omaha, Nebraska.

The next halt was at Denver, Colorado; then he took an overnight train westwards – two splendid hours crossing the Great Salt Lake at sunset, where the scenery recalled for him the Algerian countryside between Biskra and Toggourt. At length, just after 9.00 a.m., he reached the snowy altitude of the Sierra Nevada; then the train plunged down to sun and palm trees. 'California!' is the exultant beginning to a letter to Johnnie.[5] In Sacramento he loved the 'gleaming whiteness of the buildings . . . the soft clear sky seems so bright it seems the whole firmament is one big sun'.[6] The Tuesday Club of Sacramento hosted his talk, given on the 19th, with the governor's wife in the audience. On to San Jose, via San Francisco (which disappointed him); here he met his bachelor cousin Victor Martin, who lived with his mother. Victor, who was to become a Benedictine monk after his mother's death, showed great curiosity about what 'K' stood for in the letters to Johnnie. San Jose College heard him talk on the crisis in Europe. He then took the coastal railroad to Los Angeles.[7]

Here he met a number of movie people, whose company he always enjoyed. They included the leading Armenian-American film director Rouben Mamoulian, who proudly told Oliver that, when growing up in the Armenian community of Tiflis, Georgia, he had received his school-leaving certificate from none other than Oliver's old friend Alexander Khatisian, at that time the city's mayor. Other movie celebrities he met included Marlene Dietrich, Josef von Sternberg, Dick Cromwell, and Jesse Lasky; also Rodgers and Hart, who were then working on *Love Me Tonight*, with Maurice Chevalier. They talked about their picture with Oliver, and he suggested a whispering chorus for 'The son of a gun is nothing but a sailor', an idea they took up, to his gratification. Mamoulian took him to see the set for the recently finished *Dr Jekyll and Mr Hyde*, and Oliver pointed out the misspelling of 'Guiness' on the inn-sign. He went on to watch Elissa Landi, Tom Douglas, and David Rawlins, and lunched with Ivor Novello ('OOOllliver . . . '). When he got round to speaking, it was to the Jewish Institute of Los Angeles. In Pasadena he spoke three times, once on the 'lost generation' in England.[8]

From LA he returned to San Francisco, and on to Salt Lake City, where his university audience heard him on the European crisis; and the Ladies Literary Club of Grand Rapids, Michigan, was treated to the same subject. He managed to see a school production of R. C. Sherriff's *Journey's End*, well directed and with talented performances.[9] Heading east to Maine, he spoke at Bowdoin College, Brunswick, on British politics.

At Hudson, Ohio, he talked to the boys of the Western Reserve Academy. These he found delightful, even captivating ('I have a hankering to be a schoolmaster again. They are all so charming.'[10]) He made plans to return. A brief visit to Toronto followed. The Canadian political atmosphere was repressive at that time under Prime Minister R. B. Bennett, and Oliver was happy to get out. An engagement in Buffalo followed, which he describes as a bright level town of friendly people;[11] the University Club heard him speak on Europe. Here too he caught a play, *Bird in Hand*, a comedy written by

his Oxfordshire neighbour, John Drinkwater. After addressing the Park Church, of Elmira, NY, he spoke to the boys of
Colby College, Waterville, Maine, before he took the train to
Boston. His schedule included a speaking engagement on
26 February at a lunch at Boston's Copley-Plaza Hotel, but
the Daughters of the American Revolution had decided that
he was a communist, and arranged the cancellation of the
lecture. Another meeting had been arranged at the Ford Hall
for ten days' time. Baldwin says that this meeting was
organized in consequence of the cancellation, but this is
autobiographical embroidery; the original contracts show
that the Ford Hall meeting was scheduled before he set sail
from England.[12]

Oliver visited Dr Clarence Ussher in Worcester, and
renewed memories of Yerevan in 1921. Following a visit to St
Paul's School, an embarrassingly over-elitist school in
Concord, NH, he went on to talk to the Women's Club of
Sewickley Valley, Pa., on the lost generation. His final
appearances were in Massachusetts. During a brief break
before his last lecture he returned to the Western Reserve
Academy, at the invitation of the principal. Here, at the
school where he had been so charmed, he put in a few days
as a kind of adviser and counsellor to the boys, something
which all parties seem to have found worthwhile. At the end
of the tour, in mid March, it was time to do some accounting.
His lecture fees had averaged $250, and in all he had earned
around $6,800, which, after expenses, translated into about
£1000 on his return to England: more money than he had
ever made in his life.[13]

Oliver had had a magnificent time, and loved the people
and the landscape, so excellently observed from the train.
American domestic arrangements impressed him too. He
later wrote 'I want to learn why her houses are so comfortable and so nice to look upon. I want to learn why they are
warm in winter and cool in summer, why her toilet arrangements are so much better than ours, why the poorest of her

people can have central heating whilst we are content with one coal fire in the living-room.' To Johnnie he expressed a kind of childish delight at the pink and violet loo paper he found in America. With the people themselves he developed an easy rapport: they were 'wonderfully friendly and not a bit like they are in England or Alger when they travel'.[14]

Despite his earnings, finance was still a worry. His youthful autobiography entitled *The Questing Beast* had been published the month before. It was not a money-spinner, despite reprinting. He earned considerably more by writing articles and short stories, including detective fiction, for which there was a ready market in the 1930s. Oliver lived by the typewriter in the 1930s. On political and social topics he spread the word of rationality, tolerance, knowledge and equality wherever he was given a space.

On reading Lord Rothermere's call in the *Daily Mail* for the country to turn to Oswald Mosley and the fascist party, he was stung into a trenchant response in the *Daily Herald* (see below, in the chapter on Baldwin's journalism). However, there was clearly no long-term hostility on either side between him and the Northcliffe group, and within a year he was writing for Rothermere's papers. *Good Housekeeping*, *The Tatler*, *Vogue*, *John Bull*, the *Strand Magazine*, and others also printed articles and stories by him. He secured the help of an agent, F. Rupert Crew. In a fairly average month (December 1933) he earned £94 6s. 8d. [£94.33]. For the year ending April 1934 his income from writing amounted to £1074 17s. 5d.[15]

A Foray into Films

His also worked hard to get a foothold in the film industry and start a career there. To Oliver the films that mattered showed a connection to society, and were defined as art rather than mindless opiates. In 1932 Britain the pictures were hardly seen in this way, but Oliver Baldwin sought to change that. He cited *The Chain Gang, Earth, The Fall of St Petersburg, The General Line, Counterplan, Kameradschaft* and *Les Misérables* as fine examples of the genre, in advance of anything produced in Britain.[16]

He was given a tentative opening into the world of film-making by A. C. N. Dixey, whom he describes as 'an old political friend, of the other side'. Dixey introduced him to Zoltan Korda (brother of Alexander). Oliver was full of high hopes. A letter to Johnnie, undated but probably of April 1932, says, 'I'm going to Paris to study Korda's direction of a new film . . . I am to direct when I get back – a proper film. I am told I ought to make xooo a year next year. Then you can buy new Rolls. Y.O.K.'[17]

In July 1932, Korda's company, London Film Productions, confirmed his appointment with the company for two years at the rather un-Rollsish salary of £600 per annum.[18]

Oliver worked hard for Korda, spending some months in Paris; and though the hopes of a career in films turned out to be misplaced, something was achieved. He was a valuable asset to Korda since he spoke fluent French, and he worked on *La Dame de chez Maxim* as both assistant director and translator. Parts of it were shot in England, and in autumn 1932 production moved to Paris, where shooting continued in two versions, with a French and an English cast. Oliver noted the fascination with which the French observed the shooting of the English version, whereas the English lounged around indifferently when they were not performing.[19]

He contrasted the waste and expense of Anglo-Saxon/ Hungarian film-making with the austere excellence and careful organization and preparation of René Clair, of whose work he was a lifelong admirer. An old friend of Oliver's was working with Clair as *maquilleur*: none other than Arshavir Shakhkhatuni (Chachatouni), Town Commandant of Yerevan in 1920, now keeping his Constantinople pledge of 1921 to stick to films.

Oliver fell out with London Film Productions Ltd – he even issued a writ against them in May 1933, alleging non-payment of salary, but the action does not seem to have come to court – and he left their employment. Whether because of temperamental clash, his own impatience, or the trickiness of his employers, practical film-making was not his line of business.

If he had failed to make a career as a film-maker, he could at least succeed as a cinema journalist, and he had two quite successful (if brief) periods of film reviewing. He worked first for the BBC (from September 1933 to June 1934) and then for the socialist weekly *Clarion*, founded by Robert Blatchford and now in its last year of publication. He was with them from March to June 1934. His BBC work – he was a kind of proto-Barry Norman – was a fortnighly slot on Wednesday evenings, initially from 6.50 to 7.05 p.m., entitled 'Films Worth Seeing'.[20] For each talk he was paid 12 guineas. His talks ranged fairly widely, and included social criticism, as for example in his review of the film of Noel Coward's *Cavalcade*. He sometimes interviewed film actors and actresses, including the two Fairbankses, Alma Taylor and Stewart Rome; these interviews, despite giving the impression of spontaneity, were all scripted. He took part in a direct broadcast to America at midnight on a cinematographical anniversary, and on another occasion the broadcasters became actors, and the audience was invited to guess who was playing the part; Baldwin played Henry V, in the scene between the king and Catherine – something one cannot imagine happening in Broadcasting House or Television Centre today. He was always keen to broaden what he sensed was the narrowness, not to say the provinciality, of English taste; to encourage his fellow Britons to warm to 'foreigners'. One of these was the distinguished German Jewish Shakespearian actor Alexander Moissi (1880–1935), who had worked with Max Reinhardt in Prague, and at London's Globe Theatre in 1930 had performed the Prince in *Hamlet* in Schlegel's translation. Baldwin persuaded the BBC to get Moissi to participate in an arts programme.[21] Oliver relates a story of the funeral of Moissi, in Austria, following his tragically early death, just two years after their meeting. The deceased great actor had inherited the Iffland ring, a handed-down talisman, worn by the greatest German actor of the day, a tradition started in the days of Goethe and Schiller. From Moissi it had been passed to the new leading German actor Albert Bassermann, who was not Jewish. At the graveside Bassermann drew it from his finger and threw it into the grave, declaring that he was passing it back to the greatest German actor, with the implications that Moissi had been a great German artist, and that under Nazi tyranny the ring's significance for the continuity of art was dead.

In late 1932, while Oliver was absent in France working with Korda, the Farm House establishment moved to a new location in Oxfordshire, to Little Stoke House, North Stoke. This was to be Oliver and Johnnie's home for the rest of Oliver's life. The house became famous for its charm and its owners' hospitality: for Johnnie's giant aviary, where rare birds flew around as if in a private zoo, and for its large and well-stocked garden that went all the way down to the river, where there was a landing-stage and a bathing place. From the outside the house looked smaller than Farm House, being built only on two floors, but it was actually somewhat larger, since it had depth. With three bathrooms, it was easier to accommodate the all-important weekend guests. In Little Stoke House, Oliver and Johnnie would run, in the words of Rosamond Lehmann, 'a very hospitable and prodigal household'.[22]

*

The spiritual matters which had been central to his play *From the Four Winds* were a powerful draw at this time, and Baldwin decided to spend time in Algeria writing a radically new version of the life of Christ. It was to be based only on the gospels, with the backing of historical accounts of the time. The author would concentrate on the actual circumstances of the protagonist and his message, ignoring the theological accretions of St Paul and the Church Fathers. Jesus's life was to be placed in a Mediterranean context – in this case Algeria, which Oliver knew well. Baldwin saw Jesus as the originator of Christian socialism; he viewed him as an exceptional but not divine middle easterner, and very far from the authority-figure by whom the ruling classes of the western world had sought to legitimize their power, and whom they had patronized as one of their own. This was a typical Arian or Socinian view of the life of Jesus: a human being, not a hypostasis of the divine essence. The author left for the Villa Aurelian in September 1934, and stayed there writing for six months.

On his return more journalistic work was offered to him. Despite his attack on Rothermere, the *Daily Mail* was in conciliatory mood – quite possibly not unconnected with the fact that he was the prime minister's son – and offered him a fortnightly column. His anti-fascist work included a well-timed but somewhat hyperbolic pamphlet addressed to the King of Italy deploring the seizure of Ethiopia (then known as Abyssinia). He also wrote some plays for the West End, in an attempt to take advantage of the staging of his play in 1931, but he had no luck in getting them taken up by any management. Then, in late 1935, the real world of politics called him, as the country prepared for a general election.

Campaigning in Scotland

Parliament was dissolved on 25 October 1935, and the prime minister, Stanley Baldwin, called a general election for 14 November. Attitudes in Britain had become polarized, owing to the increasingly warlike atmosphere in Europe.

Oliver Baldwin had been offered a seat in Paisley. Several things seem to have led him to a Scottish constituency. One was his own Scottish, Macdonald ancestry, and the fact that he liked being in Scotland, feeling very Celtic there. He was also drawn by his friendship with James Maxton, Independent Labour MP for Glasgow Bridgeton, whose austere but approachable and communicative socialism appealed to him.

He enjoyed campaigning in Paisley:[23]

Electioneering in Scotland is very different from England [he wrote in the *Daily Mail*]. It seems to me that here the electors are more polite to the candidate. They send up written questions instead of shouting abuse . . . The audiences up here look so intensely interested in what one says, and obviously do not care to miss a word, which shows, I think, that they are keener on politics than the English outside Lancashire and the Durham coalfields. An election meeting up in Paisley gives the lie to that strange belief that the Scot has no sense of humour, for if you give him an inch he'll take a yard and toss repartee backwards and forwards with the candidate until the meeting degenerates into a Music Hall turn. And the interjections are really humorous. They are kind to their candidate's wit as well, and were appreciative when, after my referring to a certain 'lawyer', a man cried out, '"Liar", you mean,' and I was able to reply, 'You must excuse my English pronunciation.' . . . At question time the other day a man quite solemnly asked whether if I were elected a member of Parliament I would see that Paisley were kept top of the League at football. The someone blew a referee's whistle and politics were finished for the evening . . .

He found other contrasts with campaigning in England:[24]

Here there were no public houses to watch while Tory councillors bribed the electors with beer . . . No begging or whining for free drinks in exchange for a vote; no misrepresentation and sheer rudeness. No stones from the slag heaps flying your way. One old man, a stranger, came up to me, held out his hand and said that although he should vote against me he hoped I'd have a 'bonny fecht'. And when we lost, what a grand wind up with the co-operative choir singing 'Will ye no come back again?' I did . . .

Baldwin's 1935 election address began with an economics lecture. He acknowledged the improved conditions of the previous five years – the increase in employment which had come from an increase in export trade. But he pointed out that the export boom had come about because of Britain's departure from the gold standard, and the subsequent devaluation of the pound sterling; and he pointed out that the defence of the pound had been the main reason for the formation of the National government in 1931. So the panic of 1931 was shown to be an artificial one, 'organized in the interests of a private corporation which is known as the Bank of England'. The threat heard in 1931, of a complete collapse of the currency, merely because the Labour government had wished to maintain a decent standard for the unemployed, 'was nothing more than a means of driving a Workers' government from office'. He compared the economic situation with that of anti-socialist Italy, where despite a deficit equivalent to £125m sterling and vast daily expenditure on warfare, the lira was remaining steady.

So the first priority was his old hobby-horse, nationalizing the Bank of England, returning it to the state ownership it had enjoyed during the war. Labour would also, he said, abolish the Means Test, and give work to some of the unemployed by government contracts – although he pointed out that full employment would not occur until the system had changed from capitalism to socialism, 'which can only occur if the majority of the people desire it'.

Other points concerned education, building houses for rent, nationalization of mining royalties (and eventually of the mines themselves), support for the League of Nations in its use of sanctions to end 'this shameful war of aggression in Abyssinia'. His final point demonstrated the pacificism of the times. He proclaimed that the Labour Party was definitely against the National government's policy of rearmament to assure peace. This was because an arms race would only end in universal war 'and the crippling of our people by unnecessary taxation for the benefit of the holders of armament shares'. Efficient defence was dependent less on increased expenditure than on improved organization and the development of modern techniques, he believed.

Finally Oliver roused his electorate to the banner of progress, and defined the election as a contest between the forces of vested interests, land- and money-power, and the 'ideal of the Cooperative Commonwealth'. He called on voters to support him in laying the foundation for a new state in which service of the community for the community might take the place of the system of private greed and gain which had brought sorrow to so many. Here was a trenchant summary of the socialist ideals he had first heard at the knees of Aunt Georgie, and first read about in his cousin's biography of William Morris.[25]

The Paisley declaration brought the following result:

| Hon. J. P. Maclay | L | 22466 | 50.4% |
| O. R. Baldwin | Lab | 22077 | 49.6% |

L maj. 389   Turnout. 80.3%

Paisley was now a highly marginal constituency. Oliver was not dissatisfied. It had been a worthy fight. He was grateful too for a note from the new chairman of the Labour Party, who, like him, came from a privileged background – Clement R. Attlee. The Labour leader wrote to him on 26 November, saying 'You put up a splendid fight at Paisley.'[26]

Less than two months after the general election, Rudyard Kipling died, severing a deep and ambivalent tie with the past. His home had been a haven for Oliver in his late teens when things got tough at Astley; Kipling's household had been an alternative family to his own, and less stressful. The famous author and patriot had inspired Oliver with the concept of soldierly duty, and had been delighted by the boy's responsiveness. He had given him a bronze statuette of Kim, which had belonged to John. Oliver's enthusiasm and competence had been in some ways a compensation for the tragic loss of his own son. Kipling had written delightful letters to his young cousin. Yet after 1923, when Oliver formally espoused socialism, Oliver and he were barely in communication, if at all. Socialism was anathema to Kipling, as was imperialism to Oliver. In a way, too, they had outgrown one another; the manner in which each had leaned emotionally upon the other during the pre- and post-war years could not last. It is likely too that, with Kipling's conscious revulsion against homosexuality, he had no wish to contemplate Oliver and Johnnie's Oxfordshire menage. This anxious ignorance on Kipling's behalf might have increased with the realization that his daughter Elsie's marriage to George Bambridge (Oliver's contemporary in the Guards) was proving to be a *mariage blanc*, and George's insistence on the tall handsome male staff at Wimpole Hall wearing knee breeches and powdered wigs might indicate tastes in other directions. In old age Elsie Bambridge burnt all her own and George's diaries and papers. Without question they contained answers to many family riddles.

Five months after Kipling's death Baldwin created a minor storm in the columns of the press, following a lecture he gave on Kipling. Baldwin was engaged from time to time to talk on his cousin, and had prepared a set of lecture cards for the purpose. His line on Kipling was that he had a sense of inferiority (or 'inferiority complex'), and that this led him to compensate for it in various extreme manners. Baldwin noted that he had written a number of anti-democratic poems between 1910 and 1914, which showed a preference for force and hatred over the democratic process. This was especially true with respect to Ulster. The First World War was (according to Oliver) an answered prayer. John Kipling could now be his father's fantasy-soldier projection. But the loss of John shattered the father, and drove him to deeper levels of rage and despair. From this dark hell of hate, there emerged, Oliver declared, the 'wickedest story in the world' – 'Mary Postgate'.

This story deserves a closer look, since it lies at the heart of a serious debate on good and evil. The central character is a middle-aged spinster, Mary Postgate, companion to a certain Miss Fowler, the daughter of a minor court official, and aged almost sixty. The ambience of the two spinsters reeks of fussiness, frustration and controlled aggression. Miss Fowler's nephew Wynn, a solicitor – also an unattractive, bossy and aggressive character – is killed in a Royal Flying Corps accident in the early pages of the story. Miss Fowler finds herself unable to grieve for her nephew, and excuses herself from going to his funeral. In the course of a general tidy-up, the two ladies decide that Wynn's things should all be burnt in the garden incinerator. 'My plan is to burn every single thing' said Miss Fowler decisively – as if fire were the only way to cope with her incapacity to feel, and with the dirt and nuisance of everyday existence. One senses a vague kinship with Hedda Gabler in her burning of Eilert Lovborg's manuscript.

Mary Postgate pushes the items through the incinerator's grill. Then she decides to go into the village to get some paraffin. While there there is a sudden war emergency, a crash, a bomb and a child dead. Returning with the fuel (playfully termed by Kipling 'sacrificial oil'), she goes into the now twilit garden to start the fire. As she does so, she discovers, close by, the German pilot, who had been critically injured when his plane had been forced down after it had dropped the bomb which had killed the child. The German's own injuries are terrible, and, unable to move, he begs for her help, calling out, in a kind of international language (a broken French-English), '*Le médecin. Toctor*'. But despite the pleas uttered in excruciating pain, Mary Postgate only replies that she has seen the dead child. She stokes – almost strokes – the fires of Wynn's belongings. 'She thumped like a pavior through the settling ashes at the secret thrill of it.' The spinster is enjoying herself, prodding through the grill, perhaps for the first time in her life, and becomes elevated to orgasmic relief by the ignored German's dying agony a few yards away. The sacrificial oil had metamorphosed into a personal lubricant. Later, before tea, Miss Postgate takes a luxurious bath, and after it, as she relaxes glowingly on the sofa, Miss Fowler notes her looking 'quite handsome'.

Oliver Baldwin, by condemning the story, perhaps showed more perception than the Kipling-devotee critics who have rushed to defend it. Oliver caught the element of sexual frustration, followed by sado-masochistic release, in Mary Postgate's behaviour. His own liberated sexuality would have recognized the post-orgasmic relaxation of the spinster settling down on the sofa, looking good after the bath which had consummated her act of deathly cruelty. Other critics and commentators have tried to claim that this unattractive short story was merely a description of the way people behave, thereby ignoring the strong assenting and prescriptive element in Kipling's writings – as if on this one occasion Kipling were writing art for art's sake. Or else the claim has been made that the story was a metaphor for the spiritual harm that Germany had done to Britain. Any meaning, however far-fetched, has been adduced by Kipling's admirers to blot out the manifest and obvious one, which is that of the story's clear sexual and sadistic content, something which was present in its grotesque yet unaware reality (as opposed to being acted out between two fully aware consenting sexual beings). Curiously too, Kipling-devotees see no place for a central convention of war: that captured or wounded enemy personnel should be humanely treated, and have their wounds attended to, rather than be used as unconsenting sexual toys. Oliver Baldwin, as a sexual being (and one who had written about sado-masochism within a consenting sexual context), who had come to terms with the varieties of sexuality, was able to perceive the brutal, pre-moral element in Kipling's easy assent to Mary Postgate's use of a dying German for sexual gratification. Kipling, aware only unconsciously of sexuality and the sexual side of sadism, could write of the effects of frustration, sex and sadism, but could not investigate their nature or speculate about their causes. If wickedness is made up in large part by unawareness and turning away, then Oliver Baldwin was right to categorize 'Mary Postgate' as a wicked story.

In July 1936 Oliver said what he thought of 'Mary Postgate', and set the letters column of the *Daily Telegraph* buzzing.[27] He overstated his case, and declared that the story had been written in reaction to the death of John, when in fact it had originated somewhat earlier. But his main point is a valid one: that jingoism grew to dominate Kipling's mentality, and drove out the good things he had written concerning humanity and the natural environment, and the harmony between man and nature. Elsie Bambridge wrote fiercely, a commentary on the volatility of family affection, which was happily not the last word on the subject: 'With reference to the supposed intimate knowledge of my father, Mr Rudyard Kipling, by Mr Oliver Baldwin, I should like to point out that my father has not seen or spoken to him for certainly 10 years prior to his death. It is therefore clear that Mr Oliver Baldwin's statements about my father and his feelings are of little value.'[28] Nevertheless Oliver was more perceptive than the devotees in the matter of the cruelty found at the heart of this gruesome story.

Baldwin and the *Daily Mail*; assignment in Spain

Some months earlier Oliver had gained a formal contractual position with Associated Newspapers. In December 1935 he signed an agreement with the *Mail* group, which also included the *Sunday Dispatch* and the *Evening News*, to write for the papers from its stable. These papers were the providers of much of his journalistic income.

Oliver had a difficult relationship with proprietors and editors; he needed their money, but complained about their interference, although he can hardly have been so naive as to expect those organs of capitalism to take kindly to his social-istic commentaries, except in terms of indulgent patronage. Maybe he enjoyed his rows with the press; maybe they gave him a sense of righteousness. At the same time, in their by-lines the despised organs could be lavish in praise for his journalistic ability.

Thus, beside an article of his in the *Daily Mail* of 23 March 1936 he was described as 'The Prime Minister's gifted Socialist son';[29] and four weeks later, on 18 April, beneath an article on what Machiavelli had really said – the *Mail* giving its readers a rare treat of political theory – he was elevated into 'the Prime Minister's brilliant son'.[30] The *Mail* was in fact over-selling Baldwin. Although he wrote well, it was hyperbole to describe his work as brilliant. Maybe he knew it, and his curmudgeonly complaints express guilt at not being able to live up to the *Mail*'s hype. Maybe too part of the irri-tation was about being known as the prime minister's son, and not just as Oliver Baldwin.

The earlier of the two articles appeared as a challenge to the *Mail*'s readership. Written just after Hitler's reoccupa-tion of the Rhineland, undertaken in defiance of the terms of the Treaty of Locarno, it began with tough talk, but ended weakly. Headed 'Stop this Nonsense – Now', in it Baldwin predicted a world war: 'Step by step our rulers are moving towards an inevitable outbreak of hostilities . . . It will be war, a real bitter grinding war, followed by international rev-olution.' The cornerstone of Europe's sickness was the Treaty of Versailles, assisted by the tariff barriers, gambling and speculation, 'and the vast canker of unemployment'. His proposal was 'a real economic conference', and he proposed, inviting controversy, 'let the place be Berlin'. The Treaty of Versailles and the 'aggressive' Treaty of Locarno should be buried once and for all. He believed that people were still deeply against war, and that the British people would not stand for a war against Germany or anyone else. The article correctly prophesied war, but sent out the wrong signals, insofar as its tone tended towards appeasement; though it is a melancholy truth that he was probably right in saying that few British people were in 1936 prepared to fight Germany.

With the unstable political situation in Spain, Associated Newspapers decided in March 1936 to send him to Madrid and Barcelona as a special correspondent.

On receiving details of his Spanish assignment, Oliver hastened to write to Johnnie (24 April):[31]

M.O.B.P.K.K.
> Off tomorrow by Golden Arrow. Expect to be away about 10 days at outside – probably less. Terms £5.5.0 per day + all expenses – not bad. Address Ritz Hotel, Madrid. Behap & I'll be back soon – like election time isn't it?
> A & A.Y.O.L.K.

He held a vague suspicion that he was being sent to Spain to find evidence of plans for a communist *coup d'état*. This was possible, but a more likely explanation is that the paper had sent him out because he was a competent journalist, with the added cachet of being who he was.[32]

On arrival in Madrid he found elections calmly in progress for an electoral college to choose the new president. Whoever won, Baldwin believed, power would reside with the left; in this case, in the hands of the Trade Union leader Señor Caballero. Oliver interviewed him – 'the idol of the Spanish working classes and the terror of the well-to-do'. Personal sufferings and threats had edged him with bitterness, and strengthened his determination to destroy the capitalist system. 'He is undoubtedly an extremist, but he knows the mentality of his people so well that he will not move without their solid support. With him agitation goes hand in hand with education, and his knowledge of contemporary revolutionary history has forced him to insist on a discipline amongst his followers which is alien to their very individualistic outlook . . . His mind being orderly, he has little use for anarchists who, in Spain, are the chief cause of revolutionary trades unionism, but he does not underestimate their force nor their danger to his ultimate ideal.'

Baldwin contrasted him with the prime minister, Señor Azana, candidate for the presidency. 'He is tall where Caballero is short, voluble where Caballero is silent and diplomatic where Caballero might be ruthless . . . I was struck by his complete calm and sense of humour . . . He was full of hope for the future of his country and to my question as to whether he were not disturbed by secret organizations of the right or left, replied that in Spain nothing was secret as people always spoke too much anyway. The prime minister is looked upon by the right as a Kerensky who will eventually have to give way to a Lenin, but they are beginning to realize that support for a Kerensky is safer than an attempt at restoring the monarchy. The biggest surprise I had was when I asked permission to visit the leading fascist in prison in order to find out his point of view. In a few seconds he placed the written permission in my hands and in answer to my amazement at this unusual acquiescence, replied with a bow, "You see I an a liberal."'

Next day he was outside the prison. A number of fascists had been arrested on suspicion of planning a coup. Smart cars – Packards, Hispano-Suizas, and so forth – were depositing relatives at the prison gates. Oliver noted the regime's open attitude towards political prisoners. He then met the fascist leader, José Antonio Primo de Rivera. Did he have any complaints about life in prison? Only that his country was not a serious one – if a man were condemned to two years he should serve his full sentence and not be let out for a favour. 'Here, I thought, is a real conception of a disciplined state.'

Oliver questioned him about his supporters. What was his programme? National Syndicalism [a kind of totalitarian workers' movement]. Had he many supporters? About 80,000. Were they all well-to-do? No: they included shopkeepers and artisans. Was he surprised that a newspaper man could come and see him? Not in the least: anyone could come. 'So I hoped he would be as lenient to others if he ever ruled the state as the present government was to him and left him to his friends . . . This then was the ultimate hope of big business and the right wing, those people for whom everything in Spain is in chaos and who living in their own narrow circle recount fantastic tales one to another . . . It seems in Spain that everyone views events according to his political complexion and that a balanced view can only be formed by an outsider. In this one is reminded of a poem by the Spaniard Ramon de Camporamos who says that in this traitor world, nothing is true nor untrue; all is according to the colour of the glasses with which one covers one's eyes.'

Baldwin then travelled to Barcelona, the Catalan capital and stronghold of anarchism. The city was in shock following the assassination of the police chief. Oliver made the point that, on the declaration of the republic, the anarchists had been offered control of the new Catalonian government, but 'their strange doctrine forbade them from facing facts and accepting the responsibilities of ruling'. They had declined as a result, and individual anarchists were drifting to the avowedly revolutionary party of Andres Nin, often described as Trotskyite. Catalonia differed from the rest of Spain in being a land of small-holders who had never known the extremes of poverty. The region's anarchic spirit had assisted it in gaining devolution, but had made it almost impossible to maintain it.

Oliver witnessed the funeral procession for the murdered man, an impressive display, with a taut sense of occasion which snapped twice. He speculated on the assassins: maybe anarchists seeking revenge, or gangsters exiled from Madrid now working for the 'Spanish phalanx [Falange]'. The May Day procession a few days later was a tame affair, with 20,000 on the streets. By comparison in Madrid, he noted, there were 80,000 on the march. His prediction that Señor Azana would be elected president was correct, 'and there then lies before Spain the task of returning to normal now that the enthusiasm after the victory of the Popular Front has subsided' – a prophecy which was not untrue, but which took forty-five years to be accomplished.

Baldwin's journalism on the eve of the Spanish Civil War was a moderately interesting reflection of the situation: a slab of meat which was not really shaped or cooked in a coherent manner, and not related to other ingredients. Oliver never made the connection between what he saw in Spain and the civil war itself, which for decades afterwards was a traumatic memory for most leftists. After his visit Spain ceased to be of any real interest to him. Its situation did not fester in his mind, as it did with others of his party. It was almost as if he were turning his back on the tide of leftist sentiment about the war, ignoring the views and experiences of fellow-English such as George Orwell, John Cornford, W. H. Auden, Stephen Spender and others who fought fascism in the International Brigade. His separateness from other leftists and from the consensus of radical opinion is striking, as is his down-playing of the impact of the events in Spain on the course of fascism in Europe. Maybe the problem was that many of the international leftists were past or present communists, and Baldwin had derived his moment of political illumination from having been at the heart of an anti-communist uprising in 1921. It remains hard to square his side-lining of Spain, despite having been there, with his forthright condemnation of fascism two years earlier in the *Daily Herald*. Perhaps he was miffed not to have predicted the civil war – a rather basic oversight for one who believed that his Macdonald heritage had granted him some ability to foretell the future. Perhaps he misread the force and violence of fascist ideology in Spain. Or maybe he just realized that he was too unintellectual and unglamorous to associate with the artistic and literary crowd who made up the International Brigade.

Towards SB's retirement

In the first year of the Spanish civil war, while fascism was testing out the weaponry later to be used across the continent of Europe, the British people were consumed by the gripping soap opera of their monarch's abdication. The issue had a constitutional dimension, but much of the popular interest revolved around novelettish concerns and incidental trivialities. Stanley Baldwin, of course, played a central and stabilizing part in the events, which have been lengthily rehearsed elsewhere.

Oliver was deeply sceptical of the regnal qualities of Edward VIII, believing that, had he stayed monarch, he would have 'pushed us into some form of republicanism'.[33] One of the aspects of Edward's background which Oliver criticized was the choice of his tutor, H. P. Hansell. Oliver described him as without doubt an admirable man, but one who knew nothing of 'the political world or the rise of our democracy'. He bracketed his distrust of Hansell with the later choice of tutor for Princess Margaret, C. H. K. Marten, 'that most reactionary of Tories'. (Marten had prevented Oliver from addressing the inaugural meeting of the Eton Political Society, on account of his advanced views.) Baldwin believed, reasonably, that there should have been an element of balance; but his choice of a second tutor for Edward, when he was Prince of Wales, was weird: he held that his own socialist mentor H. M. Hyndman should have had the job. This notion was evidence either of deep irony or of a loss of touch with reality.[34]

Edward VIII abdicated in December 1936, and George VI, the new king, was crowned on 12 May 1937. It was, in its pageantry and celebration, the peak of Stanley Baldwin's career. Oliver sent his father a touching, if curiously stilted, letter of congratulation (13 May): a letter showing great loyalty, avoiding any hint of awkward matters like the Hoare-Laval Pact, or the inappropriate choice of Sir Thomas Inskip as minister for coordination of defence.[35]

My dear Father,

As yesterday was, outwardly, the greatest day in your life, may I say how thrilled I was to hear of the real affection with which you were greeted during your passage through the streets of the West End yesterday – and I say the West End purposely because I know had it been the East End your reception would have been as great, and because of many political difference[s] – the greater.

You have indeed had a glorious ending to your rule, which has been of so much more importance to our people than that of any British King, and I am glad for your sake. All of which means that I hope you are happy and do not regret for one moment the events of the end of last year, which rid us of one who I am sure would have caused civil strife in our midst before many years had gone by. And don't we both take off our and bow low before Mother whose faith in you has been so really grand, and without which neither you nor I would know our possibilities or – (in my case only) – superfluity.

If we only had the sentimental grandeur of the French, I would urge the erection of a tablet for you: 'S.B. qui a bien mérité de sa patrie,' and I shouldn't mind if an American would add: 'et comment?' which the French might not understand, but we should. God bless you.

Oliver

One cannot help wondering what SB's reception would have been had he passed through the East End. But the son's letter had touched his father. He wrote back from 10 Downing Street (16 May):[36]

Dearest Son,
    You can never know what happiness your letter brought to
your mother and me: it went straight to our hearts and will
remain there always. And God bless you too.

A month later SB resigned and, after briefly being styled
Sir Stanley Baldwin KG, he was elevated to the peerage as the
1st Earl Baldwin of Bewdley. Oliver, as the heir, took the
courtesy title of Viscount Corvedale, a name chosen by the
new earl because it reflected the Shropshire origins of the
Baldwin family. He wrote to Oliver, in his quiet mysterious
but slightly humorous vein: 'Our Corvedale title has given
great joy in the area . . . the syllables are co-equal and co-
eternal.'[37]

Oliver continued to work as a journalist and short-story
writer. For the *Mail*, he covered the by-election in West
Birmingham, in which Richard Crossman stood as a
Socialist against the Tories' Walter Higgs (29 April 1937). He
followed Crossman about, but found little enthusiasm in the
election, though he thought that the electors were being
offered the choice of 'two first-class candidates – the sincerity
of both is the brightest star of a dull electoral firmament'. At
the last moment the communist Harry Pollitt appeared –
'unasked and unwelcome' – to offer his support to
Crossman. Baldwin seems to have liked Crossman; he noted
his kindly charm. The ladies, he reported, thought he looked
'like Bing Crosby, when he has got his glasses off'. He
correctly predicted a Tory win.[38]

His contract with the *Mail* was terminated in December
1937, and in that month he signed a contract with the *Daily
Sketch* (in the same group), for 60 articles per annum,
starting in April 1938. Many of them were ephemeral pieces.
The *Sketch* initially liked what he wrote, and encouraged him
to write more. The management suggested that he should
rent a house in London so that he could have easy access to
government and generally be in the centre of things. Oliver

(who by now had ceased to use the house in Graham Street) rented 17 Chester Square, SW1, a somewhat ambitious property, showing again a rather tenuous link with the realities of personal finance. When relations between him and the *Sketch* stagnated, on account of his cool attitude towards Neville Chamberlain, and the group realized that it was less interested in his work than it had anticipated, the contract was not renewed and Oliver was left with a big house and little income; so for six months there was a cash crisis. He blamed Associated Newspapers, and there is no doubt that they were in part responsible. But Oliver himself seems throughout his life to have believed he was on the threshold of a big break, that round the corner the new Rolls (for Johnnie) was already being polished by some stripped-to-the-waist youth, ready for collection. Unfortunately its wheels never crunched the gravel of Little Stoke House.

One notable event which took place in the Chester Square house was the concert put on by Oliver in honour of his father, on 15 December 1938. It was a family affair, apart from the presence of Lord and Lady Davidson and Lord and Lady Birkenhead, who almost counted as family. As well as SB and Cissie, three of Oliver's sisters were present – presumably Di, Margot and Lorna – as well as his brother Windham, who was with his wife Elspeth. The programme was cheerful, celebratory and undemanding: Joe Batten was at the piano, and Marriott Edgar recited his own compositions, which had names like 'Sam', and 'Albert and the Lion'. Graham Squiers told Black Country stories; Mark Hambourg played the piano. Other artists included Parry Jones, S. Major Jones, Hubert Harben, Percy V. Bradshaw, George Baker, Norman Allin and Strube. Names which most people today would find hard to place, but (in Oliver's words) 'it was a wonderful evening and made the old man very happy.'[39] The following day SB wrote to his son, 'I enjoyed every minute of your happy party last night . . . In the excitement of leaving I don't believe I said Good Night to Johnny, whose work as caterer was beyond praise. Bless you. Your loving old Father.'[40] It was a felicitous way for son and father to affirm their affection for one another, and for the son to show gratitude to his father. Curiously, the event is not mentioned in Robert Rhodes James' book on Lord Davidson, entitled *Memoirs of a Conservative*. Tory historians – and indeed some writers on the left – and sexually conventional moralists appear to find difficulty in facing up to the fact that Oliver, SB's socialist homosexual son, was actually fond of his father, and that the affection was reciprocated; so they have written out of the script all expressions of the good and positive feelings which flowed between the two.

CHAPTER 11

Tempted to Prolixity

Baldwin wrote a short, sharp and telling essay on leftist theory in 1929, in collaboration with Sir Roger Chance, the author of a study of political philosophy published the year before and entitled *Until Philosophers are Kings*. The joint 50-page essay was called simply *Conservatism and Wealth*, and it demonstrated that Baldwin wrote best when denied the opportunity to indulge at length, and that the restraining – or encouraging – hand of a collaborator could be beneficial to the structure and style of his work. The pamphlet starts as an attack on Edmund Burke, whose organic, romantic view of human society was seen to possess certain superficial charms but which was ultimately identified as anti-democratic and harshly restrictive of political rights. The authors give us two memorable quotations from Tory theorists: Walter Elliot's 'Biology is the logos of Toryism'; and Lord Hugh Cecil, on the ethics of the New Testament, extolling 'the emphatic teaching of the blessedness of poverty.' The authors have no time for Burke or Cecil. But Disraeli is a different matter. The dynamic leader of Young England is viewed as understanding British society clearly and with a pristine eye. His early travels around the Mediterranean had convinced him that in Britain we had created a society 'which had mistaken comfort for civilization' (*Tancred*). Disraeli was a Conservative who believed in the working classes. This set him very much apart from other Tory theorists. Eighty years on, Baldwin and Chance were appalled at the lack of civilized options for working people. They quoted Upton Sinclair: 'We go to work to get the cash to buy the food to get the strength to go to work to get the cash to buy the food to get the strength to go to work to –'. Despite the praise for Disraeli, the essay is an indictment of Tory attitudes to wealth. It ridicules the four elements seen as essential tokens of Toryism: symbolism, empiricism, continuity and realism, which on examination turn out to be void, vapid and anti-democratic. In turn the authors call for an increase in inheritance tax, a surtax on unearned incomes of more than £500 per annum, and state control of banks and the UK credit system. This tough, testy pamphlet repays re-reading today, and might energize the left into re-assembling the beginnings of an intellectual case for its stance.

Baldwin's youthful autobiography *The Questing Beast* appeared in February 1932, published by Grayson & Grayson, a firm well known in leftist circles. This was his third book. Much of it is interesting, vivid and well told, although the author's vagueness about details can be irritating. It was to some extent (like most autobiographies) an exercise in self-justification, perhaps legitimized in view of the abuse he had received for unfilial impiety. A Latin proverb stands as epigraph to the first chapter: *Audi alteram partem* (hear the other side). The book received a few favourable notices, notably in the *Observer* (28 February), which was amused and amusing about the author.

The reviewer, identified only as H. W., spoke of Oliver as 'shockingly and typically English in his reticence', and described the book as 'almost a classic of understatement as to his own emotions and experiences'. This was undoubtedly true, partly because, although Oliver had a showy and dramatic side to his personality, he also had a secretive one, due partly to the fact that he risked jail if his sexual proclivities became known, and partly because there was a kind of subtle self-deprecating ironically humorous side to him. In a paradoxical manner showiness, and a tendency to portentousness and self-dramatization, co-existed in him alongside a capacity to vanish down a corridor like a puff of smoke.

The Questing Beast was dedicated to Johnnie. The dedication reads: 'J. P. B. Homo antiqua virtute ac fide' ([To] JPB, a man of ancient virtue and honour; the Latin is not strictly grammatical, since nominative 'homo' should be dative 'homini'. But accurate grammar would lose the winking subtext of the form 'homo'.) Johnnie was not just a loved companion who looked after the home and garden, and with whom Oliver had, despite occasional tiffs, a deep and mature understanding. Oliver also saw him as a repository of ancient virtues, an individual imbued with uprightness and integrity. The words of the dedication, *virtus* and *fides*, are typically Ciceronian, representing the qualities of the Roman Republic at its most effortlessly noble and high-minded. Here they may seem a little severe; but they represent how, at one level, the author perceived his companion: as the embodiment of essential virtue.

Much of *The Questing Beast* concerned public events and policies, and Oliver's reaction to them. The *Observer* reviewer noted the author's 'puzzled earnestness' in his search for the right way forward in life – an earnestness which had led him to renounce the political faith of his father. The pages on life at Astley are full of incident, but the reader is kept at a distance.

Oliver is brilliantly focused on his schools – devastating about Eton. On the war he is brief, and down-plays both his competent leadership and inner anxiety, both of which his letters made clear. His awakening socialism is clearly delineated: the seeds planted by Aunt Georgy while he was at prep school, the sense of disillusion after the war, and the awareness of the injustices in society, which seemed intolerable. It becomes hard to deny that his path of political unfiliality was the only honourable one to take. Relations with the family are discreetly sketched, and his parents receive only gentle comments. The central issue which led to the break with home is (we conclude) just an objective disagreement about public policy. The book also conveys the inner process of a developing individual: a man becoming whole. The discretion was also shown towards friends who are routinely referred to by their initials: however, it is possible to identify a number of these with the aid of the index to Kipling's *History of the Irish Guards in the Great War*. Despite reprinting within a month, royalties from *The Questing Beast* were not large.

In October 1933 the same publishers brought out another book of his, which proved more profitable. It was called *Unborn Son*, and it went through seven impressions from publication to mid 1935. It is hard to see today why it should have been so popular, and even controversial; the author says that a banner appeared in the Strand, London, with the legend 'Should Baldwin's Book be Banned?'. The author here delivers a rambling collection of homilies to an eponymous unborn son, often in an awkwardly patronizing tone.

The title indicates its author's yearning for fatherhood, and the book represents his acting out of that urge. His frustration at not having someone to whom to be a mentor is palpable. In contrast to the narrative vigour of *Six Prisons*, and the amusing autobiographical themes in *The Questing Beast, Unborn Son* seems mostly to drone on. It re-runs many of Oliver's hobby horses, with half-digested ideas from psychology and science wrapped up with magical sub-Kiplingesque explanations of 'why we're here' derived from some mythical sage living in an Algerian oasis. Much of the book's heart is in the right place. Despite a predictable and even mechanical aura of mysticism, it stakes out territory which is rational, sensible, enlightened, and in favour of disclosing rather than withholding information. But it is weak in construction and lacks self-discipline: a strange state of affairs for one who took such pride in his military bearing. There is no list of contents and no index – always a bad sign.

It roams over child development, education, and sex. (Here Baldwin includes a original passage indicating that masochism and sadism are OK as long as they are not taken too far, warning that bondage sessions can lead to unintentional death.[1]) He makes a plea for understanding the sheer complexity of sex and human relationships. The homosexual author is circumspect in what he says on homosexuality, and in one place mentions a rather gruesome medical 'cure', which represented the unpunitive thinking of the time. He is careful not to invite the interest of the constabulary in his own establishment. On the matter of the law as it was then framed, he drops the mask: 'Our laws in England on sex are archaic and hypocritical, founded on ignorance, prejudice and fear.'[2]

There follows a passage on travel, part of which drew on his recent American tour. The author also chugs across the Pacific, exploring the exotic locations of Honolulu and Samoa, and occasionally charming us with details such as that in Tahiti boys wear scarlet hibiscus flowers behind their ears.[3] One can sense the kinship that Oliver felt with those Europeans such as R. L. Stevenson and Gauguin who had escaped the pressures of European bourgeois life to find peace and harmony in the elemental world of the Pacific Islands. The travels take his reader, in a rather routine manner, across India, and through large parts of East Africa, to beloved Algeria, and to the Greek Islands.

Sometimes Baldwin imposed sufficient self-discipline on his writing to come up with a few good paragraphs. After the ramble across continents, he returns home thus to politics, economics and the nature of patriotism, matters on which he had pondered deeply:

1. I consider it finer to live for your country than to die for your country; chiefly because I am incapable of deciding which country I like best. I see so much good and so much bad in all of them. I do not own a square inch of England, but because I was born in it and have absorbed its atmosphere, I want it to be a good and happy place.

2. I am not impressed by the possession of vast tracts of land that make up 'our' Empire, or by the fact that we rule over millions of alien people by the power of military force.

3. My object in public life is to see that the vast mass of the people in this country get enough to eat, are decently housed, sufficiently clad, have congenial work, and access to those forms of recreation and knowledge that they prefer. And that is the 'patriotism' I advocate. To me it is the primary material duty of public life and expression, and anything that stands in its way I oppose.

4. For holding these views I am unpatriotic; because I do not consider that materialism, flag worship, tradition and pride of imperial possession should come before that which I have expressed in the former paragraph.[4]

Here is the essence of Baldwin's politics: socialist and egalitarian, while eschewing grand designs and inept Hegelian-Marxist theories. It was realistic, it sought justice for all, and expressed a hatred of violence; and it correctly saw a materialist outlook, and sentimentality dressed as tradition, as belonging to the right and not the left. It nevertheless did not spell out the point which appeared in his election manifestoes, which was that he challenged the structure of capitalism (which he saw as unreformable), and sought a socialist society, with all major enterprises managed and run by the state. He viewed the mainsprings of conservatism to be fear and selfishness.

Unborn Son also contains sixteen pages outlining a theory of currency reform, which, apart from opposing the tying of sterling to the gold standard, add nothing to the debate on public finance.

Rather better is the odd *aperçu*, such as this reflection on the teaching profession:

Always surrounded by ever-flowing youth and getting older and older and more intolerant yourself. If you teach the richer classes you have long holidays, and that is the compensation. You would teach English history from the same book until you knew it by heart; Latin from the same old Caesar you covered with ink in your own youth; geography from some old map that had not been altered since the last war – but you would not notice it as long as it showed the capes and the rivers and the mountains. You would see your old pupils return, and find they were looking for a job, and you would have the sad realization thrust upon you that not a single thing you taught them will be of the slightest use to help them in finding one. But you would cheer yourself up over a glass of port to the tune of the old school song, and let fall a silent tear in gratitude that though your teaching has been useless, it has been no more useless than it has always been.[5]

This was as close as Oliver got to historical inevitability. The wry wit was alas rare.

Oliver Baldwin's fifth book, his alternative life of Christ entitled *The Coming of Aissa*, was properly shaped, and is still just worth reading today. Grayson & Grayson published it in 1935. Here Jesus is portrayed in a local Mediterranean/Near Eastern context, and the story is thus freed from its European overlay. Baldwin's purpose was to clean off the heavy brown varnish. The overlay of the defining faith of Europe was scraped off to reveal an Asiatic Palestinian religion, with a vague cousinage to the mystery religions of Lebanon. Names were changed to more authentic, less western-sounding ones; so Jesus became Aissa (= Isa), Nazareth was El Naseerta, Pilate, Bilatus and John, Yohana. The context undoubtedly became fresher as a result, though some names could be perplexing without local knowledge: thus, Aissa spoke the 'tongue of Echcham' (= esh-Sham, i.e. Damascus), the Romans were known as the Blad Eroum, and Egypt appeared as Misser, the semitic name for that country.

The book was dedicated to W. J. Brown, Labour MP for West Wolverhampton, one of those who, along with Oliver, had signed the Mosley Manifesto of 1930. Brown had been enthusiastic about Baldwin's play *From the Four Winds*, with which it shares a family resemblance.

The book's major departure from orthodox Christian belief lay in the author's refusal to accept the divinity of Jesus, on the grounds that the notion was absent from the gospels. So there are no scholastic theological contrivances like the Trinity, or strange doctrines like the eternal pre-existence of the Logos. Other heterodoxies include a denial of the virgin birth, and no birth in Bethlehem, no flight into Egypt and no taxation by the emperor, all of which were rejected as accretions. Aissa's mother becomes the young second wife of Joseph; Aissa himself is given three half-brothers. Aissa is given no pedigree: Baldwin ridiculed the desire of the early church to make Jesus a son of David as altogether modern in its snobbishness. Nevertheless the book is not a work of debunking. Though the author finds no place for devotion, his work expresses wonder at the life he is portraying. His understanding of the life of Jesus bears many similarities to the Socinian view: the admirable principle that we should only believe and follow what we can understand with our rational faculties.

Many of the early scenes are convincing, notably the episode of the young Aissa disputing with the rabbis in the temple. As one would expect from an author in and out of public life, the political background to the events is coloured with vigour and directness;[6] we are made aware of the Jews' servitude to the Romans, and their indebtedness to the wealthy of their own people. In the period before Aissa's ministry, with no guidance from the gospels, he is pictured earnestly seeking a better way of conducting life, and discovering the primacy of forgiveness. These elements give the early chapters vitality and coherence.

Pressure is put upon the young Aissa by his parents and brothers to conform. They show no understanding of his individuality, and finally place scissors under his bed – a symbolic act which may have been an Algerian folk tradition signifying a form of scapegoating within the family – 'and he knew they thought him mad and a hindrance to their existence'.[7]

Aissa gets the message that he has to leave. His departure from Mary and Joseph would have had a certain resonance for Oliver. Once away, Aissa goes on a vast search across Asia for wisdom. First he travels to Iran, where he meets a Zoroastrian holy man named Nisaya: 'What do you seek?' 'Strength and counsel.'[8] The wisdom Baldwin puts in the mouth of the Iranian sage is warmly expressed, but adds up to little more than the Neoplatonic notion that all religions are one, and that the delights of the body are illusory, eluding 'the embracing love of the whole.'

Travelling further east, he meets an Indian sage, Bahrtri-Das,[9] an elderly Brahmin who lives in poverty contemplating life and death, but who is at the same time a happy man. Here the young postulant learns more about vague Neoplatonic notions such as perfect being, perfect knowledge and perfect ecstasy – ideas which leave one's mind muzzy for lack of definition. Apart from identifying the central conflict in life as that with oneself, the Indian sage's teaching makes little impact. Leaving India, Aissa heads for China, where the sage Pu-Shang teaches him of the sayings of the Lord Buddha, and of his search for enlightenment. The two engage in some thought-provoking exchanges: thus, Aissa asked Pu-Shang whether there was a chance of changing men's natures. He receives the insightful reply, 'Men's natures are the same; it is their habits which cause dissension.'[10]

Aissa returns, and once back in Djeleele, he gathers round himself a band of friends. There is much excitement at the appearance of a prophet who has appeared in the country, one Yohana ben Zachary, who was to be found by the river El Laordun. (Properly al-Urdun.)[11] Yohana's message centred on justice, peace and repentance, especially on social justice, with condemnation of pride, covetousness, and oppression of the poor. Aissa is moved. As the two meet, and the postulant is baptized, the author presents us with a moment of symbolic power.[12] Baldwin was not frightened to use images usually held to be more appropriate to the mystery religions: 'Then they moved to the water, and there were cries of exultation, and Aissa saw Yohana, like a pagan god, the sweat pouring from his face and body, seizing the people and immersing them in the waters, calling out to Yehovah to save them and claim them for his own.'[13]

We follow Aissa giving the Sermon on the Mount, and in discussion about the nature of the Kingdom of God. We witness the drowning of the Gadarene swine, which occurred not because they were filled with devils – that was an ignorant and superstitious tradition – but because they had suddenly taken fright and bolted.[14]

Aissa appears as a healer and miracle worker, but also a man of challenging morality. Baldwin brings out to the full the forgiving nature of Jesus' teaching. 'The brotherhood of man could only come through love, and with that in men's hearts peace and plenty would descend upon their world.'[15] All the time his enemies, especially the religious establishment, lie in wait. The author seeks to differentiate individual disciples, making a point of the loyalty and the affection for Aissa of Yehuda ben Simaoun of Keriouth (=Iscariot). The death of John the Baptist is handled in the idiom of watered-down Oscar Wilde.[16]

The passion narrative[17] begins with the conflict of Aissa and his disciples against entrenched religious authority. The Pharisees are seeking a way to destroy Aissa. They accuse him of blasphemy. They plan to find out where he is based, and then lure him away. One of their number goes out on this mission. In the city, he meets a follower of Aissa, and declares that he and the others of the establishment are interested in learning more about Aissa. The follower is taken to the house of the chief priest, where the establishment also declares its intention of following him.[18] The priests and scribes affirm their devotion to Aissa's teaching. They ask what they should do to show support. Well, contribute, was a suggestion of the disciple Yehuda ben Simaoun of Keriouth. They manage to find 30 pieces of silver between them, and then indicate that they would like to visit the master. So Yehuda tells them where to find him: by the Mount of Olives; in the garden of Djathsemene.[19] They will know Aissa by the greeting which Yehudah gives him.

In Djathsemene Aissa is praying with intense and terrible foreboding. The disciples are sleeping. A band of men with torches is seen moving across the valley. The familiar confrontation takes place, with the added element of the shock and disbelief experienced by Yehudah, on realizing that he has been deceived. They seize Aissa, and take him away.

The following day Aissa is taken before the religious court. Kiapha appears uninterested in the alleged blasphemies, and so his enemies arrange for him to be sent before Bilatus. The Roman governor does not take Aissa seriously as a political threat.[20] So a factional demonstration is arranged, a display of unrest that the civil authorities cannot ignore. Wearily, and still unconvinced, Bilatus bows to the pressure; the scourging, and the crown of thorns follow. He is handed over for crucifixion.

Yehudah is appalled at the priests' deception. In fury he seeks them out and confronts them, but they turn away contemptuously. He hurls the 30 pieces of silver on the pavement. They ignore him, but gather up the cash. Yehuda curses the Roumi for their part.

The procession to Golgotha, and the crucifixion (upon a tau-cross) are described with merciless clarity. After the death of Aissa, Yusuf of El Ramaia takes Aissa's body, with the governor's permission, to his own tomb.

Yehudah, tormented by the chain of events which his action had unleashed, flees to the place of the cross, and with great sobs embraces the empty death-tree of his leader.[21] He knows the place of the new tomb, and runs there. With immense effort he rolls back the stone, and on entering finds the body and kisses the cold face of Aissa, begging for forgiveness. Seizing the body from the tomb, he takes it back to Golgotha, where he holds it high, proclaiming that it was the sacrifice of the people of Yerushalem. Now he curses not the Roumi, but those of his own people who had performed this deception. Through rain and thunder he takes the body far away until he finds a deep ditch, and there he buries it in a place known only to himself. Thereby he achieves some contentment, happy to realize that Aissa's teaching concerns the way men should live, not doctrines or mysteries: almost exactly the Socinian conclusion.

Oliver always held that *The Coming of Aissa* was his best book. It is hard to see why, to his conscious mind, it should appear so, except that, as a sceptical agnostic, he took religion more seriously than the average church-goer. *Aissa* is readable today – just. Although it was brave in its heterodoxy, in evoking period, place and character it cannot compete with (say) Dorothy L. Sayers' theologically orthodox *The Man Born to be King*. *Aissa* was original for 1935. Today it appears as worthy rather than accomplished.

Whatever his own opinion, Oliver's best book remained *Six Prisons and Two Revolutions*, the story of the exploits in Armenia. Owing to a half-hidden sense of failure towards the Armenians, and an awareness of the bad faith of his country, any sense of achievement which the earlier book might have brought seems to have become repressed into the half-world of his unconscious mind. Maybe *The Coming of Aissa* constituted a kind of reconciliatory force, bringing light and forgiveness into the catastrophic darkness associated with memories of Armenia, so clearly evoked in the narrative he wrote of his exploits, where we feel his ever-present fears of annihilation, and sense his guilt at his nation's guilt. There was no theological redemption in his version of Jesus' life – that would have been untenable magic – yet there was personal reconciliation. There was peace too in the evocation of the Algerian/Middle Eastern way of life, in expressing the primacy of forgiveness, and in confronting and coming to terms with the anger and aggression within oneself, and not projecting it on to others: no 'all your fault'. Perhaps the final, personal quality which led him to rate *Aissa* highly was the ambiguous but real satisfaction of his Socinian-like conversion: rediscovering the faith he had been taught, and reacted strongly against, in childhood, as an external guide to lived life, a key not to believing but to doing, devoid of mysteries, sacraments and other pagan charms.

In 1936 Oliver's last published book, *Oasis*, appeared. He himself admitted that it was a fairly gloomy and depressing work. The title drew attention to one of his central concerns: a place – mental or physical – of peace and calm, where the desert of hostility, dust and din, paralleling the unpeaceful world of those who criticized his views, and what they saw as his lack of filial piety, would give way to harmony and understanding, and perhaps too to a rediscovery of an inner lost childish joy. But despite a title hinting at spiritual refreshment, the initial impression of the book is of great constriction, of grinding self-absorption and self-obsession. For pages on end there are no paragraph breaks; the text goes on relentlessly. The appearance that this gives to the book, combined with the author's harping on subjects over-familiar from *Unborn Son*, suggest the outpourings of a bore who harangues one on a street corner, for ever saying, as one is on the point of leaving, 'And another thing . . .' The reader never reaches any oasis, nor, one suspects, did the author; everyone is left stranded in the desert. Maybe the book has a slightly better structure than *Unborn Son*, and some of the anecdotes are telling. But the oasis turns out to be a mirage.

Like *Unborn Son*, *Oasis* is in part an (unwanted) advice manual. The text contains a set of letters to a girl on the threshold of maturity. The oasis itself was a small Algerian village. Here there lived a small rather ill-tempered community. There was M. Duguet, with a large house, and

Sidi Maklouf, the wise holy man who lived a donkey-ride away, a guru-figure of a type Oliver was over-keen on. Other characters included Miss Penman, who visited for some months each year from Dorset, Mr Jones, a retired bachelor schoolmaster who was her special friend, along with a few expatriates and misfits.

Amidst the sub-soap opera accounts of the carryings-on of these people, the book also gave Baldwin the chance to test out hypotheses about politics and current affairs, and to attack narrow British social attitudes. To this end he introduced a mysterious 'square-set, clean-shaven clever-eyed man in his fifties who was fond of a good story.' He turned out to be a French Jesuit, specializing in espionage, and he gave a prediction of the course of world events, which turned out to be, like most of Baldwin's crystal-gazing, interesting but hardly prophetic.

'Spain and France will go to the left; Italy will have a revolution, starting in Milan; Germany will pick a quarrel with Russia after arranging an alliance with Japan, and then France and Russia will crush Germany like a nut and Germany also will have a revolution.'[22]

This was probably written in 1933, and even allowing for the fact that the speaker was a French Jesuit, it is significant that Britain was allowed no participation. (The United States was securely isolationist at the time, so could not have been expected to play a part.) Baldwin, like his father, saw little place for Britain in world affairs at this time.

Oliver also offers assessments of some of his political colleagues – Jimmy Maxton, Leslie Hore-Belisha ('as a companion he is witty and well-informed; as a politician he is less witty and even better informed'), Oliver Stanley, Oswald Mosley ('had he stayed on the left he would have been Socialist prime minister; having gone to the right he will die on some self-erected barricade'), Lloyd George (whom Baldwin reports as saying of Sir John Simon, 'He has sat so long on the fence that the iron has entered his soul'), Attlee ('one of the best of men and has a pretty wit which he reserves for the company of his friends, being too shy to try it in the House'), Stafford Cripps, Sir Archibald Sinclair, Sir Sam Hoare ('he is likely to be prime minister one day, as a permanent stop-gap'), Anthony Eden ('would make a devout Catholic, and an excellent Papal Nuncio'), and finally Harold Nicolson ('an admirable foreign secretary, or viceroy or prime minister'): reflections which have some wit and generosity to them, even if the predictions – always rash – tended to be wide of the mark.[23]

When focusing on the main Algerian topics of the book, the author contrasts British social and sexual attitudes with those of the Mediterranean peoples. To this end he tells the story of one Levanthia Legge, born forty years earlier in an English country rectory,[24] a spinsterish lady who arrives in the village after the death of her parents, whose small legacy had enabled her to travel. She becomes secretly infatuated with one of the local Arabs, a charmer called Abdullah, of great good looks and dignified bearing. However she denies the truth of her feelings to herself. There then arrives in the same village a lively, articulate American woman, who can speak easily about feelings, and who, as an uninhibited go-getter, makes all haste for a night-time assignation with Abdullah in the sand dunes. Levanthia Legge is horror-struck, and plans Abdullah's murder, playing on the affections of a suitor, whom she persuades to undertake the killing. In haste she leaves the town the following day, returning to England.

Then one day she receives a letter from Algiers, and the shock of it kills her. It is apparently a loving and unsuspecting communication from Abdullah, begging her to see him again. He has just left hospital and affirms that he is waiting for her. His letter ends, 'When I lay by thee and kissed thee it was but a hundred kisses I could give; but every pore in my skin was a mouth and every mouth was kissing thee always till the dawn came and the cool wind made me cover up my thousand mouths with my burnous.' Many women, the narrator notes, in Europe and America have read those words at different times written by the same hand, but on none did they have the effect that they did on Levanthia Legge.[25]

As a sub-Forsterian essay the story is moderately convincing, and with its contrast of the warm natural human spirit of the Mediterranean, affectionate but opportunistic, and the arch, in-turned, ill-tuned spirit of much of England of the time, it made a point.

For the rest, *Oasis* contains long, turgid autobiographical passages about being a misfit in a family and being the odd man out, and the consequences therefrom. (Though the comment that 'few things can be duller than having children exactly like oneself' shows that he can lighten up if he tries.[26]) Despite the plentifulness of whinge, matters with a sparkle sometimes get a look in, such as the author's rudimentary interest in developmental psychology.

*

It is surprising, after the taut narrative of *Six Prisons and Two Revolutions*, that Oliver Baldwin's books should be largely ineffectual and self-indulgent. (Two more remained unpublished. The first of these was a text written for Sir Allen Lane, and for which a contract was signed in July 1937, entitled 'What Is This Socialism?', a jaunty title which was inappropriate for the subject matter, which was given an unrigorous treatment. Lane was right not to publish, even if he behaved unethically in turning it down once the contract had been signed. The second was another volume of reminiscences, written in late 1951, entitled 'Golden Rod' and which covered Baldwin's autobiography up to 1948, containing some interesting material, but served up with more unwanted passages of advice to a young relative.) The prospect of filling 250 pages brought out a response of prolix self-indulgence, whereas a demand to write a 1800-word article produced tautness, and often vitality and memorability.

Moreover, Oliver needed something to say, which he had had in *Six Prisons*, and to a great extent in *The Questing Beast*; and he had a powerful story to follow for *Aissa*, though the latter would have been improved if he had explored the by-ways of the gospels, and relied less on including many almost verbatim passages from those texts. *Unborn Son* rambled ineffectually. Readers of *Oasis* would feel they had been dealt more than a desert mirage if the author had written even a chapter on his travels in Algeria, or on his observations of Mediterranean ways of life, instead of alternating between a 'literary model' and the advice stuff. His refusal to be natural, and his preference for striking an attitude, deadened his writing, as did his yearning to be a mentor. As a result second-hand copies of his books are today usually to be found relegated to the 50p rack.

CHAPTER 12

The Discipline of Brevity

From the mid 1920s until the Second World War Oliver was primarily a journalist. His best pieces concerned socialism and Labour policy, and were written for left-leaning papers and periodicals such as the *Daily Herald*, the *Social-Democrat* and *New Britain*. He also wrote frequently for Associated Newspapers in 1935–7, despite the initial attack on Rothermere. A regular column in the *Mail*'s stablemate the *Sunday Dispatch* in 1937–8 was entitled Searchlight on Politics. His work with the Northcliffe group continued for six more months in 1938 with a column in the *Daily Sketch* called Let Us Discuss. He reviewed films seriously in 1933–4, and continued to write on general matters concerning society and social attitudes. If one weeds out the ephemera and word-spinning, a quantity of writing remains which deserves a second look.

Politics, peace, socialism, and the fascist threat

Oliver Baldwin wrote a single, almost unclassifiable article for the German press, on the eve of Germany's first election after 1918. At the time the author was not yet living by the pen. The text is headed 'For Mr Zimmermann of the German Press'; there is no record of whether or not it was translated and used. Part of its significance lies in the fact that the author had participated in the conflict. It opened rhetorically: 'On the eve of your elections I, a former enemy, speak to you across the sea and the land. What chance is yours! What opportunity! You a country on the threshold of democracy. How little you know of the power of Democracy, you who for so long have suffered under the autocratic will of princes. For you now there is one hope, one great yearning – Peace.' Oliver envisaged the new Germany guided by its women in rebuilding the state. They could raise children in a new and different manner. They should be gentle in teaching *Kultur*, and allow an international spirit break the bonds of narrow nationalism, so that the child could become man, free from 'the prejudices of kingship and worldly dominion'.

He identified the main enemy as fear. Fear of poverty had led to revolution; fear of aggression to war. There was mutual fear between France and Germany, and between both and England. But there was room now for optimism: 'The past has lived in darkness. The dawn is approaching. As in the early hours before dawn, the spirit weakens, so it is with us, but we must not lose heart. Each and all of us has a duty to his neighbour as well as to himself, and it must not be a material duty: it must be a spiritual one.'

The churches had failed, he continued; their actions during the war were the evidence. It was the people who should lead. 'In them and them alone lies the new world based on a new comradeship, a new outlook, a new hope not for what can be received but for what can be given. During the war we learnt one lesson, that of sacrifice. Without hesitation we sacrificed the lives of youth. We did not think, did not question. If we can do thus when our nerves are stretched to the utmost, why can't we do it now? . . . We can strive together to make the new world . . . Our sacrifice must be for the spiritual uplift of humanity. All that we do, all that we vote for must be for something better, some advance in theory and practice, some better basis of our society.'

What were the alternatives? 'Nationalism, so dear to the heart of youth and age, reminiscent of the child's love of pomp and ceremony, titles and rewards. Republicanism, so often a half-way house, so often dull and lifeless. Social Democracy that offers you a hopeful future if only its ideals remain high and humanity its guiding force . . . Communism – sometimes a hope of a great future, built on despair, believing, like the Jesuits, that the end justifies the means. So often a doctrine of force that is the antithesis of beauty and love.'

Writing as their brother, 'a molecule in eternity', he advised them not to let their vote be influenced by desire for material advancement or personal ambition; such would be folly and arrogance. They should vote rather for 'the future of a free people who are determined that the life you order for your children be a better one than that left to us by our fathers. Our values have become so warped. We are apt to look upon science as the threshold of true civilization. Because a man has flown to America: because a motor-car has raced at 250 km an hour: because we can speak by wireless from Berlin to Casablanca we lie back in our chairs and think the millennium is nigh. This is not civilization. Civilization is a state of society in which war is unknown: in which imperialism is the playful idea of children: in which force is the savage relic of a barbaric nature. International comradeship must rule the world, and a humble spiritual outlook embracing sympathy, gentleness and understanding is the only road that will lead to a happier race.' He ended this humane appeal by urging the people to vote for humanity before profit, and to strive in an international spirit for the true advance of civilization.

On politics and policy in Britain in the 1930s, four articles give a general impression of his standpoint. He wrote a piece for the *Spectator* of 30 June 1933, which seems to have been his only work for that journal. His text was much improved by the paper's sub-editors. Under the title was 'Why Young

Men are Going Labour', he sought to explain why children of the middle classes were breaking with family voting habits and supporting Labour. They were 'generally the first members of their families to sever their traditional political allegiances'. Why Labour? Because all papers now discussed socialism. That was not so before 1914. Moreover no one of the older generation really knew what socialism entailed. Now, if today's generation enquired, they realized 'that the sorry state of things has not been brought about by land nationalization, state control of banking, family allowances, national investment boards, cooperative farming and distribution, and the abolition of the House of Lords'. Capitalists prophesied eternal prosperity; the situation as predicted by socialists was the one that turned out to be accurate.

Governments victorious under a tariff policy have trotted off to proclaim free trade: the National government, 'originally formed to keep us on the gold standard . . . is now doing its best to keep us off it.' 'These inconsistencies may seem all right to the calcium-lined brains of age, but youth finds them exasperating.' Behind their facades, the two capitalist parties were really just doing the same thing, upholding the sanctity of rent, interest and profit. Socialism, by contrast, appealed for three reasons. It was a saner method of economic living; it was more ethical; and it was different. The link between the issues of production, distribution and consumption was the problem of money; and 'money intended as a means of exchange has become a private monopoly'. Socialism's job was to de-throne money monopoly (i.e. nationalize the Bank of England), and to control the methods of production, distribution and exchange in the interests of the majority. Its attraction lay in the fact that it offered a decent wage for a job, and a pension in retirement. In passing, Baldwin looked at communism and fascism, 'both of which advocate violence. These creeds attract those who despair of humanity or those who hope for personal power.' Conservatism 'offers youth an empty platter though nicely gilt and of antique workmanship'. Liberalism offered the same, without the gilt. But youth had seen the vision of the new Jerusalem, 'and finds the stones at his feet ready to be lifted into place by Socialist hands.' The article generated some lively correspondence, all of it hostile.

A powerful piece entitled 'What of Dictatorship?' was published on 5 July 1933 in C.B. Purdom's *New Britain*. The editor had asked for 'something really sharp and striking . . . we cannot go the way Sir Stafford Cripps indicates . . . the dictatorship of labour is incredible.' The article took as its starting point Cripps's extraordinary threat to invoke the Emergency Powers Act if Labour were returned at the next election. This act contained dictatorial measures which paralleled the wartime Defence of the Realm Act. Under the Tories, Baldwin viewed the act as having saved the British Empire for the bankers; under Labour, it would lead to the suppression of all liberty. The measures themselves constituted 'a threat to all those liberties for which English Radicalism has stood since the seventeenth century.'

Oliver was also concerned to see exactly what a new Emergency Powers Act might entail – to be on guard for liberty, so to speak. 'If it is dictatorship as to our personal liberty, we will have none of it. If it is to prevent the continued control of our means of livelihood by high finance, we shall welcome it. If it be to introduce national planning we will accept it, but if to advocate forced labour – no. If it means more restrictions, the muzzling of the press, increased censorship of art, preventing democratic elections, it must be opposed.' He peered deeper into the meaning of dictatorship. Would it embrace the abolition of the hereditary second chamber and of plural voting, and would a change in the slow legislative process and antiquated procedure of the House of Commons be seen as the antithesis of democracy?

Then he launched into a well-rehearsed but still effective tirade against an old enemy:

The word Dictator sounds offensive to democratic ears
because of its associations with unpleasant tyrants, but I doubt
if any dictator has been as powerful as the governor of the Bank
of England. Whether the government of this country has been
Coalition, Tory, Labour or National, the Bank has decided on
the number of unemployed it needs, on the taxation it requires,
on the money it will issue, on the debts it will collect, on the
interest it will receive, and the appointments of men to serve on
any commission that involves expenditure of public money, on
the houses it will allow to be constructed, on the municipal
work schemes it permits. It controls our whole economic
existence; it allows us money to pay the mid-wife and money to
pay the sexton, and its raises its eyebrows with a pained look
when we suggest it is a tyrant.

There is the real Dictator for you, ever present and ever
protected. Protected by the House of Commons, by the press
and even by a guard of soldiers from the Royal Household in
return for which latter privilege it allows the officer of the guard
a free bottle of port. It has brought this country to its present
sorry state and has made more money out of people's misery
than it did in thirty years before its deflation policy of 1921.

There were other dictatorships too, to watch out for. One
was that of Trades Unionists 'for their mentality is essentially of the right wing, a dictatorship of one class, one
interest and one narrow material conception. This mentality
is also amazingly subservient to the past, to tradition and to
exterior vanities.' Baldwin did no more than mention the
proposed dictatorship of Mosley, as though the personal
friendship of early 1931 still told for something; he warned
instead of his able lieutenant, Lord Trenchard.

At this time he wrote two articles about fascism in Britain,
one for *New Britain* and the other for the *Daily Herald*. Here
one should recall that, besides Mosley, another good mind
he knew had, he believed, been seduced by the lures of
fascism: the distinguished Caucasian scholar and Unionist
MP for Belfast West, W. E. D. ('Bill') Allen, alias James

Drennan. However recent revelations have shown that Allen was more likely to have been a British intelligence agent planted inside the fascist brothel.

The piece for *New Britain* (appearing in the issue of 26 July 1933) was entitled 'An Open Letter to British Fascists'. It acknowledged the attraction of fascism, which appealed to 'one's sense of discipline, orderliness, rhythm or noise'. (This point would have had a particular meaning for Baldwin, who, as Kipling had noted in 1916, had an instinct for drill.) But then what? 'Do you intend to go round the country showing your intellectual level by attacking Jews who happen to be more intelligent than yourselves? Do you intend to beat up socialists because you cannot counter their arguments with better sense? And if you are going to do these things, what do you intend to do next? To abolish Parliament?' If people were drawn to discipline and order, there were alternatives, Baldwin pointed out, which they could take 'without banging inoffensive opponents on the head'.

If people wanted to keep things as they were, then 'throw your energies into the Conservative Party and strive manfully to recruit little "bourgeois" into "Young Britons"'. If they wished to dethrone money power and use the land of England instead of letting it go to waste, 'then join the Labour Party'. If they wished to run with the hare and hunt with the hounds, or less energetically, to sit comfortably on the fence, then they should join the Liberals. If the urge for discipline and marching and shouting continued, 'you can always join the Territorials, the Hikers or the Church Choir'. If a comprehensive philosophy was wanted, then help make a New Britain, 'in which there is a real and definite understanding of the destiny of mankind but [which] realizes that our brains are given us to use for a common end and not for selfish purposes. One in which patriotism does not consist of waving flags, self praise and denunciation of the foreigner, but of pride in a country which has used its land, its factories and its laws to give a more equitable share of the means of livelihood to a well-educated, happy and contented people.'

Fascism had its smart supporters, notably Lord Rothermere, who, in a notorious *Daily Mail* article entitled 'Hurrah for the Blackshirts!', appealed on 15 January 1934 to the British people to turn to Mosley and fascism. Oliver Baldwin's splendid reply, full of invective and appearing under the headline 'NO FASCISM for British Youth', was printed in the *Daily Herald* just two days later. It was a superb demolition job of Rothermere's arguments. The *Mail*-man had said that Britain needed to be protected from experiments, but Baldwin pointed out that the biggest experiment of all was the fascist one. Rothermere had not spelt out what fascism stood for. What was it, then? 'First and foremost, the expulsion of all Jews from positions of trust and importance. Secondly the persecution of all political opponents, and the internment of their leaders in concentration camps. Thirdly, the breaking up of the Trades Unions, and lastly, we imagine, an aggressive imperialistic and foreign policy. And for the unemployed? We are not told.' It seems they would be mobilized into a civilian army at a military wage, so that the regime could boast of decreased unemployment. Physical force would be used by the hooligan element, dressed up in black shirts, against imagined opponents. In India, there would be such aggression that revolution would break out, to be barbarously crushed. Britain would assert herself in the world 'in such a way that only an international war can result'.

The article was fairly heavily sub-edited by the *Herald*'s staff, and the order of fascism's priorities was for some reason changed in the printed version. There, the persecution of political opponents was placed first, the breaking up of trades unions second, the baiting – the *Herald*'s word – of Jews and their expulsion from positions of trust and importance third, and an aggressive foreign policy last.

Baldwin then looked at fascism's economics, and concluded that 'at last, a big right-wing newspaper-owner has realized that capitalism is crumbling away, and the only possible way he can think of to postpone its end is to adopt fascism – that is, the forcible continuation of capitalism in the face of common sense, common humanity and the ethics of Christianity.'

'It may be that the Mark of the Beast is the Swastika. If so, we are heading rapidly for the final struggle . . . so that we are each thrown into one camp or the other – the camp of national and individual profit-making, persecution of minorities and selfishness; or the camp of those who imagine our little world can best be run on tolerance, with the fruits of the world for all, and not merely for the few.' Baldwin almost welcomed the cry from his opponents; it would mean that many who had been marking time on the outskirts of the ranks of freedom and democracy would return with renewed zest to old allegiances, glad that at last there was something clear-cut and vitally important with which to contend, something which old socialists had always prophesied – that when the struggle really started it would be the capitalists, the land-owners and the financiers who would fire the first shot, and overthrow the constitution. 'Let us know when you intend to start.'[1]

A few days later a letter from a reader in Battersea was printed in the *Herald*, acclaiming Oliver's piece as 'the most inspiring challenge to fascism and Rothermere that I have ever read.'

Broadcasting and the BBC

A more relaxed tone was evident in Baldwin's articles on broadcasting. He was fond of the BBC, but laughed at the silly conventions with which it surrounded itself during the 1930s, and he found the pseudo-militarism of its corporate image slightly sinister – the fact (for instance) that all ground-floor staff had to spring to attention when a top executive entered the building. Oliver had made his first broadcast (from Birmingham) in about 1925, in a state of high anxiety, but he soon became cool and professional. His film-reviewing slot gave him a heavy work-load; he had to see the films, and write his scripts; and when people wrote to him care of the BBC, he had to pay for the postage for the replies himself. All broadcasts went out live.

One of his stories concerned the actor Richard Arlen, just in from America where he had been unwell. He was still confused, and lost his place in his script, so that the two of them had to improvise. As soon as the scheduled broadcast was finished, 'he burst out with "I'm so sorry, I'm afraid I messed the whole thing up." But he said something stronger than "messed", and we were still on the air.' Oliver enjoyed the atmosphere in the canteen at Broadcasting House, but he brought up his impression of 'the atmosphere of OGPU which overshadows the building itself'. Once he asked a studio attendant how many engineers were trades unionists. The man said that he did not know. Was he one? No. The studio attendant then reported the whole conversation in writing to the powers that be, 'for which I hope he got promotion'.

Oliver could nevertheless reveal himself as almost a radio groupie. In 1934 he wrote a whimsical piece about wireless knob-twiddling in search of Little Orphan Annie. She eluded all the stations that he found; but discovered instead were the multifarious sounds of Europe and the Mediterranean. These included balalaika music, a talk from Breslau on 'The Ancestry of Famous Germans', songs by Fauré and Debussy from Lyons, French accordion music from Algiers, the tones of the Hardangar flute and dulcimer from Oslo, songs in Flemish, non-stop waltzes from Vienna, tzigane music from Central Europe interrupted by a familiar English voice declaiming 'A deep depression from Iceland is filling up . . .', a gym class for women from Heidelberg, and so on and on: the piece is amusing, flighty, and stays just this side of obsessional.

After listening to a number of foreign broadcasts, Baldwin wrote in November 1934 that he was convinced that the BBC was the leader in the field. But: 'the BBC, from top to bottom, is impregnated with an atmosphere of age and respectability, which is more in keeping with horsehair sofas and plush picture frames than with the modern furnishings with which the building is fitted. To watch the artists arriving at Broadcasting House is to realize that they are made to feel rather that they have come for a course of extra drill than to express their art; and the way they are bound with red tape, ushered (to use a polite term) here and there and left hanging about like lost umbrellas is surely a bad preliminary to the delivery of their best in music, song or speech.'

He spoke up for radio presenters and newsreaders in 'The Truth About Announcers' (written in March 1934 for *Radio Pictorial*), noting the knowledge and tact that their job required: knowledge of foreign languages, and the possession of a sympathetic and well modulated voice. The announcer laboured under several disabilities: 'worst of all, after six o'clock in the evening he has to dress up in a stiff shirt, stiff collar and patent leather shoes.' He was apt to become a talking robot, and is only able to show originality when there was a hitch in the programme. Oliver did not rule out women announcers, and pointed out that a deeper, contralto voice sounded better on air than a soprano.

In probably his last article on broadcasting, of June 1938, he made a plea for the relaxation of censorship at the BBC, as well as for the end of bossiness towards artists (the corporation seemed like 'a cross between Miss Pinkerton's Academy for Young Ladies and the junior division of the OTC'), and more liberty. And could not a well-known nature lover, Grey Owl (who was actually something of a fraud), 'tell children not to hunt wild animals to their death for "sport", or are the fox-killers still to be all-powerful?' Religious and political broadcasting had to be reformed; and we could start brightening Sundays by exchanging the average parson 'for a few moral talks by Bernard Shaw, Professor Joad or Bertrand Russell'. On the matter of accents, Baldwin wondered why the Scots accent was considered respectable, while an English countryman's dialect was not felt to be suitable for announcing. He looked forward to hearing poetry read in the national tongue, rather than in 'the bastard dialect of the richer public schools'. Nevertheless, Baldwin concluded, we were lucky with our BBC. 'Sir John Reith has been open to much criticism, but he has, on the whole, served us well.'

Women and women's issues

Oliver Baldwin wrote fairly frequently about women, in a tone which was almost always enlightened and emancipatory. Only occasionally did a half-line of prejudice or crusty thinking slip in. In lighter pieces, he celebrated women's achievements and the time he had spent in female company.

'I Take My Hat Off to These Women' (probably of 1935) was a breezy look at the history of women's emancipation, from its beginnings in the late eighteenth century, possibly (he thought) under the influence of the French Revolution, but more probably owing to the encouragement of radical male writers. The struggle had been long. In the nineteenth century, women seeking emancipation were ridiculed by men who, 'though they possessed intelligence, became bigoted and narrow-minded before this question of feminine assertion'. There were the writers: George Sand, George Eliot, Jane Austen and the Brontes of course, but Mrs Aphra Behn and Mrs Lynn Linton should not be forgotten, the latter 'a strong opponent of feminism, but although she wrote against it her arguments were nullified by her skilful proof of woman's capability as a creator'. He noted the painters Angelica Kaufmann and Rosa Bonheur. Mrs Bloomer, who rode her bike without a skirt, deserved a mention for introducing the garment which bore her name. 'This was the most daring innovation which even ridicule could not kill, in the same way that the post-war habit [i.e. post 1918] of women wearing trousers and shorts defied all objections and pointed out the strange legal anomaly in our country that whereas a woman could wear trousers with impunity, a man in woman's clothes is immediately arrested'.

In the courts 'our women justices . . . have had to fight bigotry and even rudeness from some of the old molluscs of our provincial benches.' He reflected on women in the arts: amongst actresses he recalled Mrs Siddons, Eleanore Duse, Yvette Guilbert, Ellen Terry, Sarah Bernhardt and Ruth Draper, and in ballet, Pavlova, Adeline Genée and Isadora Duncan. Among musicians he named Dame Ethel Smyth, the cellist Madame Suggia, and a host of opera singers. Explorers, scientists and nurses were given their due. And then there was 'the ordinary working-class mother, the woman who year in, year out, lives a life of perpetual sacrifice.' He looked forward to 'the day when a statue of the English working-class mother is erected in London, in exchange for one of the more commonplace of our deceased royalties or military officers.'

In 'Women and the General Election' (1935), he encouraged questions on real issues, like maternity and health care, education, school age, sentencing policy for juveniles, and equal pay. Candidates could also be asked why more houses were not being built for letting rather than for sale, why slum clearance was going so slowly, and asked for more clinics to prevent 'the awful loss of maternal mortality'. They should be checked for policies for 'many of the abuses that prey heaviest on woman-kind'.

'I am Glad to Meet these Women', published in *Everywoman's* in April 1938, was more relaxed. In past times, Oliver said he would have liked to have met Black Agnes of Dunbar, Joan of Arc or Madame de Staël, but not Catherine the Great or Marie Antoinette ('I like neither cruelty nor stupidity, in man or woman'). Of his own women friends, he mentioned Beatrice Webb ('a practical idealist and a woman of courage') and Rosamond Lehmann, whom he described as 'a truly handsome woman . . .' Of her sister Beatrix, he wrote: 'her performance in *Mourning becomes Electra* has at last made people realize what a really great actress she is. [She] would be wasted in any other profession than that of the drama; she would be smothered by the materialism of life, for she is like a reed flute on which emotions are constantly and easily playing'. He also enjoyed the company of Agatha Christie, who 'possesses the admirable quality of being able to be silent when there is nothing worth while saying'. He valued the friendship of Merle Oberon. Within the family, he singled out Mrs Mackail (Margaret Burne-Jones – hauntingly beautiful, and three times painted by Sir William Blake Richmond).

Other female friends included Dame Margaret Lloyd George, her daughter Megan, the Duchess of Hamilton, and finally 'that fine novelist Naomi Mitchison. Mother of countless children – at least they seem to be all over the room, the house and the garden at the same time – she still finds time to exercise her passion for social justice and use her great intellectual gifts in the pursuit of "what ought to be". She is not restful. She feels too deeply; she is too indignant at times, but she shakes you up. There can be no lack of interest when Naomi Mitchison is about, but she can make you feel your own laziness and waning fervour. Therefore she is good to know, for she is a tonic and a signpost to duty, a woman of essential use to those of us who are apt to lose faith or feel that the battle is scarcely worth the waging.'

In 'Are Women Fit for Politics?', of January 1934, he declared he was uninterested in tales of gossip, influence and intrigue, noting rather that 'when our forebears met around the oak tree and held a moot, women came to such meetings. Edward I had summoned abbesses to his deliberations. Today in many parts of Wales sons are named after their mothers instead of their fathers, which is a relic of the old matriarchal system – John Ann Maria Jones or Evan

Maggie Richards.' The suffragettes were just agitating for the restoration of former power and privileges. Baldwin noted the massive contribution made by women in local government and local affairs, especially in dealing with family matters. There were calls for better sanitation in working-class areas of some towns. The procedure at the House of Commons however was unsympathetic to women's needs, and 'parliamentary work is too tedious and unsatisfactory for them'. As regards debating itself, Baldwin said that women were quicker at 'cutting the cackle and getting to the horses', but he spoilt his case, allowing prejudice to creep in, by saying that women as a sex were illogical. (The logic of this remark was itself faulty, since it contradicted his point about women's capacity to cut through debate, which indicated a command of reasoning.) He paid tribute to Susan Lawrence as 'an outstanding figure in the last parliament'.

Women had got much further in films in America and continental Europe than in Britain, he noted in 'The Film Industry as a Career for Women'. How could they find a way into the business? Make-up and wardrobe, he suggested, both of which were technical rather than decorative matters (the former in the matter of knowing how to alter the whole expression, the latter requiring a knowledge of historical period). Both were still dominated by men. Script-writing was another possibility; here a ' film sense' was needed, an intuitive appreciation of tempo and rhythm, essential to a smooth-flowing script, as were a good dramatic sense, an understanding of comedy, and power of visualizing what was written. In France women had got ahead as film cutters. He also mentioned the business side of films. He referred only in passing to the chance of becoming a star. 'Remember that a pretty face or figure means nothing today. What is needed first and foremost is that indefinable thing – personality.' There were further possibilities of work in the publicity department, or as an art director. The main thing was to get qualifications that would lead to the jobs.

Film journalism

Oliver broadcast and wrote serious film journalism in 1933–34, first when the BBC put out his fortnightly 'Films Worth Seeing', and later in writing reviews for the socialist weekly *Clarion*. At the BBC he put his own democratic maxims into practice: he called for listener response, and encouraged his audience to write to him ('I like receiving your letters because they are interesting and helpful for my decisions as to what pictures you prefer me to talk about', he declared in January 1934). He showed sympathy for the needs of the deaf.

Politics were never far away. He mocked the British Board of Film Censors, who, in June 1934, stopped the production of a film on the life of Judge Jeffreys, 'on the grounds that a picture casting reflection on British Justice – capital letters – could never be passed for public exhibition. And this to save the face of one of the most unmitigated blackguards in English history who died over 200 years ago. Therefore, until the film companies get rid of this incredible board, the "free" people of Great Britain can never see a film of the Tolpuddle Martyrs; nor of Charles I's trial; nor of Chief Justice Parker (eighteenth century); nor the Star Chamber. I think the best thing for our film companies to do, if they won't alter the board, is to pack up and go to a free country as soon as possible – if they can find one these days, though seeing what has come from America and France in the way of films lately they might do worse than go there. No wonder *David Copperfield* is to be done in America, and *Oliver Twist* as well, because Charles Dickens' ideas of justice and those of the British Board of Film Censors might clash.'

The 1933 film of Noël Coward's *Cavalcade*, starring Diana Wynyard and Clive Brook, was, he acknowledged, extremely popular. But both the upstairs characters and those below stairs (pictured 'with the usual incredible stupidity') were depicted as mere victims of events. 'A cavalcade of England should show what caused the Boer War; how the majority of its people lived; how the great inventions brought new means of livelihood to its inhabitants; how the armament race reached its goal in 1914; and how the seeds were sown for the great tragedies of the post-war world.' Oliver considered that the film did 'definite harm, for it shows the frills and the tinsel and hides the truth at every turn.'

Oliver's most fluent and sustained piece of film criticism was probably his vivid notice for Robert Flaherty's *Man of Aran*, written for *Clarion* in May 1934:

Robert Flaherty leapt into fame some years ago with a film of Esquimo life called *Nanook*, and those who saw that picture will remember what a revelation it was. Since that time Flaherty has been in the South Seas, and has just finished two years on the barren Aran Islands off the western coast of Ireland. The result of his last sojourn is his new film which he calls *Man of Aran* . . .

First of all it is not a film in the proper sense of the word. It is miniature saga of the lives of the people who inhabit these islands and scrape a living from the sea. And not an ordinary sea at that, but a great hungry rolling sea that uses the rocky Aran Islands as a test of its own mighty strength. It is a sea which, by constant battering, has made shelves of the islands up which it rushes with incredible fury, casting its spray high into the dark sky and throwing itself at the last flat upon the soil-less rocks. Yet the people grow potatoes there, on those rocks. They cover them with thick layers of seaweed and then set forth to search the crevices for powdered stone, guano and decayed birds who have crept therein to die. And that makes the soil.

When the sea is calmer than is its wont, the men set out to hunt sharks in order to get oil for their lamps. We see this sequence, and although the sight of a great shark beating the frail boat with his tail makes one glad we are not there, it is later on in the film that the real thrill takes place. There are no actors, only ten figures: frail sort of things against that background of hard dark rock and that colossal expanse of sea. Ten figures, one of which is a woman with the face of a Madonna and one boy with the hands of an artist and the smile of a Cupid. The others are all men with strong faces and strong arms, tall and lithe, unsmiling but inwardly full of Irish humour . . .

The drama is at the end. Little Michael wants to go out with his father and his two friends to fish in the evening, but his father will not let him. He is too young and there is an ominous look in the sky; so Michael wanders unhappily back home and sleeps by the peat fire. Then the storm breaks. Just rain and a slight wind to start with, but Michael and his mother know what that portends. The sky is black with rain clouds, and as the two make their way down to the sea, the wind rushes at them and tears at them, and the big breakers in the distance push their white heads into the sky and set forth on their wild rush landwards.

As each wave strikes the rocks, the clouds of spray hide the two wind-struck figures from sight as they hurry to the little beach to be of help to their men should they be needed. Once on the shore, their feet covered by tongues of foaming sea, they search the distance for the little boat. They see nothing; but the camera on the cliff has found it. At last the boat is seen by the watchers below, but only intermittently; for the waves are so high and the trough of the water so deep that each sight of the frail coracle might well be the last.

I never knew such drama could be in the struggle of three men with a hungry sea. I never saw such sea photography and such good cutting of so difficult a subject. As I watched, I also was on this strip of beach: and as you watch, you will be there as well, straining your eyes and full of fear for the safety of these stout-hearted fighters. *Man of Aran* must be seen, and when your eyes have looked for the last time on these fisher-folk as they stagger ashore, leaving their boat to its fate, you will feel as if you have been through part of their trial, and the roar of the surf will drown the noise of the busy streets for you for many minutes after Robert Flaherty's masterpiece has ended.

General topics

Among Baldwin's many miscellaneous pieces there are two 1935 20-minute radio talks on Oxfordshire, focusing on its Civil War associations. An article on the religion of Oliver Cromwell (written post-1939) indicated his self-perceived affinity with the Lord Protector. Ever since childhood he had felt a strong admiration for the man whose Christian name he shared. One could however add that Baldwin's somewhat severe Roundhead image of himself was true only of his public aspect and political convictions ('right but repulsive', in the words of *1066 and All That*). At home with Johnnie, Boldie – Miss H. A. Bold – and other friends, he was more of a generous, careless, rather indulgent Cavalier ('wrong but wromantic').

The titles of some of his articles give an idea of what he was churning out to make a living: 'Why Not be a Millionaire?', 'Don't Waste Your Leisure', 'Are We Good Hosts?', 'Why I Believe In The Scot', 'Are You a Misfit?', 'How to Get the Best Out of a Holiday', 'What is Happening to Sport?', 'Britain's Crime Babies', 'The Lure of Greta Garbo', 'If Dickens were Alive Today', 'Those Speech Days', 'We Must Learn to Play', 'The Sins of Civilization'. He also wrote two articles for *Prediction*: 'Is Hitler Possessed?' and 'Was Christ a Spiritualist?' Despite the odour of hack-work which these titles give off, there was usually an original and radical observation in the texts, which made them worth reading (once, at least). 'Britain's Crime Babies' was a serious and comparative attempt to wrestle with the issue of juvenile crime.

In all this material there was almost nothing about Armenia, or his experiences in 1920–21. He wrote on the Assyrians, who are Asiatic Christians like the Armenians, for the *Manchester Guardian* on 17 August 1933, and the Assyrian leader, Agha Petros, was occasionally his guest for the weekend. In France he still kept up a friendship with

Khatisian, and with Jacques and Anya Kayaloff. But the Armenian issue, despite his enmeshment with it both in Yerevan and at Lausanne, was virtually blanked out. Perhaps he felt too deeply Britain's – and possibly his own – failure to bring Armenia help in its time of crisis, thereby denying that nation the independence, borders and security which it deserved.

'Prime Ministers I Have Known'

For *Men Only*, Oliver Baldwin wrote five short pieces on British premiers in March 1955. The subjects were Lloyd George, Stanley Baldwin, Ramsay MacDonald, Winston Churchill and Clement Attlee.

All of these, with the exception of Ramsay MacDonald, were figures he admired. He had met Lloyd George first in the lobby of the Commons in 1929, when T. P. O'Connor was congratulating Oliver on his maiden speech, something the Irishman had to hear since he had heard Oliver's grandfather's and father's Commons debut. At that moment Lloyd George came up, and said, 'You should have been a Liberal.' Lloyd George and Oliver struck up a warm friendship, which lasted until Oliver left for the war in 1940. Oliver spent at least one weekend at Churt, where his host's bonhomie and somewhat self-regarding sense of humour were vigorously displayed. In the garden Oliver was shown the fine canes of Lloyd George raspberries that he was growing. But, said his host, they would not grow next to Baldwin blackcurrants, so the latter had to be moved. Ll G insisted that Oliver tell this detail to his father.

After dinner he liked to sing Welsh hymns, play charades, or enact historical scenes. During one weekend, the house party performed the departure of the British delegation for the 1932 Ottawa Conference. Megan Lloyd George, in an overcoat and holding a pipe, was SB; Lady Carey-Evans played Oliver's mother. Gwilym Lloyd George played Lord Swinton, 'and lastly the old man himself as J. H. Thomas, stealing the limelight, waving at the crowd, talking at the top of his voice – and the last to embark.' One day Mosley came to tea, and as he left, the rest of the party (and the dog, a chow) drew up outside and gave Mosley a send-off with mock fascist salutes (and presumably a raised paw) – an action which shows how fascism was perceived in parts of Britain at the time, not as the ideological horror it later manifested itself to be, but as a silly nursery fantasy, whose adherents needed a dose of ridicule to make them see sense.

In the House of Commons, Oliver was captivated by Ll G's speaking manner, 'a joy to listen to and a joy to watch.' Clearly the Lloyd George magic had worked on him, and seduced him from analysis of the showiness and posing which characterized much of Lloyd George's conduct of foreign policy, especially concerning western Asia. Baldwin hated Curzon for what that superior person had done to Armenia; but equally to blame for denying restitution to that state in 1920–21 was Lloyd George, who by his vanity and desire to score points against the French and Italians held more responsibility for relegating western Armenia to a nation of refugees excluded from their homeland, by then an ethnically cleansed wilderness.

Baldwin wrote a clerihew on Lloyd George:

Sly, cunning, charming
A leader of men
Strong & emotional
User of men.

Baldwin had few good words for Ramsay MacDonald. He endorsed the views of his own socialist guru, H. M. Hyndman, expressed in 1912, that MacDonald was driven by personal ambition, and was a dangerous enemy to socialism, remaining basically a Liberal. Oliver held that that prophecy came true in 1931. He referred to his meeting with MacDonald on the train in the summer of that year, when MacDonald affirmed to Oliver that big business was too powerful for the Labour Party to deal with, and that the country would be irretrievably ruined if we went off the gold standard.

Thereafter, Baldwin believed, MacDonald began to show evidence of losing his senses. He would repeat stock phrases and clichés, in a meaningless manner, parodied thus by another Labour member: 'The trade cycle must have been punctured by leaving no stone unturned in exploring all those avenues.' Oliver disapproved of the fact that in 1935 MacDonald had put his own son Malcolm on the list of Labour ministers bequeathed to his successor Stanley Baldwin, to the exclusion of Lord Sankey, the Labour Lord Chancellor. But he remembered Ramsay MacDonald too at Chequers, listening to fervently patriotic Scottish songs. Oliver sums him up as 'a man of talent, directed to great opportunity, who thought too much of himself ever to attain happiness or success for the cause in which he had once believed.'

The clerihew on MacDonald went

Own worst enemy
Own worst friend
Retreats or advances -
Never can bend.

Oliver was by contrast a fan of Churchill. He admired him for his changeability, evidence of 'knowing when he had been wrong and acknowledging it openly'. For instance, in 1911 Churchill the Liberal had inveighed against the Tories for making use of the socialist Robert Blatchford in order to 'work up a German scare'. Very different from Churchill's position in 1914. Oliver first met him in 1929, a few days after Churchill had come into the Commons chess-room and said, in Oliver's hearing but without seeing him, 'Move your Baldwins', referring to the pawns. Oliver liked his puckish sense of humour. During the negotiations for the Government of India bill, someone referred to Joynson-Hicks' statement, 'We won India by the sword and will keep it by the sword.' Churchill commented, 'I never knew Jix had a sword.' At the Treasury, one of the permanent officials noted, 'They say Lord Randolph asked, with reference to decimal points, what those damned dots were for; Winston didn't even ask.'

Behind the inconsistencies, Oliver detected a pattern and a burning zeal to get things done. There was no conceit and no envy in his nature. Wit, but no malice, and with an ingenuous acceptance of people. 'At heart a Radical Imperialist, yet there is no Carson about him; he accepts the decisions of the majority with sorrow, yes; but not with the idea of future revenge . . . He prefers youth to age, and thus keeps young in thought. He likes adulation. He is naif in some things and very sentimental. He is easily moved by tales of cruelty and unkindness; by the theatre or the cinema, and by deeds of heroism and the march of a company of Guardsmen . . . I have always felt that he never quite under-stood the working class. I doubt if he has ever spent a night in one of their homes or could tell you the times of their normal meals. He would reply to this that spending nights in the trenches among his troops was good enough training to understand such men, and there is much in that, but not all. In politics he had not much use for Stanley Baldwin, but the latter had for him . . . He has a great natural courtesy and will go out of his way to do a kindness. He has no class con-sciousness . . . As a leader, he has the genius's power of del-egation, believing that to lead, one must first get the best men, give them directives and let them get on with it.' On Churchill's manner of choosing people for tasks, Oliver quoted James Wellwood on Cromwell: 'And if he hear of a man fit for his purpose, who never so obscure, he sent for him; suiting the Employment to the Person, and not the Person to the Employment.' Baldwin summed Churchill's career up as a fascinating panorama, held together by the man's faith in himself and in his mission. 'No one can help liking him personally and the reason is that he gives more than he takes . . . A political opponent salutes him.'

The clerihew on Churchill goes thus:

Egocentric, energetic
Jocular & terse
Tory Liberal, liberal Tory
Might have been much worse.

In recounting Attlee's formative years, Baldwin outlined the conventional start, and the influence at Oxford of William Morris. Attlee gained legal qualifications, but switched from law (which in Oliver's opinion was 'but the opinion of the dead as to how the living are to exist') to social work among the poor of the East End of London. All the time he kept a print of the G. F. Watts portrait of Morris above his desk or in his living room. In the East End, Attlee joined Keir Hardie's Independent Labour Party, a rival to Hyndman's Social-Democratic Federation.

Attlee lectured briefly at the LSE in 1913, before joining up and seeing service at the Dardanelles, in Mesopotamia and the Western front. He became mayor of Stepney in 1919, and then MP for Limehouse in 1922. Qualities which were often obscured by his shyness were his wit and his broad-mindedness. And: 'There is no mirthless laughter of the intellectual nor insincere grin of a woman TV announcer in his make-up . . . His knowledge of the working class is profound and, like Stanley Baldwin, he often prefers their company to that of the intellectuals who have lately been flocking into the Labour Party.' Oliver Baldwin could not call him a good judge of people, since he expected those who worked with him to have the same qualities of honesty and sincerity as himself.

The turning point in Attlee's career came in 1931, when he stayed with the party and held on to Limehouse, thus becoming leader when Lansbury resigned in 1935. He was respected by both his own party and his opponents. His friendship was not given easily, owing to his reserve, but once given 'is a most devoted one'. Oliver ended by hoping that he would end his days in the Upper House. The Attlee reflections were curiously sober, plain and straightforward, eschewing any colourful Attlee anecdotes.

On Stanley Baldwin

Oliver wrote four times on his father. Once was for R. J. Minney in about 1937; secondly, again probably in 1937, he wrote three articles on SB; for *Men Only* in 1954 he wrote on Life with Father, and for the same magazine as part of the series above on prime ministers.

He wrote with compassion and consideration about him. In tracing SB's early political development, he stressed his sensitivity, and the domination of his childhood by his stern, preoccupied father, busy tending his invalid wife. Two things gave him the impulse towards politics: one was Alfred Baldwin's entry into parliament as member for West Worcestershire, and the other was Stanley's marriage to Lucy Ridsdale, who gave much encouragement to her husband.

Oliver accepted that his father's pre-war days in the House were not spectacular. He opposed the Miners' Eight-Hour bill and votes for women, but supported Trade Union bargaining. He had problems with being called to speak, since he would arrive from the country dressed in a grey tweed suit, attire considered inappropriate by Mr Speaker for addressing the House, at least from Unionist benches.

The son traced his father's wartime post as one of the financial secretaries to the Treasury (when he donated his war-gains to the British Treasury), and his time as President of the Board of Trade, when, while negotiating Britain's first trade deal with the Soviet state, he did not even mention to his opposite number, Commissar L. B. Krasin, his son's plight as a prisoner of the Bolsheviks. Oliver applauded this patriotic action.

Oliver looked at his father's character: though he was half-Celtic, and full of Celtic instincts, 'he is afraid of that side of his nature, of enthusiasms, of ultra ideology, of the power of words and emotions and the speed of decisions, yet strangely enough his position in the hearts of the people is more due to these qualities . . . This feeling of distrust was that which made it difficult for him to work with Mr Lloyd George. Mr Lloyd George was too quick, too subtle, too dynamic and consequently, in the mind of Stanley Baldwin, unstable and dangerous . . . [SB] decided to leave the ship at the first opportunity. The chance came with the famous Carlton Club meeting and he went to it with two strong determinations – to make a speech against such leadership and then to resign after the inevitable defeat of the revolt. No one was more surprised than he when his speech proved to be the deciding voice . . . It was only his wife who was not in the least surprised at the turn of events.'

His premiership, following Bonar Law's resignation, was characterized by belief in a single panacea for economic ills: a general tariff. The idea had come from Joseph Chamberlain's 'parochial economics'. Stanley Baldwin felt he needed a mandate, and so called a general election, which resulted in the brief 1924 minority Labour administration. But following the Tory victory of that autumn, SB returned to the premiership, and over the next four and a half years grew in confidence and 'he tried to do his best to keep the ship of state on an even keel, even if he was not quite sure whither that ship was heading'.

Oliver outlined the problems that his father faced in 1924–9: abuse from newspapers, a coal stoppage and the general strike, trouble with Ireland and rising unemployment.

He made the point that there was a pattern to his father's methods in dealing with these problems. He would not read abusive newspaper articles. He was not panicked by the general strike, knowing the working class too well, and he showed his magnanimity when it was over by offering two of the strike leaders a knighthood 'which they gladly accepted, promising, I presume, never to do such a thing again'. Oliver believed that his father showed sympathy for all sides in the Irish settlement. In the face of rising unemployment he was powerless, owing to Austen Chamberlain's 1921 deflationary policy and the 1925 return to the gold standard.

The son believed that his father's 'besetting weakness' was that his sense of inferiority made him rely too much on the opinions of his ministers. He often gave the country the impression that 'the driver of the State coach was asleep on the box'. Oliver's understanding, which sounds like that filial regard which his enemies accused him of lacking, was that his father was he was 'constantly being surprised at his own success', and this generated a belief in him of the inevitability of the progress he sought, and he would not hurry for fear of disaster. 'He knew we were heading towards socialism in one way or another and he knew that nothing could stop it. His duty was to be a brake, to see that the family coach did not go too fast during its trotting career down Transition Lane.'

However, the general strike united the working class, and brought defeat in 1929. SB's election slogan of Safety First was sounded just at the moment when action was needed, and he lost.

During the chaotic times of 1931, Oliver's father did not view MacDonald's desperate measures with either pity or scorn. Once in the National government, SB smoothed the way for MacDonald in his dealings with the great and the good, 'who were so much more difficult to handle than the Trades Union rank and file'. But after 1935 SB grew tired, as had MacDonald, and resigned three months before his seventieth birthday.

On the Abdication, Oliver indicates that his father had great respect for the Duke of Windsor's feelings. But he was also devoted to the best interests of the country; and this sense of duty had always been his guiding star. This was set alongside a deep belief in democracy, and faith in the ability of the people to work out their own political future, be it to the left or the right.

Oliver paid tribute to Cissie Baldwin, 'his firmest friend, wisest counsellor, and most perfect sympathizer.' In her he had been lucky. But: it was said he was weak in foreign affairs. Here SB was driven by his horror of war. Oliver somewhat rashly quoted Pericles in this context: 'No Athenian ever put on mourning because of me.' Summing up, he said that he saved Toryism from reaction, and therefore the country from revolution, and gave a high ideal to public life.

His first article for *Men Only*, of 1954, contained an account of the summer holiday which father and son took together in France in 1913, when Rheims Cathedral made a dazzling impact on Oliver's adolescent self. The article in the series on prime ministers, of the following year, went over familiar territory, stressing SB's friendship with Labour trade union stalwarts and that he 'seemed to like the Clyde group of the ILP more than the rest of the Labour Party.' As regards the tales told about his father, Oliver vouches for the truth of only two: that he did say 'Good God,' when unveiling Epstein's statue of Rima in Hyde Park, and murmured regretfully 'She never looked like that to me' when unveiling the statue in memory of Queen Alexandra outside Marlborough House. In 1946 he bricked up half his fireplace, on hearing the exhortation of Emmanuel Shinwell, Minister of Power, to cut down fuel consumption, and sat in front of the diminished blaze wearing an overcoat. Stanley Baldwin was full of reminiscences in these last two years, after Cissie's death. Oliver recalled a conversation in which he said, 'If I had stayed in industry, instead of going into politics, I should have been disgustingly rich.' 'And do you regret it?', asked the son. 'Not a bit,' he replied.

CHAPTER 13

The Second World War: seeking service

Oliver Corvedale was underemployed for much of the 1939–45 war. He never received the command which he felt was due to him. He had been a more than competent subaltern for six months in 1918, and had gone on to gain further military experience in Armenia. He had discovered his potential as a soldier. Now, on the day that war broke out, he volunteered his service. But the War Office, then and later, showed little interest.

To Oliver, as to many other people, Chamberlain's government was out of its depth in the crisis. As he put it, 'Birmingham business and foxhunting highchurchmen cannot deal with suicidal mania.'[1] At the time he was keeping a diary, and it articulates the anxiety of those times: hourly news-bulletins on the wireless, and a pervasive atmosphere of tension and depression. On the morning of 3 September he was giving Rosamond Lehmann a lift from Reading to her home in Ipsden. He stopped the Chrysler by a hill overlooking her village, on the Woodcote Road, and they heard Chamberlain announce that Britain was at war with Germany.[2]

Corvedale was puzzled, as were many, during those first months of the war. Where was the action, except in Poland? Some shipping was sunk, but nothing else seemed to be happening. On the 11th he went to Astley to see his parents. The house was full of evacuees. His brother Windham told the story of a man who had heard on the wireless of the bombing of Warsaw, and who had then ridden furiously through Stourport shouting, 'They're bombing Walsall!'

In a mood of frustration he went to London, following up his letter of volunteering, looking for a post in intelligence. On 4 October he met the DMI (Director of Military Intelligence), but a few days later he was told him that there was no job. The excuse he was given was that he might make a revolution of his own. This response left him unimpressed. His cool and imaginative friend W. E. D. ('Bill') Allen was now fairly obviously an agent. The secrecy that Allen had maintained while apparently acting as an intelligence 'sleeper' within the British Union of Fascists was no longer necessary. Oliver, not part of any inner circle of intelligence, felt sidelined.[3] Further visits to Colonel Craig and Quex Sinclair, head of the Secret Service, also proved unfruitful.

Corvedale had kept up his contact with the Armenians, and their situation in the early months of the war was a matter for concern. He held several meetings with Jirayr Missakian, the only member of the Dashnak party living in England, whose brother Shavarsh edited the Paris-based Armenian newspaper *Haratch* ('Forward') until the German occupation, when the journal closed. The issues for the Armenians, especially the anti-Soviet ones, were complex. Before Hitler's invasion of the USSR, the Nazi-Soviet pact stood. Theoretically the oil-fields of Baku were available as a resource for the Wehrmacht. The Allies were alarmed, and at one stage considered the option of bombing the oil installations. The USSR was making aggressive noises about gaining Kars and Erzerum – unforgotten districts where Armenians had a strong claim. At the same time the idea was floated for an Allied land invasion using Turkey as a base – presumably to be carried out by a force which would include Turkish troops – which would have meant the obliteration of Soviet Armenia. The invasion of Transcaucasia from the west was the pet project of Bill Allen, who was also keen to engineer Georgian independence from the USSR with Turkey's help. Should the anti-Soviet Armenians cooperate with the Allies and watch Armenia wiped out; was there a possibility of Turkish-Dashnak cooperation; or should anti-Soviet Armenians stay neutral? These questions were part of the dialogue. No final decision was reached, but matters were clarified when notions of bombing Baku and invading Transcaucasia were dismissed as madcap adventurism. Oliver mulled over the points with Missakian. The Englishman sensed a fairly undisguised wish within the British establishment to find a pretext to attack Soviet Russia. He commented, 'They will have us at war with Russia, if they can, these fascists.'[4]

It is possible that Oliver's long-held radical political opinions stood in the way of his being offered a role in the British war effort. He was later told that he was passed over because he had worked on the early issues of Claud Cockburn's radical journal *The Week*. But there were other matters to be taken into account. One was that he was the son of the former prime minister, and so he would have been an expensive hostage if captured by the other side. There was also the point that he was homosexual, and though many British gay men served with great distinction in the war, it is possible that, to the top brass, one who was now living so openly in an established ménage with another man in Oxfordshire might be thought to be 'unreliable'.

Eventually, on 10 January 1940, he received instructions from an 'I.P.' (intelligence person) at the Foreign Office to proceed to Paris on a mission. He left the following day, and was there for three days, before returning to England.[5]

On his return, after recovering from a debilitating hepatitis infection, he still complained about not having a job. 'Had I been a fascist or a Tory I should doubtless have been employed in the army', he noted. From off-the-cuff comments made by the military he observed that he was seen alternately as a 'bloody Bolshevik' or 'the son of the man who let us down'.[6]

Nevertheless Oliver's Foreign Office connections still carried some weight, even if the War Office was unproductive, and in May 1940 he made a second trip to France, flying from Hendon to a secret aerodrome near Versailles. He then took a taxi to Paris, where he stayed at the Hotel Westminster. After a day or so he took the train to Marseille, and sailed in a French boat to Alexandria. The ship berthed briefly at Algiers, so he was able to catch up with news of the Villa Aurelian. He carried with him a letter which proclaimed him to be the accredited correspondent of the Britanova News Agency in the Near East. It is possible that this was a real news agency, but it seems more likely that it was a convenient cover for intelligence work. In Cairo, the Continental Hotel became his home on and off for the next two years.[7] His job was linked both to the War Office and the Foreign Office, and related to minor issues, such as rounding up German spies, and attempting to strengthen Allied interests in the region. Letters reached him via Colonel Thornhill at the British Embassy.

Social life seems to have been tolerable in those early war days: there were visits to, amongst others, Napier Alington, Peter Haddon, an actor who had become briefly engaged to Doreen Arbuthnot after Oliver had broken off with her, and Bunny Isaac, an old friend from the Worcestershire Viginti cricket team, as well as Russell Pasha, the chief of police, and Christopher Scaife, a lecturer at Cairo University who wrote passionate verse about brawny Neapolitan dock-workers. He enjoyed the company of young officers such as Geoffrey Makins. Oliver also found a black kitten, which he took to the hotel to live in the kitchen, and gave the provisional name Black Kootie.[8]

He also lectured, in both Egypt and Palestine, on various military matters: to OCTU and the 60th Rifles, on the effects of shell fire, drawing on his 1918 experiences. Senior officers continued to murmur that this chap was indoctrinating the men with bolshevism.

The fall of France (16 June 1940) posed serious problems for the Allies in the Levant. Who was loyal to the Free French, and who accepted the authority of the Vichy regime? Corvedale's job shifted to monitoring the Syro-Palestine frontier, and guarding oil installations in Haifa. He was in Palestine at the time of the arrival of the immigrant ships full of Jewish refugees from Eastern Europe. Though basically sympathetic to their plight, he sceptically noted that the sinking of the *Patria* was 'very well managed'.[9]

His letters also show concern about conditions at home, especially for Johnnie who was largely on his own at Little Stoke House. So he wrote home in a manner both entertaining and morale boosting: 'Did I tell you James Fraser rang me up in Cairo & spent a day with me – no curls & no fat & much nicer & very keen on his job – such a change'. 'Clifford Lewis from Dinard days, friend of Bob Orme, came up to me. He has lost his looks but is very nice & is a private in the A.S.C.' 'We are are all so full of admiration out here for the way you are standing it all & tell Ernest that even I who have no respect for the way our people vote am full of admiration for their courage & hope & believe that peace will come as a result of their marvellous obstinacy.'[10]

In January 1941 his directionless war was given a sharp shove. He was told to proceed to Nairobi and thence to Khartoum, in order to participate in the campaign to expel the Italians from Eritrea. He reported to Captain George Steer, who was to be his commander and would become a friend.

Oliver's job was to liaise with the local population, and to experiment, initially on the plains of Omdurman, with a powerful sound system, consisting of loudspeaker horns which could make the voice travel for two to three miles, and which was to be used for propaganda and for winning desertions from the enemy.

He went into action with his sound equipment in Keren, Eritrea. British forces had started badly in East Africa, registering a number of defeats in 1940. Only at the end of that year did fortunes change, with the dislodging of the Italians from Kassala, Sudan. Commanded by the Duke of Aosta, Viceroy of Ethiopia, they were still well entrenched in Keren, defended by a formidable range of mountains, and by some of Italy's best troops.[11]

Corvedale's HQ was some three miles to the rear of the army. A witty account of his activities appeared in the *Daily Telegraph* in April 1941. '"Broadcasting House" was the inscription on a board in the front of a native grass hut only a few hundred yards away from the outlying defences of Keren,' wrote the special correspondent, Alan Moorehead. 'This was the headquarters of the broadcasting propaganda unit . . . Through five powerful loudspeakers, nightly talks were given to the enemy troops on the crests opposite in Amharic and Tigrean, the principal Abyssinian languages, and in Italian. The bluff, moustached captain who commanded the unit is the son of a noted Conservative statesman, and was himself at one time a Socialist MP. The unit's post, well in front of our main position, was an obvious target for the Italian artillery, and it was impossible to reach it by daylight. But as night fell the members of the unit crept up the sandy fold of the hillside to their post.' Then the speech would begin – an enormous voice booming across the valley, appealing to the men's pride to come over and fight for their own king and flag. This was followed by an Italian-speaking officer giving the latest news of their 'dictator-led defeats', and similarly appealing to them to come over. 'Afterwards, with heartbreaking inappropriateness, there would rise over the grim valley the lovely, lighthearted note of a Rossini opera. Finally, as the sky began to pale, the captain approached the microphone. "This is Broadcasting House," his words sounded across the valley. "We are closing down for the night, but will be on the air this evening just after sunset."'[12]

In all, Oliver says that over 200 of the enemy came over as a result of this ruse – 'a better way of making war than killing them'. Moorehead concurred with this judgment in the account of the campaign he gave in his book *African Trilogy*. He noted the scepticism of the British commanders, who feared that the sound system would draw fire. 'Apparently it had the reverse effect. It used to stop the war . . . Corvedale got deserters, as he richly deserved to. Everything here to do with propaganda and the fifth column was in fact being handled with a dispatch and vision that had not yet reached Cairo.'[13]

One night Oliver tested the apparatus to see if it was working. He touched the microphone with a pencil. The resulting noise sounded like a squadron of tanks clanking through the valley.

In a moment of reflection, Corvedale found time to give expression to the activity of these months in a poem, which he dated 'Before Keren, Eritrea, March 1941'. He dedicated it ('without his permission') to Alan Moorehead, War Correspondent. The opening well encapsulated his change from drift to purpose:[14]

> Stung into action; so long thoughtless, and preoccupied:
> We had not paused for poetry nor rhyme.
> No paeans of glory from our untuned lyres;
> No prayers to God before our life expires . . .
> Because we were too old, or far too young, before our time.
>
> Therefore I ask my God, when peace shall lift the veil from God
> And we, once more, shall start to build anew;
> That glorious music may come from this earth,
> That our lame poesy may have re-birth,
> If poets be only spared . . . and God, there are so few.

The initial attacks on Keren were unsuccessful but British forces entered the town on 25 March. Oliver did not delay there, but started off on the road to Asmara. There he was stopped by a burst of rifle fire. In rage – and fear, he admits – he stepped forward to ask what it was about, and seeing an officer wearing a French kepi, led fly a torrent of abusive French. The Legionnaire's commander, Lt Col Koenig, had thought the party consisted of escaping Italians. There were profuse apologies. Oliver and he made a Legion compact, that as a result when he next met an officer of the battalion he should buy him a drink. Some months later he claimed a bottle of wine as his reward in Homs, Syria.[15]

Allied forces entered Asmara on 1 April, and General Platt, the officer commanding, wired Cairo with the news, concluding his cable with the words NOT REPEAT NOT APRIL FOOL.[16]

Once in Asmara, it was Oliver's job to censor anti-British articles in the local newspapers, and to write for them himself. He changed the slogan of one paper from *Credere, Obbedire, Combattere* to *Pensare, Riflettere, Vivere in Pace*, and physically altered a number of the giant painted slogans of DUCE into PaCE. But he was ticked off fiercely when he suggested that there might be a screening of Charlie Chaplin's classic *The Great Dictator*. Oliver implies that lingering pro-fascist sentiment was responsible for this decision. After a week or two he was given the post of General Platt's unofficial intelligence officer. He was astonished by the amount of pro-Italian and pro-fascist sympathy that he found among fellow British. One such man had held a position of authority in the Sudan, and his action had nearly led to the loss of that country; he was now in charge of the civilian admin in Asmara.[17]

Oliver also noted the lethargy of the administration in interning the secretary of the local fascist party. Eventually this individual was detained by a naive young ex-Palestine policeman, who allowed his charge to go to the loo unsupervised. Down the pan went a shredded list of members. Fortunately Oliver was able to rescue carbon copies from the waste paper basket.

The Italians were now stuck fast in the strongly defended positions of Amba Alargi and Gondar. Corvedale's job was to discover the true defensive situation of these fortresses, which he did by liberal dispensation of Ethiopian Maria Theresa dollars.[18]

One day, in his office, he had an idea. His eye had alighted on a packet of the Duke of Aosta's notepaper. It was intended for the Duke's splendid and confidential correspondence. Oliver sat down and composed a letter (to be translated into Italian), addressed personally to the Italian commander of Gondar. It divulged the Duke's secret intention to surrender on 11 May, with 'honours of war' (a phrase which he felt would appeal to the Latin temperament), and requested therefore that Gondar should surrender on the same date. He planned to trace the Duke's signature from the many examples in papers in his house. Several copies were to be made: one would be dropped from a captured Italian aircraft, and others would be sent through the lines by messengers. The brigadier liked the idea, and agreed with Oliver that it was a good way to shorten the campaign. But he had to show it to General Platt, to receive his sanction. Oliver was excited and elated, and found it hard to sleep in anticipation. He went eagerly up to the brigadier next morning and asked, 'Well, sir?'. The brigadier raised his eyebrows. 'General Platt says it would not be playing cricket.'[19]

Amba Alargi surrendered on 16 May. (Gondar held out for another six months.) Corvedale was ordered back to Khartoum, and was sorry to leave 'the finest bunch of staff officers one could wish to serve with'. He was proud to have participated in 'the first victory of the war', but ruefully noted that there was no campaign medal, and that those who won the victory in East Africa wore the same ribbon as the men who had spent the war in Cairo.

Oliver himself was now back in Cairo, preparing for the invasion of Syria. He was to be based in Jerusalem, and would be in charge of French propaganda. At the same time he was promoted to major. He wrote and had printed some pamphlets, which were dropped by aircraft in July 1941. The gist of them was that the French were fools to fight for Hitler, which was what their support for the Vichy regime amounted to. After a quick campaign British forces were in Beirut, but despite the appeals to oppose the Vichy regime, sentiment was markedly anti-British and pro-Axis.[20]

Autumn 1941 was a grim time in the Near East. There were no victories; and Nazi forces were smashing through Soviet territory towards the North Caucasus. Oliver was recalled to Cairo to write a section of a pamphlet on Turkey.

Then he received a piece of curious information. Some Armenian parachutists had been found half-buried in the snow near the Syrian-Turkish border. They were, like Missakian (and indeed Oliver himself) Dashnak party members. A section of the party had unquestionably bound itself up with Mussolini's grand designs, though the party's central bureau in Cairo remained uninvolved. Oliver says that the Dashnaks had been chosen by the Italians to be dropped into Syria and to radio back military information. Corvedale, as the only non-Armenian member of Dashnaktsutiun (and one more honorary than real; his party dues were seriously in arrears), seemed the right person to sort the matter out.

He was summoned to Beirut, and ordered up to the frontier. He was given a pass by Brismis, the British mission in Syria, and travelled with a former junior member of the Armenian government. Oliver's party included the captured parachutists, and they set off to see if they could find what had been buried. The captives could not, or would not, identify the whereabouts of any items. Oliver grew threatening. Still they could not say where they had landed. Oliver decided to search on foot, giving himself a severe blister in the process. But it was worth it; he found a miniature wireless set, maps showing French troop dispositions, a revolver, a code-book and the address of the German agent in Switzerland to whom they were to report if things went wrong. This individual's identity had long been sought.[21]

Oliver had a few more minor adventures, before his return to England. One was a weird plan to capture a certain Herr Oppenheim, active in southern Turkey, and to deliver him trussed as a parcel to the security chief in Beirut. This would have meant crossing into Turkey, something Corvedale had no qualms about, but his superiors viewed with alarm. It seems that his knowledge of Turkey, and his hostility to that country now that the Allies were courting it, made the bosses feel it was unwise for him to stay. So he left in early 1942 for Khartoum and then travelled via Kano to Lagos. From there he embarked for Freetown, and then came home on a troopship.

Once home, a real sense of purposelessness and disillusion set in. The War Office had no job for him. He was told he had been overpaid by £300, and was also informed that he was being demoted back to lieutenant, since his promotion to major had been only a local matter. May and June 1942 were months filled with boredom edging into rage. Then he went to Matlock for an Intelligence course. In October, he was posted as Staff-Captain (I) to the Irish Command in Belfast, and remained for two months. Here he was to await the landing of the Germans in the south of the Republic, and then, with Dublin's permission, to proceed to repel them.[22]

The mood changed again. In November 1942 he learnt that American and British troops had landed in Algeria. Here was a chance, Oliver thought. He was the only British-born serving officer with property in Algeria, he had lived on and off there since 1920, he knew the political scene there, and could write Maghrebi Arabic, which is different from Egyptian. Soon he was told to report to London. But more disillusion awaited him. He was indeed to proceed to Algiers, but with two junior officers as a cable and wireless censor, a job he knew nothing about. The only small recompense was in learning the job.

He left in November. On board were Americans, Canadians and British, and Oliver's sociability, and his offer to get some entertainment going, broke down the initially difficult atmosphere between the different nationals. He also taught classes in French and Arabic, and lectured on a variety of topics from Russia to elephant-hunting in Malaya.

Once in Algeria, Oliver hoped to go and live in the Villa Aurelian, which he somewhat rashly assumed was his, even though his uncle had not formally made it over to him. But wartime regulations prevented him from gaining access to it. Much of the fault was his for not having had the foresight to make the legal position quite clear. He was compelled to billet himself on a friend, at the army's expense.

Oliver witnessed the curious activities of various factions in Algiers during those months, unrelated to the war effort: the stratagems of French monarchists, the strange persistence of fascist sentiment and laws, and the ignorance shown by both Americans and British as to who their real friends were. Only in April 1943 were Jews, Gaullists and pro-British prisoners released from Algerian jails. Oliver was convinced that sentiment in the French Algerian administration was basically pro-Hitler until the arrival of Harold Macmillan as British Civil Commissioner.

Corvedale himself, despite his wide personal knowledge of Algeria, was given almost nothing to do. Since there were no facilities for sending non-military telegraph traffic, there were no cables for him to censor. So he spent the time revisiting old haunts, chatting with friends, and generally whiling the time away in a manner which in peacetime would have been very agreeable, but in wartime, for someone with his sense of service and public duty, was profoundly frustrating.[23] He did however find an opportunity to give further lectures. The Americans seemed keen to learn about front-line loudspeaker propaganda, which Oliver had pioneered 18 months earlier, but the British authorities objected to the release of his expertise to their transatlantic allies. So an American major and he had to meet clandestinely, so that he could reveal what he knew of the subject.

He was given a more intensive censor's job in April, then asked to serve as liaison officer to a Turkish staff delegation, despite protesting that, since he had been held as a spy in a Turkish jail, he was the last person fitted for such a job, since he would have to lie if he were asked if he had ever been to Turkey. But the arrangements were final, and the meeting went off smoothly enough. Work in the censor's office continued until Oliver, troubled by a kidney stone, was told to return home. He embarked for Britain in November 1943, at the conclusion of a singularly unprofitable tour of duty.

He had the operation in March 1944. By April the zest for life had returned and he looked around for another job. In June his name was put forward as a testing officer with the War Office Selection Board (WOSB; 'Wosby'), to select potential officers from the ranks. Initially failure dogged him, but when he was sent to a selection board near Leeds, he was highly recommended, and got the job. This work was congenial. Eight men would be selected, and the testing officer would watch them work and be open to any confidences they wished to express. He was part of a team whose job it was to test officer material for powers of leadership, capacity to control anger, and quickness of thought, together with ability to show cooperation, drive and general initiative.[24]

In August and September he was posted to Edinburgh. A letter to Johnnie read, 'It is shocking weather, but I had a lovely 2 hours walk the other evening with one of the candidates, who was a most pleasant & ingenuous child of 18. He was in my group & I passed him – but not as a result of the walk.' He was then posted to Hereford, where the work was even more rewarding. Corvedale was proud when one of his groups, on exercise at the Highland Fieldcraft Training Centre, a place for intensive training hidden deep in the Cairngorms, gained a 100% pass. He was still working for Wosby, dividing his time between Hereford and Betchworth, Surrey, when victory was declared in Europe. For Viscount

Corvedale the last 12 months constituted a satisfying end to a war which otherwise, despite his strong desire to serve, had been largely frustrating.[25]

*

On the personal level, when Corvedale had arrived back from Eritrea and Beirut in 1942, he had been delighted to return to Little Stoke House, after a two-year absence. His first instincts were gratitude and delight. This to Johnnie: 'What a wonderful home coming. What a happy house; how beautiful the garden. How marvellous you are; how nice the Craigs: how young Ernest looks: how well Luvelizabeth cooks & Mary cuts bread & butter. How sweet David looks, but oh, how wicked & rich is your French friend . . . '[26]

Once back in England, it was clear that, despite the weight of war and privation, social life could, for some of the time at least, continue in a lively, positively raffish manner:[27]

MOPKK

Had your letter & went to Bob's party yesterday . . . At the party was the Bogus Countess covered in paint & Woolworth pearls, her daughter & son in law, a Sir Jocelyn Lucas MP & wife, Henry & hideous Karl, an American or two and of course the bounding cockatoo, red face, yellow crest & yellow waistcoat. Also his sister – pitch black . . .

A year later, as Oliver's frustrating time in Algiers drew to an end, he wrote briefly and triumphantly to Johnnie: 'I'm coming home!' After this second return from Africa, Johnnie received a mild reproof from Oliver in July 1944: 'Just had a letter from Phil who says you are worried & lonely. Now you've no business to be worried nor lonely . . . Behap. WE have so very much to be grateful for, when you think.' Johnnie found coping with evacuees at Little Stoke House stressful. Oliver's remedy was somewhat harsh: 'I do hope the refugees are not too much. If they get on your nerves get rid of them at once because nerves produce Angra-Pangra & old Mother Naggins.' From Hereford he wrote in an undated letter: 'I may not be able to get down to "Little Nag House" this weekend . . . John Tillotson is back & Michael Redgrave sent his love.' The need to keep Little Stoke House as an oasis of peace, and as free as possible from quarrels and rows, was still paramount for Oliver.[28]

The issue of finance was one which troubled Oliver throughout the war. Already on 31 August 1940 he had written: 'I am afraid we shall be badly overdrawn till after the war but I don't see how we can help it.' The anger he expressed about being reduced in rank on his return from Cairo had as much to do with finance as prestige. In August 1942 Oliver wrote to Johnnie: 'Try & keep things down – drink bills especially, if you can.'[29] Three months later Oliver had paid back to 'the Pay people' £167, considerably less than he had expected, but a significant sum to a man with an overdraft. He urged Johnnie to get on with the sale of a small property they owned at Mayfield. Stanley Baldwin, living self-lessly in cold wartime near-isolation at Astley, sensed that his elder son was in difficult financial straits, and sent a touching letter to Johnnie in July 1943. In a letter clearly marked Private, he wrote:[30]

My dear Johnny,
    I know nothing of Oliver's finances and I have often wondered how they are these difficult days.
    I used to send him a small present at Xmas and birthdays but for some time I have had no address and I know there are difficulties about sending money out of the country. Would it be useful – and acceptable – if I compounded for these missing little gifts and sent £50 to be paid in to his account. You know him better than I do and I should be grateful for your advice. But respect the word Private!
        Yours always
            Baldwin of Bewdley

Oliver was promoted to captain in July 1944, which eased the financial strain. (He was further promoted to major six months later.) Plans were also afoot for selling Little Stoke House itself, and moving entirely to town: 'I have been thinking what fun we'll have in our London house with all our furniture & you without the worry of outside & the garden & chickens – just the house & your car & the motor-boat off Hammersmith for Sundays perhaps.' Their Oxfordshire home had 'served its time but I want you to be as free from worry as possible to enjoy your 12 suits I shall give you after the war.' He for his part would only go to the club on Wednesdays and Saturdays – leaving Sundays for 'our parties'; though Johnnie would be limited 'to 150 telephone calls a day'. Oliver's playful mood reflected his fulfilling job with Wosby, and the scent of victory in the air.[31]

The death of his old Irish Guards comrade George Bambridge some months earlier cast a shadow. But even this brought forth a heartfelt letter from his widow, Oliver's cousin Elsie, in response to Oliver's letter of condolence, showing that the angry words of 1936 were forgotten now. Addressing him as 'darling, darling brother', she said she was replying to his letter first, and would always cherish it. 'Do let us be nearer after the war. You have always meant most to me of the family & that George knew . . . Thank you darling for your understanding.'

Despite the loss, the mood remained good for Oliver, and it appears to have translated itself in March 1945 into a generous tribute to Johnnie, in the form of another near-Ciceronian expression of high-minded esteem for his life-long companion:[32]

MOBPKK Just to say my admiration for your courage & perseverance is greater, if possible, than ever. You make me realise how true it was when you said, twenty years ago, apropos of something or other, 'I am a soldier's son.'

Stick to it, MOK, just a little longer, & then you shall have a real rest. I have heard of people in war time doing the work of two men – you do that of four, & always for others. Bless you.

AYOLK

VE Day found Oliver Corvedale in Betchworth. About a month later, as the war was ending, and the celebrating, relieved and released people of Britain were moving rapidly towards the first general election for ten years, Oliver received an urgent telephone call, telling him of a greater loss. His mother, Lady Baldwin, had died on 17 June. Oliver hastened to Astley.

He left no record of how he felt on his mother's death: whether the strength of her bond with him was reflected in his sense of bereavement. But he sent Johnnie an impression of the funeral: 'pretty grim', but 'SB was wonderful . . . I watched SB & his face had the same worried & puzzled expression on it he always had when Mother left the room to go upstairs – sort of "Where's Lucy going to now?" Yes, where indeed? I'll tell you details when I see you.' Oliver had received a number of letters of condolence – 'very kind of them all'.[33] Then he travelled north to campaign in Paisley.

*

One curious sidelight to the wartime years was the touching friendship which had grown up between Johnnie Boyle and Lady Baldwin (also known as The Empress), who was then living with her husband at Astley, a house changed from being an expansive comfortable Edwardian family home into a cold, wind-blown tenement-like establishment, with little privacy, where evacuees far outnumbered owners. This was a burdensome duty for Lady Baldwin, though not a passive, put-upon duty (such as that evinced by Aline Solness in Ibsen's *The Master Builder*) but rather an active duty derived from devotion to the ideals of patriotism and winning the war. She seems to have managed psychologically rather better than Johnnie at Little Stoke House.

In her wartime difficulties Lady Baldwin appears to have gained strength from her correspondence with Johnnie. She had opened her heart to him as long ago as December 1923, when she had memorably written, 'Thank you for loving my Oliver'. She had corresponded sporadically thereafter, but more frequently from 1939. Of course, Johnnie was punctilious in expressing gratitude for any social favours; he would send her flowers, and remember her birthday, things guaranteed to make her feel flattered and wanted.

In many ways, he was an ideal son-in-law. Thus, on 20 June 1939, she wrote: 'My dear Johnny, What lovely, lovely flowers & how I am revelling in their beauty. It was dear of you to think of sending me such a welcome gift. I just love them, I always say that if I had only 6d a day 1d would have to go in flowers.'[34] And in April of the same year, when she and Lord Baldwin were away in Canada, she wrote, part jokingly, but one wonders whether with an element, however small, of underlying seriousness, 'Don't let Noll marry any strange female when I am away he frightened me about a woman who was divorcing her husband.'[35] There is a hint here that Johnnie was her unconscious guarantee that she would not lose her beloved elder son to a rival female.

At the same time, there was a certain *quid pro quo* in Johnnie's gifts to Lady Baldwin, since she briefly paid the gardener's wages for Little Stoke House. Johnnie was under instructions from her not to tell Oliver of the subvention. Financial constraints meant that she had to stop even this small contribution in late 1941.

By December of 1939 Lady Baldwin was thanking Johnnie for a Christmas box of crystallized fruits, and complaining of having caught the cold of the century: 'the evacuees leave windows and doors open . . Also we have cut down the fire in the hall . . . I may remain in my present state for the duration.'[36]

In July 1940, Johnnie wrote to her saying he was suffering from depression. She wrote back, accepting his depression, and saying that she personally had found the answer in prayer and in her belief that prayer was answered, and in a curious belief in visions.[37]

Lady Baldwin shared with Johnnie the scant pieces of news of 'Noll' which she received. And in November 1940 she told him about a massive burglary that had taken place at Astley, on a Saturday evening while she and Lord Baldwin were sitting listening to the news. ('I couldn't sleep for 3 nights thinking of it & feeling them about my room.'[38])

In October she was discussing wartime domestic economy with him: 'I hope that you have laid in a store of tinned food as I have, but you are such a good manager that doubtless you have. – Sardines are a great standby & fried in batter if you can't get fish are delicious. Also Country market peas are wonderful . . . '[39] In March 1941 she gave Johnnie news of the injury which Betty had sustained while dancing at the Café Royal, when it received a direct hit ('falling debris all around blood coming from her face which had been cut but thank God a thousand times nothing worse . . . '[40])

Two years later, in May 1943, despite listing the difficulties of life in wartime, she could nevertheless exclaim to her correspondent: 'What a marvellous spring this has been I never remember such a colourful spring & such depth of colouring. Keep cheerful . . . '[41] A few months later she wrote again, saying that her younger son Windham had received a tax rebate on account of being on active service; she suggested that Oliver might try for the same – 'Especially as Noll in not now able to carry on his usual occupation of writing to help his living.' Her sensible maxim was, 'I always believe in not being done for want of making an enquiry.'[42]

Lady Baldwin's last letter to Johnnie, of January 1945, began characteristically: 'How very kind of you to send me a wire for my antique birthday so old that I wonder it is not forgotten!'[43] She gave him news of Betty and Windham, and after speaking of SB's distressing attack of shingles, she ended with her love, thanks and affection: an appropriate conclusion to a touching and unusual friendship, of value and significance to both parties.

CHAPTER 14

Viscount Corvedale, MP

Corvedale had left Betchworth to travel to his mother's funeral. Then, while still a serving officer, he went on to fight the election in Paisley, the seat he had narrowly lost ten years previously.

He had been reselected in May. Nineteen thirty-five was the last time the electors had been given the chance to vote; since then, 'we have undergone much and suffered much'. In his election address Corvedale offered himself first as one who had served them as a soldier. Then, in the form of an acrostic, he set out his view of Labour policy and ideals – **B R I T A I N**:[1]

Brotherhood – the continuation of the spirit of mutual service which enabled us to come through our ordeal so magnificently;

Rehabilitation – a progressive policy of housing which will not be impeded by land grabbers, speculators or other anti-social interests;

Intensification of our efforts to defeat Japan and liberate our prisoners and colonies;

Trade Boards – the control of exports and imports to maintain our people in employment and our needs as consumers;

Agricultural reform – by the control of prices and thereby the safeguarding of both the producer and consumer;

International affairs – the stressing of friendly relations between Russia, the USA, France and ourselves. The insistence of a more democratic outlook on the part of our Foreign Office officials;

Nationalization of the mines and of credit and currency – to prevent the financing of our enemies, the periodic and artificial currency crises and to enable our national credit to be used not for speculation but for development.

The war, Oliver reminded the electorate, was not over, and peace was yet to be won. He believed that a Labour government, with its wider democratic outlook, would be a better assurance of peace than 'a capitalist government over-concerned with international financial and business interests'.

He recalled too, the ex-servicemen and their dependants, whose cause he had supported in his four previous campaigns. He made reference to his work with the Comrades of the Great War Movement in 1919, and reflected that it was a grand thing today that 'we can be free to exercise our choice of parliamentary representation'. He ended with a touch of non-party universality: 'Whichever way you may decide I wish you all great courage for the difficult task which lies ahead of us all.' There was humility in the manner in which he signed off as 'Your servant, Corvedale'.

In an interview with the *Paisley and Renfrewshire Gazette*, he said that the Labour Party was fighting the election on the principles of common sense and common humanitarianism. Socialism was, he believed, the only way to give people a decent standard of living. The 10,000 houses required in Paisley needed planning; and planning needed controls. Asked about the essence of socialism, he described it simply as the intention 'to help other people'. This he considered a higher ideal than that found in capitalism. In socialism there was something really to hope for and to live for, 'a greater ideal and a greater hope.'[2]

His 1945 campaign was more staid than the earlier ones. Johnnie was still a supporting elm. Oliver, leaving for 'what I feel will be my last election', wrote, blending gratitude, practicality and playfulness: 'I shall not forget how you helped me yesterday with your encouragement and I shall be thinking of you every day up there. I want you to have a few days off in London to see your friends . . . I shall be back in Hereford on the 6th July and then we have to wait three weeks for the result, although one ought to have a pretty good idea of what's happening by then. I shall be staying during the actual campaign at the Adelphi [Hotel, Glasgow] . . . Now we'll have a happy day in the country. Cast care aside and oh, behap you dear little fat. I don't express what you want, but it's there and you know it and now get out your little lighter and burn it up and send it up in smoke to heaven.'[3]

In the course of the campaign he repeated to Johnnie that he was feeling his age, and would not do another election. As a result of the operation of the preceding year he found it difficult to speak for long without exhaustion and back-pain. The campaign nevertheless released his political instrincts. The Liberals had sent one of their top people (Sir Archibald Sinclair, later Viscount Thurso) to campaign, showing the importance they attached to holding the seat. Letters home could show a touch of the old excited spirit: 'Just back from Paisley. Grand meeting 2000 – packed in cinema.' After nominations had closed, he was pleased to note he had both a Tory and a Liberal opponent, so the anti-Labour vote would be split, 'but I should like to beat the two together.' He insisted on being a considerate campaigner: 'I refuse to go about Paisley in a car in case I knock over a child.'[4]

At the declaration the Paisley result reflected the emphatic swing to Labour found across Britain. Oliver's victory was decisive; as he had hoped, he gained an absolute majority over the other candidates. The results were:

Viscount Corvedale	Lab	25156	55.6%
T.G.D. Galbraith	C	14826	32.7%
Lady Glen-Coats	L	4532	10.0%
A. R. Eagles	Ind	765	1.7%

Labour majority, 10330   Turnout, 73.9%

Viscount Corvedale was almost a Labour elder statesman now. Back in the House of Commons after 14 years, he looked with a critical eye at some of his younger colleagues. There were 'band-wagon boys' such as a young Labour member who, having been asked to stand by both Labour and Tory, simply tossed a coin to make the decision. Then, more tellingly, in the first week of the new parliament, Oliver was lunching with Arthur Greenwood (the Lord Privy Seal) in the members' dining room. A tall presentable young man asked if he might sit with them since the place was crowded. Of course, they said, and soon the young man was talking fluently about himself, having no clue as to who they were. It was not hard, he said, to achieve one's life ambition. 'Look at me, for example.' He had been determined to get into Parliament, and all he had had to do was to ask for a seat from one or other of the parties, make a lot of speeches, and hey presto – he was an MP. Oliver noted that he was very talkative and sure of himself. He was also in a hurry, and left before the others had finished the meal. Greenwood and Corvedale looked at one another, and asked the waiter the name of the new young Tory member. He turned out to be a Labour fellow![5]

Not all were opportunists. One new member, who became a minister in 1947, had been converted to socialism at the age of 16 by a speech which Oliver had given in his home town.[6] The member for Paisley gained a sense of fulfilment in seeing the evidence of his work as a practical communicator of ideas and ideals – it was an aspect of (to use Erikson's terminology) the generative side of his personality.

Viscount Corvedale participated even less in the business of the Commons during his second period as an MP. His parliamentary interventions were limited to putting down questions, often on constituency matters, for written or oral answers. He asked about the looting of Allied supplies in Greece, and in November he focussed on Paisley matters, with a question to the minister of supply about the employees of a local firm, who were about to be turned out of their houses after being directed to employment there, in the course of which they had left their original dwellings, to which they could not now return since they were occupied by others. Corvedale saw this as bad faith. Could the minister do anything about the situation?[7] No, sir. He received the same answer when he returned to the issue on 20 December.

Also on the 20th, in the course of a debate on housing and standards of public housing, he put down a question to the minister of works about the standard of doors in housing schemes, which he sought to improve. The minister was none other than Harold Wilson, who replied sympathetically, but pointed out that there were problems in the supply of timber.[8]

Oliver showed that he was not afraid of raising issues which might be controversial. Thus, on 23 January 1946 he asked the foreign secretary whether he would, as a tribute to the gallantry of the Greek people during the war, take steps to arrange for the return to them of the caryatid taken from the Erechtheum in the acropolis of Athens, and now in the British Museum. Hector McNeil, the minister, replied briskly, No, sir.[9]

Other parliamentary interventions (there were only 16 in the whole of Corvedale's second period as an MP, from July 1945 to December 1947) concerned non-controversial matters such as housing and unemployment in Paisley. In December 1946 he sought to bring the mentally handicapped into the national insurance scheme, giving them the same rights as the blind. The minister was sympathetic.[10]

In March 1946 Oliver was appointed Parliamentary Private Secretary, first to Fred Bellenger, Financial Undersecretary to the War Office, and then to the Secretary of State for War, Jack Lawson. He also took on the massive, and apparently unpaid, job of assisting hundreds of de-mobbed soldiers of all ranks re-enter civilian life. The work was extremely interesting, but at the same time arduous. With monthly all-day surgeries in Paisley on Sundays, he was finding political life very stressful. Six months after the appointment he wrote to

Johnnie, 'I am overwhelmed with stuff. From 2.30 to 6.15 in one unending stream of applicants. I can't compete with the stuff, unless I give it all up and apply to the Chiltern Hundreds . . . I'm not as well as I was & I find the trips to Scotland exhausting.'[11] The following year he wrote: 'I really prefer NOBODY at weekends – just U.U + myself.'[12]

His work in the War Office and as a PPS could be described as virtually thankless. It gave him no financial reward, and it was not in any way politically glamorous. But his efforts received warm acknowledgement both from Lawson and Bellenger. Lawson wrote that Oliver's 'constant consideration and friendship' had helped him immensely. Fred Bellenger wrote in October 1947:[13]

My dear Oliver,

On Friday I fly over to Belfast & hope to be away for a week. When I come back I want to see you & have a heart to heart talk.

I wrote to Will Whiteley [a Labour Party agent] telling him that you have done more service for the Govt. than many of those loud voiced "young men" who are supposed to be the only hope for a Labour Govt. (Amazing how the "Evening Standard" & "Daily Mirror" think alike.).

But Oliver, I cannot thank you too much for your patient, friendly attitude to me while you have been associated with me as my P.P.S. Don't forget I had the foresight to choose you – & how right I was!

I will show you my letter to Attlee & his reply when I see you. How I could talk if I were less loyal than I am. But there have been some grievous mistakes made. Indecision amongst those who still remain & I fear it will go on like this until we are submerged in the torrent that may overtake us.

But you have been a good pal Oliver & I cannot thank you too much.

Let us meet for a meal when I return.

Yours

Fred

Up in his constituency, there was the odd moment for reflection. Here, one day, Lord Corvedale noticed that conditions were changing. At a cricket match in which the visiting South Africans were playing Scotland on the Paisley ground, he glanced at the children who grouped themselves round the boundary. They were not the waifs of the old days, but were well clothed, well fed and well shod youngsters. It was a moment of quiet satisfaction.[14]

Following Lady Baldwin's death, SB was very lonely, and in these sad days Oliver saw a lot of him: more than ever before.[15] The son sensed that his father had been hurt by the political attacks made on him during the war, and he acted as a sympathetic listener, hearing of his woes and petty humiliations, such as when the former premier was forced to stand in a train corridor all the way from London to Stourport. SB spoke to his son of the pain he felt when Astley's great wrought iron gates, monuments to the skill and industry of a local blacksmith, had been ruthlessly taken away for scrap. Together they talked of old friends in the Commons, father and son united as never before, with their shared sense of the value of ordinary people, especially West Country people, and of the intricacies of British constitutional machinery, matters which united them more deeply than any difference in party might divide them.

This mood of reflection found an echo when SB wrote to his son in 1946:[16]

> I was anxious for him [G. M. Young, the biographer] to do a history of the inter-war years which I thought would be an introduction to such biography as could be written after my death, and I thought it would be a good thing to get the material into shape – e.g. the Abdication history for use when the time came when that history could be written. Poor old Winston: I am glad he asked after me, I always thought that when the end came it would be quick: he used to look awfully ill way back in the India Bill days which now seem prehistoric. The happy Death should follow quickly on the completion of a

man's job. If Ll. G. had died in 1918 what a reputation he would
have left behind him!

We gave Louis Mountbatten a degree in Cambridge: our last
meeting had been on Derby night in 1936 when we dined at
York House with K. Edward VIII to meet Mrs. Simpson.
Prehistoric again.

They often spoke of the abdication (although Oliver's
papers contain no significant insights into the affairs of 1936),
and Oliver would entertain his father with stories in
Worcestershire or Black Country dialect. And, aware of his
approaching end, SB had taken a great interest in religion.
Oliver mentioned that he had written a life of Christ, and,
since his father had not read it, he sent him a copy. Next time
they saw one another he asked him how he was progressing
with it. It lay unopened. He wanted nothing to disturb his
faith, least of all a text reflecting his elder son's heterodox
beliefs.

Father and son met for the last time at the Athenaeum in
November 1947. Oliver told SB that he had been awarded a
peerage in the New Year's honours. The 1st Earl Baldwin was
delighted. But the honour was never bestowed since SB died
on 13 December. If he had lived for another 19 days father
and son would have served on opposite sides both in the
Commons and the Lords.[17]

With SB's death there ended one of the closest and at the
same time unusual father-and-son relationships in or outside
politics. The two were always personally close, and warmth
and affection inform every sentence in the letters from the
father to the son, as do a certain respect mingled with
affection in the son's correspondence to his father. And not
only in the letters: references to the two in the eye-witness
press also speak of the good relations, and Oliver's memoirs
echo the same theme. It is only inferential historians and
social gossips, and odd theorists writing about the decline of
British power, who cannot accept the fact that the socialist son

was fond of his Tory father, or that the father was anything
but humiliated and distressed by having a son who was (as
they saw it) arrogant enough to profess socialism – and who
added the outrage of being homosexual to his dissident
political beliefs – who invented the myth of Baldwin father-
and-son hostility. It is refreshing, after such fantasy – an
unconscious exploration of antagonism beneficial only to the
commentator – to return to the letters from father to son, and
the few which exist from son to father, and sense the real,
warm and life-giving nature of the relationship between them.
Oliver himself channeled any unconscious negativism
towards his father into the path of political disagreement. By
publicly espousing political dissent he freed himself of the
natural, unconscious, Oedipal anger which had been so powerfully present in the moody surliness of his adolescence.
With the rage and chaos thus allowed to be diffused from his
mental equipment, he could engage in the life-enhancing
friendship with his father which actually occurred.

We may also wonder how Baldwin *père* coped so generously with his son's radical political beliefs. In occasional
comments he let fall the impression that he half-saw himself
as the Fisher King fishing for the last time, or the corn god
who would himself be harvested in the following season.
Consciously, it was his temperament to be inclusive rather
than exclusive. His openness to his elder son's radicalism
derived too from his wide and deep understanding of English
history, especially of two periods: the Civil War, and industrialization. No one who understands the seventeenth century,
with its profound clashes of ideology, not just of Royalist
versus Parliamentarian, but of the liberties of the subjects
against the flawed majesty of kingship, can ever entirely reject
the feelings and the sentiments of the other side. SB, with his
devotion to crown and constitution, could not disregard the
part played by the common people in creating the ground-
work from which modern British politics derives. He knew
that the people were as important as the kings and queens in

forging Britain. In rarefied moments the country may be perceived in a magical, elevated and even etherial light, an enchanting landscape lightly trodden by the characters of a mystic masque; but this has to be balanced by the real and hard events, and the suffering consequent upon agricultural starvation or industrialization. For his elder son to adopt the cause of the people was therefore nothing exceptional.

But the cause of the people was hard and burdensome. In the final phase of his parliamentary life, despite his quiet success as Lawson's and Bellenger's PPS, Oliver Corvedale had manifestly not been a great Commons man. He had worked hard, and had enjoyed the spirit of Westminster; and he was well liked in his party. He had found Parliament a great institution. But he lacked the political skills of his father: the knowledge of when to dissemble, and when to go for the jugular, of when to cheer and when to bay; the ability to 'carry the House with you'. He had been a good constituency MP, assiduously looking after Dudley interests in 1929–31, and those of Paisley in the later period. But the greater themes were lacking – themes which were subjects of his journalism at its best. Never did he make a speech as good as his impassioned *Daily Herald* article 'No Fascism for British Youth'. Maybe the Commons chamber was always a bit intimidating; maybe it aroused in him those anxieties and insecurities which he associated with the second worst period of his life, his time at Eton. There is a strange quality almost of timidity in his lack of interventions, and an uncertainty even in the mildly eccentric ones. He never came near to setting the place alight. He had been content to let it be a vehicle for constituency matters, for his humane social aims, and for the odd wry aside on international affairs. He had felt more at home in the smoking and dining rooms than in the chamber itself. The social business of the house is in a sense as important for parliamentary work as the chamber itself; but nevertheless, Viscount Corvedale's ineffectiveness in the chamber during the post-war years remains puzzling.

CHAPTER 15

A Most Unconventional Governor

Oliver succeeded to the Baldwin earldom on his father's death in December 1947, and was compelled to leave the Commons. He did not go unwillingly; he had had enough of the lower chamber. He had been offered, and accepted, a barony in the New Year honours, planning to call himself Baron Mitton, after a parish in Stourport with strong Baldwin connections. However, he was now the 2nd Earl Baldwin of Bewdley; and without a job. He made discreet enquiries.

In late January 1948 he received a note from Arthur Creech Jones, Secretary of State for the Colonies, requesting him to look in and see him about a proposal.[1] This turned out to be an offer of the post of Governor and Commander-in-Chief of the Leeward Islands – Antigua, Montserrat, Barbuda and St Kitts-Nevis-Anguilla. Lord Baldwin accepted the offer without demur, and was appointed to the position in February, at an annual salary of £2750. Almost at once he left for the Caribbean, arriving in Antigua on 23 March.[2] A wit in the House of Commons declared that there had been no more amazing political appointment since Charles II had made Sir Harry Morgan captain-general of Jamaica.

The new governor had two companions on his journey. One was Ross Hutchinson, a friend from theatrical days in the 1930s, of fairly pronounced Tory views – he was to stand as a parliamentary candidate for Lewisham South in 1950 – but nevertheless a frequent visitor to Little Stoke House. He had spent the war as a signals officer in the navy, and was now doing nothing very much in Old Sodbury. By nature he was courteous and efficient, and also a good pianist, excelling in the lighter repertoire of Gilbert-and-Sullivan and Lionel Monckton. Over drinks at the club, Oliver offered him the job of private secretary.[3] In a few days he had packed, and was by the quayside in Bristol. The other companion was Gerald Bryant, the 17-year-old Welsh houseboy from Little Stoke House, who was to be steward and head chef of Government House, and Oliver's valet. He had been expertly trained in domestic duties by Johnnie; at the same time he was a wild goodlooking argumentative adolescent tearaway. Oliver's letters to Johnnie sometimes manifest a mildly obsessional edge about Gerald, as if both writer and recipient had a special place for him in their affections. ('Gerald is as happy as a king and is friends with his two cabin compan-ions. He has already won a £ in the sweepstake on how far the ship goes per day . . . Gerald is playing cards with the Chief Justice of British Guiana.'[4])

The trio travelled by ship to Trinidad; the new governor hated flying. On board, Ross Hutchinson entertained the passengers with his playing and singing, and towards the end of the voyage he persuaded his lordship to join in: the two of them gave a lively rendering of 'Sing hey to you, good day to you' from *Patience*. From Trinidad to Antigua they had to travel by air.

From his imperial posting his excellency wrote weekly letters to Johnnie Boyle – surely he was the first imperial governor to keep in regular touch with a 54-year-old boyfriend. The letters show a manifest enjoyment of his new post, especially of its challenges. At last he had a job which was commensurate with his abilities, which was in a warm climate, among congenial people, and where his sense of application and public duty could find fulfilment. The main topics covered in these letters are the industrial relations on the islands, the social and ceremonial matters which attached to the role of governor, and incidental episodes, where

Gerald and his friends often feature. There is also reference to the water shortage on Antigua, and to his own remedy for it.

The political legacy which Lord Baldwin had inherited in the Leeward Islands was far from easy. The islands' economy was 85 per cent dependent on the export of sugar. The budget showed a deficit; and there were three strikes current (of dock workers, and of sugar workers in both Antigua and St Kitts). Settling these strikes became his priority almost as soon as he had been sworn in as governor. Socially, the 120,000 population of the islands was dominated by the 2,000 whites, who maintained a strict form of apartheid in their dealings with the black majority.

It is not surprising that the sugar industry was racked with labour disputes. Harvesting cane sugar is a complex and dangerous matter. It is seasonal, so the workforce is left unemployed for much of the year. The cutters can easily themselves be cut by sharp leaves and cut stems. Moreover the sugar has to be transported rapidly to the processing plant, otherwise it partially dries out and loses much of its value. In these circumstances the defensive, entrenched positions of all parties become understandable.

Within a week of touching down in Antigua, Oliver wrote to Johnnie of the first few days:[5]

On going down the gangway one spur fell off, which I did not know, but I inspected the guard and in getting into the car afterwards the other fell off . . . there came the swearing in ceremony, the speeches, inspection of guard, national anthem and cheering crowds . . . we have the Fleet in, and we have given 3 cocktail parties of about 20 each and been entertained on the flagship and Canadian cruiser. Tonight we are giving dinner for 20. I am going to church this morning to please the bishop and this afternoon to Clarence House where we hope to spend next weekend. Yesterday at 3.45 I settled our dock workers strike and next week I shall try my charm on the other strike – the sugar workers. There is a great deal to do, and I find the owners thinking I have a bomb in each pocket and the black workers expect me to bring them a new world. All very difficult . . . I am just off to church and will finish this after. There are humming birds in the garden and lovely coloured finches fly through the house and sit on the tops of the chairs. The service was interminable but they had a special prayer for the Gov., which I appreciated. We are off to inspect Clarence House, but I have to see the Labour leader suddenly as the owners are annoyed at something that came out in today's Labour paper. I'm afraid both sides are children. Bless you MOBPKK

> YOK

(Clarence House, to which the governor and his secretary would repair most weekends from Saturday afternoon to Monday morning, lay on the south side of the island. It was named after the Duke of Clarence, later William IV, and dated from 1787. It overlooked English Harbour, where Nelson had refitted his ships before the Battle of Trafalgar.[6])

Reflecting later on his arrival, the 2nd Earl wrote: 'It is extraordinary how fate made me arrive on that particular Tuesday instead of later as first arranged, for the Chief of Police told me the other day that unless I had arrived the place would have been in open riot by the Thursday.'[7]

As the first letter indicated, Lord Baldwin was a 'hands on' governor. He saw it as his job to work for settlement of strikes. Previous governors would have seen it as beneath their dignity to engage in such a task. Their time was consumed on the white cocktail circuit. Lord Baldwin rejected such a pose, and would not leave industrial relations to market forces, since thereby starvation and revolution would come about. Despite the seriousness of the situation on his arrival, by 4 April he was sounding hopeful of settling the Antigua sugar strike, 'and then for St Kitts'. Other strikes too were rumoured.[8]

The following week he reported a successful settlement of the Antigua strike. He had found 'both sides very sticky, very childish and very petty. Finally the owners said they absolutely couldn't grant an increase in wages unless they put sugar up by $\frac{1}{4}$d a lb. So I told them to put it on and get shot of the business.' On the 18th he wrote: 'Tuesday last I flew to St Kitts to see if I could settle the strike there which has been going on for 14 weeks . . . I returned on Friday very hopeful and last night I was telephoned to here at Clarence House to say it was settled, so we are all delighted as the children were on the verge of starvation. AYOLK' Ross Hutchinson estimated that in these first difficult days of his governorship Oliver spent 75 per cent of his time in meetings and discussions, adding 'it must be a source of great pride to him that his strenuous efforts have resulted in all the strikes being settled within four weeks of his arrival. With his usual modesty Oliver has given all the credit to the Administrators.'[9]

Another major issue in Antigua was the chronic water shortage, a situation which he solved in a very original way. 'The drought is still on. We hope every day for proper rain', he wrote. So he decided to pay, from his own funds (which probably means from his overdraft), for a dowser, or water-diviner, to be invited from Jamaica to search for underground streams. On 19 June he was able to write to Johnnie: 'So far we have dug 5 wells found by Claud Bell, and all are fit for cattle and watering.' The search for water did not stop, and three months later he wrote: 'Our dowser thinks he has found a big stream.'[10]

This was far from the image of the usual remote, superior governor, carrying English whimsy to all parts of the globe, while maintaining an iron distinction between rulers and ruled. At the same time a necessary part of the governor's role was that of participant in the ceremonial and semi-theatrical display which attached to the position. Here, proper dress and precise movement were central issues. This aspect of the job appealed both to his 'instinct for drill' and to his love of the theatre. Moreover for someone as gregarious as he, the prospect of the subsequent party (to which all races were invited) was always pleasing.

The first official duty was the king's birthday, celebrated on 10 June. The private secretary gave an account of it. The day started with 'a parade at 0830 at which Oliver took the salute. It was really very well done and Oliver looked extremely smart in his uniform . . . This time he had made sure that his spurs would not fall off by having them screwed into the heels of his boots. This made it very awkward for him to walk down the stairs in Government House, which are not very broad, and he had to adopt a curious side-ways action rather like a crab, placing each foot with the greatest care while gripping the banisters with both hands. I followed behind, but as I had his sword in one hand and his helmet in the other I should not have been of much assistance in the case of a slip or a trip . . . . In the afternoon we gave our first big official party; two hundred of the haut ton entertained to tea in the garden, while the police band provided background music.'[11] The majority of Hutchinson's '*haut ton*' would have been black.

At the frequent less formal occasions Oliver seldom hesitated to abandon the magical totemism of imperial authority, indicating the manner in which his governorship was moving. A couple of weeks before the king's birthday, he wrote delightedly to Johnnie: 'Last Monday I went to a dance in aid of the hospital and danced one dance with the blackest woman in the room, much to the annoyance of the whites. I then departed.' However, the governor himself did not take the lead in stepping out across the colour bar. Ross Hutchinson, his Tory private secretary, related of this occasion: 'Oliver and I watched for some time, and then I led out a dusky beauty. She was extremely attractive and had a lovely figure, but, unfortunately, she knew next to nothing of ballroom dancing and contrived to tread on my feet and kick my heels a good deal during our perambulation . . . Neither of us danced with any of the whites. I expect that this has caused a tremendous amount of chat and comment, but Oliver and I both consider it a very good discipline for them.'[12]

Another semi-official episode was related by Hutchinson. The occasion was a school sports day: 'one hundred scholars of both sexes out to enjoy themselves'. Again, the scholars were black.

> The police band played for an hour and a half with, perhaps, more spirit than musical accuracy but it provided a pleasant background noise and helped considerably in creating a jolly atmosphere of gaiety. The first high-spot in the afternoon was tea. Three cakes to every scholar and, best of all, a beautiful, creamy ice-cream. There were one or two minor tragedies. The little boy who was an easy first in the 'late-for-school-race', but who had to be disqualified as he had forgotten to tie up his shoe-laces. The little girl who was convinced that she was second in the hopping-race, when, in reality, she was only third or fourth. Oliver, with his wonderful way of sensing when people are unhappy, sought them out in the grounds whither they had gone to cry and comforted them. Last of all came the prize-giving . . . A most successful afternoon.[13]

A governor who comforted black schoolchildren! However successful the tea-party was to Hutchinson, it would caused alarm and despondency among the planters. They were later to complain to the Colonial Office about this party. Their social fabric was being eroded, not by black revolutionists but by a white governor and his Tory private secretary. Was this the British Empire?

For the governor, some duties merged into unofficial pleasures and minor vanities. In the course of the drive to Antigua's capital of St John's, which was about 40 slow minutes from Government House, he experienced the gratifying graciousness of 'waving to the village people like Queen Mary'.

And, at Government House, there was Gerald, part of whose role was that of court jester, or licensed fool, using stock phrases, like a comedian: 'most discouraging', he would say in respect of the strikes, and on other occasions, 'I rather cared for that.' Once he took the governor's car to go to the Deluxe cinema, a distance all of 100 yards, with the police driver at the wheel. Oliver sternly told him 'what was and was not done'.[14] He saw the point, Johnnie was informed. A further episode in Gerald's life cast an amused eye on Johnnie's own small vanities, indicating a mixture of winning charm and steely petulance. It also includes a sample of the after-dinner entertainment current at Government House:[15]

> Rumour has it that Gerald's shopping in the town is very similar to someone else's I know of; that people's faces light up with a smile; that the shop-keepers give him things free and that he tells them off unmercifully and threatens to withdraw HIS custom if he is not attended to first. The other evening we had a few people in after dinner and we had music and played the Queen of Sheba on a Hungarian doctor and the Grand Mogul when we sit on each others knees and the end one suddenly stands up and we end on the floor. Love to Dickie. AMPKKYOLK

There were other incidental pleasures to be had: 'Last week [wrote his excellency] Ross & I went to a physical culture exhibition, which showed some wonderful torsos. Ross played the piano while they were weight-lifting like they do on stage, working up into tremolo and crescendo as they raised the things high into the air.' Lord Baldwin whispered to his pianist-accompanist private secretary: 'This must be exactly what happened a hundred years ago in the old slave markets.'[16]

A favourite relaxation was nude moonlight bathing. 'We all 3 bathe starko,' wrote Oliver to Johnnie.[17] (On this occasion the three were Baldwin, Gerald and Lord Soulbury, in Antigua working on a government report on the sugar industry.) The governor had found an enchanting spot known as Half Moon Bay. To Oliver this activity would have been the most natural thing in the world; but to the prudish planters, it would have been tantamount to participation in an orgy. It does not take much imagination to picture a pair of chill, moralistic binoculars trained on the governor and his friends – one of whom, heaven help us, was a servant – frolicking at night nude in the sea, and to imagine the subsequent spread of delicious malicious gossip among the prim, buttoned-up planter class.

A pattern was evolving. Its elements were a genuine concern for the social and economic progress of the majority population, a hatred of social distinctions based on race or class (and occasionally direct confrontation of such prejudices), and a belief that wit and spontaneity could enhance the lives of all. Above all, as ever with Oliver Baldwin, there was emphasis on creating a new spirit. Part of this new spirit might be quirky, even eccentric; but most of it was based on the idea of service, and of giving rather than taking: notions where, ironically, the best of imperial public servants find themselves in agreement with socialists of the William Morris persuasion. But a big question remained: could the new spirit be accommodated within the boundaries of what was acceptable at the time in a British colony?

With the strong naval tradition of the islands, epitomized by their connection with Lord Nelson, by Oliver's own sense of pride in British history, and by Ross Hutchinson's deep interest in the islands' naval past, the new governor took full advantage of his position to explore, and even ironically to relive, occasional episodes from the past. Under the headline '15 Men on Dead Man's Chest', *The Times* (of London) reported on 20 August:[18]

The Admiralty announces that H.M. sloop *Snipe* recently took Lord Baldwin, Governor of the Leeward Islands, on a tour of those islands which he had not visited since taking up his post in March. The church in which Lord Nelson was married at Nevis was visited. At the Governor's request, a landing was made at Dead Man's Chest [an islet in the Virgin group] by 15 men and bottle of rum. No treasure was found, but two gravestones were observed.

The Governor, the Admiralty and *The Times* could all appreciate history, irony and good humour. But the planters could not. They only experienced a growing distaste for the unconventionality of their governor.

September came, and in London an announcement appeared in the Court Circular of *The Times* of the 20th. 'Mr John Boyle will be leaving England shortly for the West Indies. His address until next spring will be Government House, Antigua, Leeward Islands.' ('And how on earth did he get that into the Court Circular?' asked Oliver.[19]) The entry – such things cannot mention every detail – omitted reference to his two companions, Dickie Payne, and Miss Bold (Boldie). Dickie Payne had entered the Little Stoke household in 1947, aged 21, as a secretary. He was a former Bevin boy from Worksop: that is, one who had chosen work in the mines to call-up. Although he was dismissed by some of Oliver's friends as 'just one of a long line, who would leave like the rest of them', he developed an acute sensitivity to and compatibility with both Oliver and Johnnie; and with his handsome charm, his ability and general *joie-de-vivre*, he soon became an inseparable part of the Little Stoke household. Everyone who met him felt better for having done so.

This trio left England in early October, arriving later that month. There was a busy round of parties for them. They travelled all over the islands. There was a minor adventure for them – Johnnie seems to have been absent on this occasion – when they were embarking in HMS *Whitesand Bay* for a visit to St Kitts. On that day the sea was agitated by a heavy swell outside St John's, as the passengers were on the point of disembarking from the police launch to the *Whitesand Bay*. Baldwin (according to Ross Hutchinson) 'took a more or less flying leap on to the ladder', and was followed adroitly by his ADC, Major Dennis Vaughan. But such acrobatics were clearly beyond the capability of Boldie, who was aged about 70. The police launch circled for some minutes, and the captain of the *Whitesand Bay* tried to make some lee for the passengers in the launch. Eventually the two vessels came alongside again, and the first lieutenant came down the ladder to receive Boldie. 'She got one foot on the ladder but seemed incapable of removing the other from the launch.' The first lieutenant pulled, and Ross Hutchinson pushed, and at last the recalcitrant foot left the launch with the intention of placing itself on the ladder. Just at that moment there was a great lurch, and it seemed that she, the ladder and number one were all going to land in the sea together. But all was well, and they continued their lively vacation.[20]

After a little over eight months in office, Lord Baldwin made a speech in which he summed up his impressions of the islands, and gave the islanders a kind of pep-talk. He spoke before the islands' Legislative Council on 8 December 1948.[21]

The world situation was, he began in a somewhat dramat-ically gloomy vein, one of gravity, disillusionment and further proofs of man's inhumanity to man. (There had been many worse years than 1948.) He spoke of the new legisla-tion being promulgated – a factories' act and a police pensions' act – to bring the islands in line with the modern world. Then he went on to review his time.

There had been the strikes. After their settlement, he had looked around. He had seen lack of employment, lack of water, and lack of sympathy between the various classes. He had also perceived 'a strange struggling yearning for improvements in social progress in the hearts of the majority'. However the instrument for the expression of this hope was 'an overburdened animal referred to always and everywhere as "government"'.

In a passage worthy less of a committed socialist than of the best of late twentieth-century Tory ironists, Baldwin continued: 'This government, apparently, has unlimited funds (most of which are kept somewhere in Government House) and it takes an unnatural delight in withholding its dollars from all deserving causes, from the provision of a decent hospital to the individual needs of the latest mother of twelve children who cannot unfortunately (or perhaps naturally) find work.'

Governments, he reminded his audience, do not have bottomless purses; 'things in this material world of ours have to be paid for'. But government was not soulless. It was full of sympathy, and understanding. He had sought by means of a bonus to alleviate the hardship of government officers, and in response he looked for positive signs of awareness of the unofficial motto of the Civil Service, 'We Serve.'

The next issue was somewhat controversial. 'Being the only governor you have had who has been in prison I naturally take an interest in that unfortunately necessary institution and I hope shortly we shall reform our prisons on the lines of open prison farms. Having worn chains myself I have had them abolished for good and all in our colony.' Oliver had had chains positioned round his ankles, but not welded, in Erzerum in 1921, as a dire psychological threat. The irony with the present was good. Like most ironies, it was lost on the whites. Their preoccupations centred around such issues as: was their governor turning prison into a holiday camp? Was he undermining native morale? Would they lose control? Was he not caving in to weak-minded ideas of equality, which would lead to the loss of profit and prestige? Was chaos in sight?

The Governor then referred to the large number of committees and commissions that had sprouted in the islands, observing that it was a pity that the money spent on these institutions had not gone to meet the islanders' needs, so that they could build their own hospital and start an insurance fund for the unemployed. At the same time it was difficult to fill posts in the administration, since so many people were employed in the commissions. One day, Baldwin surmised, he might have to make the Federal Treasurer the acting matron of the hospital.

He spoke of plans for development; and of the prospect of guaranteed markets for tomatoes, onions and pineapples. The only new industry started since his arrival, he ruefully observed, was cheese-making: a one-man industry, situated in Government House, where the Governor's pleasure was to have every day for luncheon 'the finest cheese he had ever tasted – pure Antigua goat cheese'.

Such an enterprise could be an example for others. But: 'in these islands we all suffer more or less from Leewarditis, a disease that makes people most enthusiastic about ideas and far from enthusiastic about carrying them out'. Despite the energy he had shown in settling the strikes during his first six weeks, he was frank enough to include himself in the sufferers from Leewarditis.

Nevertheless, he concluded, the heart of the people is sound, and he prayed for a growing unity, irrespective of race or colour. 'I want you to be proud that you are Leeward Islanders, that you are members of the British Commonwealth of Nations, that you are moving slowly but surely towards eventual Dominion status.' They must, he said, show themselves worthy of this goal. 'There must be more give and less take. More sense of responsibility. Less wild talk and far more thought.' He ended, perhaps uniquely for a British colonial governor, with a quotation from the *Mahabharata*: 'Greatness is to take the simple things of life and walk truly among them; and holiness is a great love, and much serving.'

This unexceptionable speech, with its themes of seeking harmony and creating a cohesive community, was nevertheless by the standards of the time exceptional. Colonial governors were not expected to foster a spirit of unity and progress. Such things might make the natives desirous of equality and rights. The tradition hitherto had been: ignore the natives, treat them as a commodity. Baldwin had sought a different relationship. The speech later became a peg on which to hang doubt and suspicion. It was a further element which showed to readers of *Crown Colonist* that their new man was dangerous.

Already before the speech of 8 December, there was a sinister and untruthful report circulating against Baldwin. It was taken very seriously by the Colonial Office in London, in the person of Douglas M. Smith. A note dated 3 December had been sent to Smith from the Secretariat of the Bahamas, putting forth the views of Sir Alan Burns, an old Caribbean hand, born in the Leewards in 1887, joint compiler of the *Index to the Laws of the Leeward Islands, 1905–12*, and now permanent UK representative on the trusteeship council of the United Nations. He may have had other responsibilities, relating to intelligence, which are not mentioned in his entries in the Colonial Office List and *Who's Who*. In the following decade he was to write a book entitled *In Defence of Colonies*. Burns, the hardline career colonialist, opined that in the Leeward Islands there was 'no government worthy of the name . . . the situation is completely out of control . . . mob law prevails.' He added, threateningly, that 'a disturbance is inevitable as soon as the cropping season begins in February, and in view of the lack of control it may result in very serious bloodshed.'[22] It was unfortunate that, owing to the antique social and political attitudes prevailing at the Colonial Office, this alarmist tissue of lies was taken for the truth.

Among Baldwin's papers there is, of about this time, a hand-written note from 'FMN' addressed to him concerning a press report. At some later date it was angrily endorsed in biro by the recipient: 'Noad, Administrator of St Kitts – sent by Sir Alan Burns to prevent the riots that did not occur.' This indicates that at some time Baldwin learnt of plans being hatched against him.

On 10 January 1949 the Secretary of State for the Colonies cabled his excellency that it 'might be necessary to come to London'. A week later, the message was urgent: Come as soon as possible. Baldwin seems not to have hurried unduly: it was 31 January before he embarked again aboard HMS *Whitesand Bay*, this time for Guadaloupe. He was dismayed at the inconvenience to his guests. Johnnie and Boldie had to be evicted from Government House, and put up in a nearby hotel. To travel on to Dieppe the governor caught the banana boat *Pacific Express*. *The Times* (29 January) had in the meantime reported a Colonial Office statement that the object of Lord Baldwin's visit to London was 'to discuss with the secretary of state some of the problems of the Islands'. Five days later the same newspaper reported the Colonial Office's statement: 'Lord Baldwin is coming back for consultations on the general problems of the Islands, including the constitution, economic development and the sugar industry. It is an ordinary consultation of the sort which happens very often.' The Colonial Office spokesman appeared emphatic in stressing its routine nature.[23]

By now the press sensed that the issue was more than routine, and that something was up. Initial newspaper reporting was downbeat. On 2 February, under the heading 'Lord Baldwin In Trouble, Sails Home', the *Daily Express*'s Guy Eden reported on the ferment that his recall had created in the islands, where demonstrators had lined the quayside to see him off, shouting 'No Baldwin, no cane crop.'[24] The following day the *News Chronicle* proclaimed, in a drolly lugubrious negative headline, 'Baldwin Recall Not Because Of His Jokes'.[25]

On 7 February the Colonial Office spokesman attempted to counter 'suggestions being made in certain quarters that Lord Baldwin . . . was being recalled at the instance of the planters or because of a speech made in the Legislative Council on 8 December'.[26] This statement was insufficient to quell a storm brewing; and a major row broke at Question Time in the Commons on 9 February.[27]

It started with Stephen Swingler (Labour, Stafford), harm-lessly enough, asking the Secretary of State, Arthur Creech Jones, how many circulars had been sent to the governor of the Leeward Islands during the past nine months. (Ross Hutchinson, as the islands' decrypter, had made frequent complaints about large amounts of unnecessary verbiage sent in code from London, a complaint heartily endorsed by the governor.) Creech Jones gave the po-faced answer his department had provided him with. Swingler then asked a supplementary about grants in aid to the Leewards, and again received an answer. Then he turned up the heat, asking 'on what date the Governor of the Leeward Islands was recalled by him; and why.' Frederic Harris and Quintin Hogg joined in the affray. The Secretary of State was given a rough ride. Jack Lawson spoke of 'rumours against the Governor' in the press. Tom Driberg demanded an assurance that Baldwin would be returning as governor. But Creech Jones would not give an inch, and merely repeated the official line about 'consultations'. (Hon members: 'Answer.' But he wouldn't.) Swingler put the boot in with the final question: 'Is he [Creech Jones] not aware of the rumours which has been circulated that Lord Baldwin is being recalled in order to be sacked as a result of the representations of the sugar barons?' All he got from the Colonial Secretary was a bland denial.

Here there seem to have been deceptions within decep-tions. The matter was not one of routine consultation. There was rather a pincer-movement of politics and sex which was seeking to make it impossible for Baldwin to continue as governor. The political aspect of this pincer-movement had been clearly expressed in the opinion of Sir Alan Burns relayed to the Colonial Office two months earlier. Baldwin's riposte to the Secretary of State was that the whites devoted their leisure to bridge parties, lawn tennis and dancing. They showed unrelenting hostility towards the governor. Stories were put around, that (for instance) Baldwin was undermining the crown because he would not salute while the National Anthem was being played. Except on his arrival, it seems that he had not saluted – because, as the king's representative, it would have been incorrect for him to do so. There was too the other aspect of the pincer movement: sex. A number of allegations were current: 'hints of strange and unnatural happenings' in Government House, as Baldwin was later to put it. The bishop of Antigua had written in December 1948 declaring that the Governor was 'very much addicted to young men and boys', and had repeated the allegation that he ignored God Save the King, and failed to drink the king's health.[28] In August 1948 HMS *Snipe* had docked on a visit: not only was the Governor alleged to have 'given offence' by making an 'improper suggestion' to the captain's steward (which the steward would not subsequently substantiate), but when the Governor and his secretary took a group of 20 ratings to Virgin Gorda for a swim and a suntan, he rebuked them for being 'too decently clad,' indicating that they should strip off. The governor and his secretary sunbathed naked. The captain of the *Snipe* continued: 'I heard of no improper suggestions to the ratings, but general conversation and behaviour convinced all officers that an unnatural atmosphere prevailed at Government House.'[29] The reception of the Home Fleet, which had paid an official visit to the Leeward Islands in October 1948, had likewise been frowned upon; the flagship, HMS *Duke of York*, had been incorrectly received, in the opinion of the Admiral of the Fleet, Sir Rhoderick McGrigor. McGrigor had sent a report to the Admiralty, asserting that protocol had been infringed, since the upper deck had been largely ignored, while the governor and his companions had gone to spend most of their time on board talking with the young ratings below decks.[30]

Other complaints and fears were aired. A certain Hilda Macdonald wrote to the Colonial Office expressing alarm at Lord Baldwin's fondness for steel bands. She had mulled over their names: Red Army, Brute Force and Hell's Gate. These bad-boy stylings led her down a quaking alley of suspicion, anxiety, fear. Might not Lord Baldwin be planning to use the bands as a kind of Leninist striking force, a personal praetorian guard to overwhelm the regular police force in order (presumably) to discard the constitution, wage tense war on the establishment and declare himself dictator? Less alarmist, Sir Hubert Rance, chairman of a government committee on the West Indies, noted in a letter to Creech-Jones a 'most unwise' arrangement at Government House, whereby, when there were no official guests, the *cook* – that is, Gerald – would *dine at the same table* as the governor and his secretary. Rance was evidently shocked at this abrogation of an important point of class.[31]

A more substantial complaint was voiced by the head of the planters, Alexander Moody-Stuart, who, while admitting that Baldwin had been always prepared to listen to him, said that, at the conclusion of a recent discussion, the 2nd Earl had declared that a piece of theatre awaited him when he was seen off on his voyage across the Atlantic. In the course of the demonstration held on the departure of Baldwin, someone threw a shoe which hit Moody-Stuart on the head. The (not seriously) injured man declared that the violent event had been instigated by the governor: his theatrical show.[32] However the actual evidence for this allegation is slim. Baldwin hated violence. The governor was a less efficient plotter than the planters gave him credit for.

Lord Baldwin arrived, unexpectedly early and unannounced, at Newhaven on 12 February. Ready and waiting was not a flunky from the Colonial Office but a reporter from the *Sunday Dispatch*, the first of a number of journalists to whom the governor gave a series of unusual interviews. To the *Dispatch* he spoke in the manner of one quaking in mock-anticipation of receiving punishment. 'I am on the carpet,' he declared, somewhat theatrically. The governor's recall was the paper's front-page lead the following day; here, his excellency, in crumpled raincoat and salt-stained trilby, gave vigorous, angry and even threatening expression to his views: 'Unless I return to the Leeward Islands, I will not be responsible for what may happen.' More than a hint of petulance here. But there was also reasonable self-justification: he pointed out that during his eleven months in office there had been no strikes and no 'native hooliganism' for the first time in a generation. The islanders had so many needs, and he had tried to bridge the gulf between the different communities. For this he had been attacked by the whites. And there was for him the powerful emotional draw of the people. As he had left Antigua, they had called out 'Good-bye, my excellency'. Oliver, showing the reporter a touch of histrionic talent, recalled their faces, and felt that they were his people. Of the future, he said candidly, 'I don't know; I may be sacked.' He told the reporter to discount any significance in the speech of 8 December, saying there was nothing wrong with it. He added, without elaborating, 'There are deeper issues than that.'[33]

What was Oliver doing in this interview? Was he trying to force the Colonial Office's hand, to out-manoeuvre the acolytes of Sir Alan Burns and make himself unsackable, by gaining the sympathy of his party and the public (that touch of recalling their faces), and by hinting at the possibility of civil disorder? Probably. He would have been angry too, and seeking to unburden himself publicly. Perhaps too he felt charged up by being in the limelight, and was determined to stay centre-stage as long as possible: though this would not have been a determining factor.

Hannen Swaffer, in his regular column in *The People*, expressed strong and measured support for the governor. 'Lord Baldwin . . . will not apologize to the Colonial Office for having been a naughty boy,' wrote this leading Fleet Street columnist. He knew his own mind, he was financially independent – Swaffer knew nothing of Oliver's remark to Johnnie the preceding August: 'I dread to think how much

we are overdrawn' – and could not be dragooned like a professional administrator. Above all there was his frankness.
He would say, 'As I am a socialist, why can't I carry out a
socialist policy and help the natives?' Three groups of people,
Swaffer believed, had been offended by Baldwin's actions:
the sugar barons in Mincing Lane, the planters, and the
Negro capitalists. Colonial governors were expected to dress
up and give parties, not favour the workers. At the same time
one sugar company which traded in St Kitts had declared a
700 per cent dividend, free of income tax. Sweeping colonial
reforms were needed to avert a crisis. The best answer to
communism, Swaffer concluded in his generous support for
the governor, was not denunciation, but a raising of the
standard of living.[34]

The following day another interview, this time daringly
frivolous, almost theatrically camp, appeared in the *Daily
Herald*.[35] Baldwin treated the paper's readers to a neo-
Firbankian burlesque. 'I am wondering what will happen to
my music festival . . . We had rehearsed *Pinafore* with
Hutchinson accompanying on the piano (only blacks in the
cast of course, for the whites wouldn't play) . . . there were to
have been prizes for the players of every sort of instrument.
We have not been able to postpone the festival . . . the people
will be terribly disappointed.' On his position as governor, he
said, rapidly changing register from counter-tenor to bass, 'It
doesn't matter tuppence to me about my returning or not –
except for my people there. I cannot tell what the outcome of
my interview may be. I am only worried that if it goes against
me you may get one of the biggest stories in years, and I
don't know what will happen in the Islands.' An interview
which began with a limp wrist fluttering concluded with a
mailed fist; and one cannot entirely put out of mind Lear's 'I
will do such things / What they are yet I know not, but they
shall be / The terrors of the earth.'

Baldwin gave a more serious press interview which
appeared on the same day in the *News Chronicle*. He spoke of

the matter as a nine days' wonder – a gas balloon. 'I am certainly not going to resign. To be sacked by a Labour government would be very interesting. If they do sack me, there'll be a riot in the islands.' He continued: 'I know why I am being recalled . . . I have been preaching socialism in my islands – to give and not to take. I put my foot wrong when I told the white population that they were doing nothing for the natives . . . I've been taught that whenever you are in a position of wealth you have duties towards people who are less fortunate. No one there knows how to behave towards the working class. What "killed" me was the servants' ball I gave. Everyone had a happy time, but you "can't have" working-class people in Government House having a party – that has never been done before.' The whites, he said, were very different from English Tories. They were 'absolutely reactionary'. 'All you are expected to be', Baldwin concluded, 'is a perfectly orthodox governor, do nothing, get your KCMG and retire and live in Cheltenham. If you try to be a human being it is almost impossible – but it isn't impossible and I go on doing it.'[36]

The interview with *Daily Express*man Guy Eden, appearing also on the 14th, was more aggressive and personal. Under the heading 'I'll Probably Be Sacked', Eden quoted Baldwin saying, very patronizingly, 'Poor little Creech Jones, he has had a bad time with Palestine, Burma and Malaya – acted like a fool.' This was Oliver himself acting very foolishly, and indeed ungratefully. The only charitable thing one can say is that the 2nd Earl was possibly drunk at the time.[37]

The same day, 14 February, Baldwin had his first interview, for just under two hours, with Creech Jones. He would say nothing about it. The *Herald* recalled a remark made in 1935 by his father, My lips are sealed; a curious motto for one who was now enjoying such a collusive relationship with the press.

On the following day, the 15th, the *Daily Mirror*'s columnist Cassandra (William Connor) wrote a marvellously evocative piece about Baldwin's homecoming – an essay both farcical and affectionate, turning the affair into a metaphor for the Britain of 1949. Under the heading 'Return of a Consul', he wrote:

'Riding up the Channel with the salt seas swinging the fo'c'sle-head of the steamship Pacific Express and about a million green bananas ripening below the decks, comes a not too new raincoat and a floppy slouch hat. Below the hat and above the raincoat, comes a fine moustache. Above the bold whiskers are two wide-set eyes. In them a twinkle. A Roman Consul is coming home. Soon – very soon – the twinkle, the whiskers, the informal hat, the raincoat and a single most undiplomatic suitcase will be put ashore at Dieppe. Then the ensemble – the picturesque, careless ensemble – will take to salt-water again, disembark at Newhaven, entrain and finally step out on to the platform at Victoria. A Roman Consul is home. There is no one to meet him. No one to welcome him. No fanfares, and no greeting smile. Only the jackdaw acquisitiveness of reporters . . . A Roman Consul has returned. It is His Excellency Lord Baldwin . . . The King's Representative is back in the heart of the greatest empire ever amassed under one flag, one sword, one Bible, the finest set of good intentions ever to survive two world wars – and comparatively little gin.

'I think it is impossible not to like Earl (or may I say Oliver?) Baldwin. This honest, affable, casually elegant and outspoken son of Stanley Baldwin, the crafty old Worcester ironmaster, who put his country to sleep for more than ten years, has just arrived back home for what Mr Creech Jones, the Colonial Secretary, rather stuffily calls 'a discussion of administrative problems'. Or, as many people think, to get the heck of a choking-off for saying exactly what he feels about the Leeward Islands. This one-time chicken-farmer ('Our revenue from eggs after feeding ourselves and our guests is about £20 a year'), this early spiritualist ('It is easy to establish communication'), this uneasy film critic for the BBC in 1934 ('Their attitude is ridiculous, stupid and fatuous'), has somehow commandeered the attention and maybe the respect of the British people who dearly love to see almost anyone

Taking on the Boss. The Governor believes that Mincing Lane, where the sugar merchants do their business, rather than Whitehall, rules the Leeward Islands, where they grow the sweet stuff. And he also says so.

'Which is exactly the kind of gorgeous effrontery that people from Birmingham to Penzance, and from Morpeth to Hornsea, love to see. The raincoat, the hat, the friendly eyes, the moustache – let us not forget the moustache – march in, unrepentant, on to what is so widely believed to be The Mat. And all the people who have ever stood up for what they think, and all the people who, with good intent, have mistakenly stood up for the wrong things and dropped tremendous bricks, and all the mugs and me who hate being ticked-off, even and especially if they are wrong, raise a silent cheer. The Roman Consul is home.'[38]

Cassandra brilliantly caught Baldwin's inner restlessness, respectable eccentricity, and slight pomposity, and projected them in superb style as a symbol for the state of the country.

The *Manchester Guardian* ran a leader on the Leewards on the same day (15 February), which took a calm and reasonable view of Lord Baldwin's governorship. Three things, it wrote, were demanded of a colonial governor, according to Sir Cosmo Parkinson, a former permanent undersecretary at the Colonial Office: just dealing, honesty of purpose, and humanity, with the accent on the last. In none of these had Lord Baldwin failed. He had been appointed in order to 'get a fresh approach'. As such the appointment had succeeded, especially in view of his 'commendable dissatisfaction with the state of his colony.'[39]

Probably on the same day, and unknown to Baldwin, Tom Driberg, who was an acquaintance but not a friend, drafted a letter to the prime minister. He wrote: 'I am venturing to write to you about the position of O.B., because it is now being privately but semi-officially put about in the Party that it is "impossible to save him" because of certain unpleasant personal allegations.

'I do so because I know from bitter personal experience how difficult it is to shake off a reputation of this kind, & how obstinately it clings to anyone to whom it has been attached, however unjustly – or even more, when there may have been some justice in the original attachment but there has been subsequent amendment of life. You will also, I am sure, be aware how often such a personal "smear" is used for political motives, or to try to discredit someone who could not otherwise be discredited seriously.'

Driberg pleaded for Baldwin's confirmation in office 'on the ground that the good he has done & can do outweighs any harm that may have resulted from his indiscretion. (When I was in Jamaica last October, I already heard rumours of his unconventionality, how the natives loved him & the whites were shocked – though not a breath of the worse calumny.) I feel that the best thing that could happen, for the Leewards Is & for him, would be if you gave him a pretty sharp talking-to, told him to behave with perhaps more patience & charity towards the irritatingly narrow-minded whites & sent him back there. The Brit public like him so well as a "character" . . . that I am sure some simple, unusual formula could be found for a public & apologetic repudiation by him of the embarrassing press interviews of last Sunday & Monday.'[40]

It was not surprising that one homosexual Labour man should seek to help another, although Driberg's language is a little effusive and self-demeaning for post-millennial tastes. Attlee wrote back to Driberg on the 16th, saying that as Baldwin was an old friend he was not likely to be swayed by prejudice against him. The essential and decisive issue was the good of the people of the colony, he averred. He would not mention to Baldwin the fact that Driberg had written.

James Cameron's column in the *Daily Express* of the 16th, headed 'I Call this Baldwin Mystery Absurd', was also in support of the 2nd Earl. Cameron's line was that Baldwin's governorship was unorthodox, and therefore praiseworthy. At several levels the Baldwin affair was proving to be a vehicle for diversity and dissent within the British political system.[41]

The governor met the colonial secretary again on 17 February. The substance of their meeting was again secret. On the same day Donald Zec, of the *Daily Mirror*, wrote of his own meeting with his excellency the governor, who 'stood against the saloon bar of the Lord Nelson in the King's Road, Chelsea, London, yesterday, wearing a blue shirt with a frayed collar and a crumpled demob raincoat.' He said to Zec: 'I don't give a damn about myself. But I am determined to make the natives pull together, to give them a better life, and create better understanding with the white people out there.' Next week, said Zec, over-optimistically, he planned to return. The governor acknowledged (for the first time) that the situation was difficult: that he had to 'hold a balance'. Hitherto the middle ground had been missing. Baldwin mentioned his distaste at having had to observe the whipping of a native in gaol. He spoke too of the social problems: the drought, the need for a hospital and for schools. '"We must raise them up, not trample them down," he said, and beat the bar counter.' The governor paid verbal tribute to the Colonial Office; they 'have been very helpful'. (One can imagine them responding 'Thanks very much.') Zec concluded that the issue of development in the islands was a Treasury matter; this was an odd conclusion, given the cautious parsimony of that institution.[42]

The same day both the *Manchester Guardian* and the *Daily Express* reported the arrival in London of a two-man delegation from the Antigua Labour and Trades Union Council, Vere C. Bird and Robert L. Bradshaw. Bird declared to the Manchester paper that 'the people are going to lose confidence in British colonial administration if Lord Baldwin is not sent back.' The admiration of these two representatives for the 2nd Earl was due to the fact that he was unlike any previous governor. 'Lord Baldwin went among the people asking questions about their work and welfare. Lord Baldwin has given a number of scholarships to the best schools in the colony and paid for them out of his own pocket.' In the *Express*, Bird praised him for always being prepared to listen (even if he ended up disagreeing), and for having invited the elderly to Government House for the Christmas party. Bradshaw stressed that Baldwin had sought the diversification of industry in the Leewards.[43]

After the meeting with Creech Jones on the 17th, Baldwin seemed more confident about the future. To the question of whether he was going back he replied, 'Well, I hope so.' The *Sunday Express* reported on 20 February that he was booked to return. Hannen Swaffer wrote a second pungent column in *The People* in defence of him. (Swaffer also put in a good word for Creech Jones, a useful gesture in view of Baldwin's own patronizing gaff about him which the *Express* had picked up.) The columnist recounted the interest which Baldwin had taken in native affairs. He had eschewed the snobbish cocktail parties given for the whites. He sought to start up new industries to relieve poverty, and stop emigration. These were opposed by the sugar barons, who only wanted big profits from their pre-existing investments, and feared that new industries might lead to a general rise in wages. Attlee, Swaffer reminded the readers, had insisted on Baldwin's appointment over the heads of Colonial Office chiefs, and would now stand by him.[44]

The following day (21 February) the *Daily Mail* had a lengthy front-page lead on the *affaire Baldwin*, written by the paper's special correspondent in Antigua.[45]

The correspondent, Richard Greenough, brought together a number of complaints from the whites, although he discounted the idea that Baldwin had been recalled because the planters had complained to Whitehall. He interviewed Alexander Moody-Stuart, head of the planters' association, who criticized the governor as a man whose 'chief pleasure seems to be upsetting the dignity and tradition usually associated with the king's representative'. The writer, apparently keen to scour the island for other opponents of Baldwin, spoke to the police commissioner and to the mayor, who declared that the 2nd Earl had 'talked much and done nothing'. Greenough made passing reference both to McGrigor's report and Sir Alan Burns's opinion, confirming the idea that the governor's recall had dual roots.

Towards the end of the article Greenough managed to find some good opinions about Baldwin. A chauffeur told him that once when he was changing a tyre, his excellency had drawn up and offered to help. On another occasion, when the governor was ferrying a car-load of official guests from Clarence House to Government House, he chanced to see an elderly woman lying sick by the roadside, and pulled up and took her to hospital. Baldwin's lifestyle was described as quiet and unpretentious, and the points were made that he tended to keep open house, with 'coloured men and women visitors calling at all hours of the day', and that he frequently dispensed with police protection.

In London, the deputation from the Antigua Labour and Trades Union Council met Creech Jones on 22 February, arguing forcefully for the return of the governor.

For the colonial secretary, the issues were complex. He summed up his thoughts, and the options open to the government, in a long letter to Attlee of 23 February. 'I have great difficulty in formulating a recommendation about the future of Lord Baldwin,' he began. He listed the difficulties. The prestige of the government had suffered 'as a result of the governor's indifference to administration and unconventional ways'. Baldwin had, Creech Jones alleged, shown little interest in practical work. (Either the writer had no knowledge of the governor's mediation in the strikes, or he did not consider it to be practical work.) Baldwin had given little guidance to his officers. He had also, according to the colonial secretary, been indiscreet in his talk and lost the confidence of some sections of the public. On the other hand, he had won the goodwill of large sections of the working people by his friendliness and by some of his unconventional habits.

'As to his personal conduct, he has denied the more serious allegations and I have no direct evidence to support them; but gossip is widespread about him and he is surprised at the range of responsible sources from which it has come and the nature of it . . . I think . . . his household has been curious, and that it would be better if less drink was consumed.'

On arrival in Britain, he continued, Baldwin behaved with great irresponsibility and indiscretion by talking to the press, even though he knew that the secretary of state wanted to have the facts from him first. More recently, 'the Navy have confirmed their uneasy impressions about his personal conduct', and Sir Hubert Rance had reported that administration had been neglected, and that he had taken no interest in matters unless the immediate interest of the workers had been affected. One cannot help wondering about Sir Hubert's views of Lord Baldwin's attempts to seek diversification of the economy. The governor, the colonial secretary continued, had won an easy-to-achieve popularity at the expense of the educated negro, coloured, and white populations. Racial feeling was higher now than in the past. Here, it would seem, was the voice of Colonial Office permanent secretaries, angry that an outsider had been awarded a plum job, and determined on revenge. Most of Baldwin's letters indicate that his popularity, such as it was, had come about through work. Neither he nor Ross Hutchinson was a slacker.

As for the effects of the affair in British politics: Creech Jones believed that a section of the Labour party was behind Baldwin. But many Tories 'as well as a responsible section of the party, have no sympathy with him.'

The colonial secretary then spelt out the options, in a somewhat brutal fashion. 'There may well be trouble in the

Leewards Islands if Lord Baldwin does not return. That might have been averted had it been possible to mention his personal conduct in any public announcement that he was not going back, but that can hardly be mentioned since he has denied all the more serious allegations and none is capable of proof . . . his resignation would result in a public outcry and possibly in temporary disturbances in the islands.' The implication here was that, in the prosecution of the government's interests, the governor was a disposable entity.

Balancing up the issues, the colonial secretary concluded that it was difficult to establish a sufficiently strong case to justify a demand for Lord Baldwin's immediate resignation. He suggested that the governor should be allowed to return for a period. The condition should be that he maintain 'the dignity and authority of his office in both his official and his private life'. That entailed doing 'everything within his power to give no colour for more gossip about his personal conduct . . . He must so conduct himself that no reasonable person would have any valid excuse for even thinking that he has those failings. He should be encouraged to maintain a less unusual household and to lead a more normal way of life.' The prestige and authority of government must be upheld, and he should deliberately seek to convince other sections of the population that what he is working for is the common good; and he should give more attention to administration.

If the PM agreed, Creech Jones wrote in conclusion, he would tell the governor so. He asked Attlee to see him. A public statement would be necessary.[46]

By the standards of the time, Creech Jones' letter to Attlee was fair. It was Machiavellian, nanny-ish, and placed government prestige (that is, the governor appearing as little more than a stuffed shirt) above a search for the best interests of the majority population. It showed that the Colonial Office was prepared to dump the governor as a queer. But it showed nevertheless that Creech Jones was prepared to believe

Baldwin, in the absence of evidence to the contrary. With that, and with Attlee's personal friendship, the outlook began to look better for him.

The issue left the headlines, and there appear to have been no more official meetings for a week or so. By early March Baldwin appeared confident that he would be returning. He gave a brief interview to the *News of the World* (6 March), in which he said that he expected to return by the end of the week.[47]

On the same day he wrote to Johnnie an urgent and anguished note expressing the strain that he had felt during the preceding few weeks. It was dated L.S.H., 6.3.48. (The mis-dating of the year indicated the stress he was under.) He wrote:[48]

MOBPKK

    I am afraid I've been through a terrible time but your first letter was a comfort. The accusations were appaling, ranging from stories of Binkie & George to strange whisperings in the garden at night & drunken orgies and sing-songs lasting till the early hours of the day. Hints at strange & unnatural happenings in the house, etc. Well the long & short of it is that Creech believes me, & Clem & the Cabinet are backing me & I'm going back. Its been a great strain & lets say no more about it: there is still work to be done. The Press got all the rumours & so did the H of C, but the Party backs me. You will love our house – full of surprises.

    AMLMOK
      YOK

————————

1. Ross has been grand.
2. What did Boldie tell the Bishop's wife about the house?

Two days later, on 8 March, the Prime Minister met Lord Baldwin for about half an hour. The colonial secretary was also present. Next day, *The Times* hinted that the meeting had gone well for the governor: 'Lord Baldwin's friends believe he will shortly return to the Leeward Islands.'[49] 'Lord Baldwin's friends' included Philip Harding, who worked for *The Times*. The *Daily Mirror* was more direct. Under the heading 'Baldwin Going Back to His Island', the paper declared: 'The unconventional Lord Baldwin has beaten the sugar barons, the diehards at the Colonial Office, and a host of critics in the Labour Party who prophesied his fall.'[50]

The same day, 9 March, Arthur Creech Jones made a definitive statement in the Commons about the affair. In what seems to have been an allusion to Sir Alan Burns's prognostication, he expressed his department's anxiety at the possibility of disturbances during the cane-cutting season: 'I had for some time been anxious lest the sugar cropping season, due to start next month, be attended by further strikes such as took place in 1948 and inflicted very heavy losses.' But: 'Lord Baldwin is shortly returning to resume his duties as governor.' Creech Jones spoke of a 10–year plan for the islands, and a proposed constitution. 'Lord Baldwin has expressed to me his unqualified regret at the nature of statements attributed to him in certain organs of the press after his arrival in this country' – a strange regret insofar as Oliver had himself volunteered liberal quantities of his opinions to the gentlemen of the press! A Labour member, Arthur Lewis, asked if there were any strings attached to his return. Creech Jones replied that he did not understand what Lewis meant. (Opposition laughter.) Oliver Stanley (Conservative, Bristol West, a former Colonial Secretary) asked what the mystery had been three weeks ago. Creech Jones answered with the same artless skill that he had shown in the response to Lewis: 'There was no mystery.'[51]

'What's it About?' asked the *Daily Express* on the 10th in its opinion column. 'The governor's recall is made more mysterious than ever by the decision to send him back. What lies behind this undignified fuss?' Perhaps one hears the voice of a frustrated Fleet Street, unable in 1949 even to hint at issues connected with intelligence and sex in high places.[52]

On Friday, 11 March, the *Daily Mirror* commented that he was returning without his halo, and hoped he had learnt two lessons – 'to shut up and get on with the job.' The colonial secretary, it said, had 'turned a Nelson eye upon his indiscretions', the nature of which the *Mirror* did not spell out. It was now time for action. The Leeward Islands could not subsist on a smile and a song.[53]

The following day, exactly a month after his arrival, Lord Baldwin left for the Caribbean. One of those who saw him off at Victoria was Basil Cameron, the conductor of the London Philharmonic Orchestra and a 'brother Savage' (fellow member of the Savage Club). The governor returned the way he had come: by ferry to Dieppe, and then by a French banana boat – the *Barfleur* – to the West Indies. The vessel was due to make a special stop in Antigua.

Both the *Daily Mail* and the *Sunday Dispatch* printed articles expressing hurt at the implication in Creech Jones' statement that their journalists had somehow misreported Baldwin. Their representatives had of course reported him very accurately; and some editors had even censored passages held to be indiscreet. Lord Baldwin had found the prospect of attacking the Leewards' white establishment and creating a row irresistible; he was suddenly again the political tyro having a go at the Primrose League, rather than a representative of the crown having a difficult time with his Whitehall department. Despite the heaviness of middle age, Oliver still retained the methods, passion and indiscretion of a young radical political fighter; and he still sought to attack mean, oppressive and puritanical figures (and that meant principally hard and superior whites of the colony, together with their supporters in Mincing Lane and the Colonial Office): men and women who would not hear of classless human betterment. He did however have the grace to say that it was 'his own fault' for having spoken to the press at all.

On 14 March the *Daily Mail* printed a sour epilogue to the affair. The news that Lord Baldwin was returning to the islands in a banana boat was 'the one touch needed to round off this distasteful farce', it opined. The last snigger had been squeezed from an episode which had brought discredit to the empire and the government. The *Mail* lamented the lack of dignity in the whole affair – which was to be found too among some of those ruling our own island. The Baldwin business had been 'enough to make a cat laugh – or make it sick'. The matter had boiled down to a contest of wills between the governor and the colonial secretary, which the governor had won. British prestige in the Leewards must be in ruins, said the *Mail*. Creech Jones could have retained some dignity if he had sent Baldwin back in a warship. 'But the personal representative of the King in this outpost of the Empire returns from the Great Capital in a banana boat. What a way to run an Empire!'[54]

In fact Baldwin, like most socialists, was looking forward to the dissolution of empire, the end of 'them' and 'us', and the growth of ideas of equality between classes and races, which emerged fully in the 1960s. Socially, the *affaire Baldwin* was an early mark of the end of deference in British society. It was a challenge to established opinion, and to the idea that 'elders and betters' (who in this case were quietly ruthless sugar capitalists, uncaring extortionate planters, and secretive civil servants) were always right. It was too a gossippy political entertainment – 'Governor on the Mat', rather more densely plotted than *HMS Pinafore*, and perhaps Oliver's best role since the days when he had impersonated Clarice Lovibond.

On 23 March he arrived back in Antigua. James Cameron was there for the *Daily Express*. The *Mail* might be sour, but the *Express* gave voice to an explosion of joy. 'He's Back – And What An Uproar / Tin Cans Shrill for Baldwin', was the headline the following day. Cameron wrote masterfully: 'Lord Baldwin, the man who caused more flurry in the

Caribbean than anyone since Drake, came back to Antigua this afternoon. There has probably never been such a scene of mad excitement in Antigua. Baldwin's arrival was a precipitation into a crowd so dense it was immovable, so uproarious it could be heard, one felt, throughout the Leewards.' Cameron spoke of the 'fantastic popularity of this man'. 'It was in keeping with the character of the whole story that His Excellency should arrive back in Antigua not in some smart plane but in a chuffing launch, preceded all the way from the French ship Barfleur to the shore by another gimcrack old motorboat crammed to the gunwale with a tooting, thumping brass band . . . That, as his launch touched the jetty-side, the Governor should wave just once to the multitudes ashore, and by that gesture touch off a racket that is still going on. The steel bands played, Red Army, Brute Force, Hell's Gate . . . As they played, what seemed like acres of people stirred and spun and cavorted in a monstrous weaving reel . . . With all this affection, Lord Baldwin will get little sleep tonight.'[55]

Within a matter of weeks the old routine was re-established: the weekly letters to Johnnie, telling of difficult embarkations to the various islands undertaken in order to settle more difficult strikes. Among the islanders, the joy unconfined at the return of the governor continued. '"Pappy's back: there's our Pappy" is the cry in all the villages when I come through.'[56] At last Oliver was, symbolically speaking, a father.

For the Islands, hope was placed in the 10-year plan. At the same time Baldwin explored the diversification of the economy: he was looking at the production of clay for commercial ceramics, and at the extraction of sulphur from St Kitts. He also entertained Billy Butlin, who visited Antigua to assess the prospect of setting up a holiday camp in the Leewards. Unfortunately for the economy, Butlin decided against the project.[57] The governor also set up a committee to look into the possibility of a comprehensive insurance scheme, covering unemployment, sickness and old age. Oliver seemed determined to combat any Leewarditis which might be seeping into his own soul.

The governor also sponsored some house-building, in All Saints. The first house finished, in September 1949, was named Little Stoke House. The others he sponsored were to be called Paisley House, Dudley House, Eritrea House and Erivan House.[58]

Baldwin's socialist belief in the reformability of humanity still burned strongly: 'I am employing a gardener at CH [Clarence House] to keep the flowering shrubs in order. He is a borstal boy who never had a chance. Gerald thinks if he makes off with his bed he won't mind too much.' Some of the joy found in the earlier letters had withered, post-return; but Gerald could still raise a smile: 'For dinner on Thursday Gerald excelled himself. His ambition seems to be to make the Administrator sick: soup, langouste, duck, queen of puddings and a savoury omelette.'[59] There was amusement too at the way Gerald's mind could wander: 'He went to get a bag of meal for his chickens, and, bless me, if he didn't feed them Persil. They nearly died and I was petrified they'd all turn white.'[60] Christmas was a time for the governor to visit the less fortunate members of Leewards society: 'I have a round – Reformatory, Prison, Lepers and in the afternoon the old people for tea. I have invited Mr and Mrs Moody-Stuart and Mr and Mrs Bird only to help with them.'[61] This move was an example both of his compassion and of his desire to find reconciliation. The idea of inviting, with their wives, the head of the planters' association and the chief trade unionist to the old folks' tea was a gesture to soften the edge of confrontation in industrial negotiation, and to remind the opposing parties of their essential and common humanity.

Baldwin himself seemed to be flourishing at this time, despite the stress of the recall. Ross Hutchinson wrote in June 1949 that his health was nothing for Johnnie to worry about. 'He is eating well and is in good spirits. All the whites are being charming – butter would not melt in their mouths – and the dinner party for the King's Birthday was a *succès fou*. I think that one or two of the ladies had had just that little tiny bit more wine than they were used to, and they draped themselves around the piano, and with any encouragement would have draped themselves around me, while I was playing. And the musical part of the evening was wound up by Oliver who played for himself and sung [sic] two or three of the "Songs of the North". A good time was had by all . . .'[62]

Time was however limited. Lord Listowel, minister of state at the Colonial Office, visited Antigua in November 1949, and, Oliver wrote to Johnnie, 'I told him to tell Creech Jones about May would suit me to finish.' Listowel had been specially briefed by Attlee to see how Baldwin was faring in the Leewards after his return. A couple of lines to Johnnie written in December allude to the deal struck the preceding spring: 'We leave here around May 30th [1950]. I am afraid that was arranged when I was in London. I offered to go but they did not dare not to send me back at the time. I shan't be sorry, the strain is pretty great.'[63]

The months after Christmas were thus final months, concerned with clearing up existing business and preparing for departure. The faithful Ross Hutchinson, a most sterling private secretary, had left in September, to work for the Tory cause in the 1950 election.[64] (Soon after his decision to go, a hen had laid an egg in his 'pending' tray, which all thought somehow apt.[65]) He was succeeded by Sidney Cunliffe-Owen: capable, amusing, and almost as competent theatrically and musically as his predecessor. Still there were chances for Baldwin to show originality and generosity. Thus, the New Year's day holiday of 1950 was rained off by a massive downpour, and so a large amount of trade from the fair traditionally held on that day was lost. A deputation of traders came to see the governor: could they have another bank holiday the following day? 'I then summoned the attorney general and he summoned a quorum of the General Legislative Council and at six-thirty we had passed the idea and I signed the proclamation. The quickest piece of legislation ever accomplished here. Then the fun began . . . The next day the town went mad . . . Everybody was happy.'[66]

Baldwin was, as Hilda Macdonald had noted, enthusiastic about steel bands, and partly as a result of his advocacy Hell's Gate gained a booking in Britain through the agency of Jack Hylton. The governor seems to have made sure that any visitor to Antigua was subtly charmed by sounds of steel.

Whatever the stresses of the past year, one element was rewarding to Baldwin in the spring of 1950: 'The sugar crop is the best for many years.'[67] And the long struggle to find water in the islands, by means of dowsing, was rewarded with some success in May: 'The new drill has struck good water, pumping 20,000 gallons a day.'[68]

On 11 May he made the official announcement of his resignation. The reasons given were exhaustion and ill-health. There is little doubt that by now the term of office was beginning to tell on the governor; a visit to Montserrat the month before found him 'really very tired', and his liver was playing up sometimes. The islanders were 'a little dumbfounded'.[69] A serious dock strike in Antigua provided a last-minute crisis; sugar piled up, and Oliver declared that it should be stored in the hospital of the former American base.[70] The strike grew so serious that Oliver was unable to send the regular Sunday letter to Johnnie. But it was solved after ten days.

Plans were soon afoot for the arrival of the new governor (Kenneth Blackburne), whom two of Oliver's colleagues had known at school and university; they described him as 'very pontifical and a die-hard Tory'.[71] And Gerald? According to Oliver, 'there won't be room on the jetty for all his girl friends to see him off.'[72]

Lord Baldwin embarked aboard the French ship *Gascogne* on 5 June 1950, and was back in Britain ten days later, just two years and three months after his departure for Antigua. There is a sadness in the fact that an appointment entered into with such gusto should have been thus cut short, and ended with a sense of exhaustion and near burn-out. Baldwin left the Leewards walking with a stick, appearing almost like an old man. His critics might say that he had been a failure, that he had fomented near-chaos and unrealistic aspirations among the natives, and that basically, the traditional Colonial Office method of appointing men who really knew their stuff was best. The brevity of his term of office was an argument for sticking with the professionals, and quietly forgetting the unfortunate experiment of his appointment.

But that is to overlook many of the issues. The first was his determination to mediate to solve the strikes, and his success in so doing. Strikes in a society where there was no mechanism of conciliation and no form of relief would have led to starvation. His methods assured that there was no chaos. The second point was that he sought to create a just and equitable society, not just to collude with the use of black labour as a commodity for the benefit of a small minority, which was underpinned by the unspoken but deeply corrupt notion that the blacks were a lesser breed. Thirdly, he had treated the elderly and the lepers as human beings, giving them his time and consideration. Fourthly, he had of course brought water to Antigua. And fifthly, the governorship of Kenneth Blackburne was less than entirely successful. In June 1951 labour relations became so inflamed that British troops were ordered to Antigua, and a state of emergency was declared there. The bosses asserted that they would starve the workers rather than give in to a strike for a decent wage, and the strikers defiantly proclaimed that they would 'eat widdy-widdy plant' rather than accept the conditions of the planters. It seemed a long way from the cooperation sought by the 2nd Earl. In April 1956 the former colonial secretary of the Leeward Islands, Charlesworth Ross, a hard-working career civil servant, a product of the system, and at the time out-going commissioner of Montserrat, wrote to Lord Baldwin on the occasion of his own retirement, with a postscript: 'Many people in M'rat and A'gua I have heard saying: "I wish to goodness we had Lord Baldwin back."'[73] To this colonial civil servant at least, the governorship had not been a regrettable experiment.

The brave vistas were given only a short time to flourish. Oliver Baldwin did not, in the manner of a protagonist of a classical tragedy, have one great flaw which brought him down. There were rather a number of issues which led to his departure from the Leewards. He worked too hard, and became too anxious and personally involved in the conditions in the islands, which was undoubtedly a good fault, but unsuitable for a man of his by now unrobust constitution. One senses his personal involvement in the references to the population as 'my people'. He had begun to drink heavily, probably as a relief for the anxieties; but large quantities of rum could bring only illusory relief. His use of the press during his recall in February 1949 was bizarre and unwise. It would appear that at first he thought that Creech Jones had material only on public matters on the islands, and that it was not until the second or third interviews that that he realized that in the secretary of state's files were allegations relating to what in 1949 were seen as sexual irregularities.

There seems to be little doubt too that what appears to be British Intelligence – or whatever unstated power or authority Sir Alan Burns held – had a part in the matters. Although Oliver had worked briefly in intelligence during the war, and had a long and continuing connection with the intelligence community (his 1951 diary lists a telephone number for MI5: WHI 6789), he seems to have been naive about its workings in the Caribbean: that the planters would most likely have had a hot-line to its local chief, something that the local blacks could not possibly have had, and that somehow he needed to keep the whites sweet, however difficult this was for anyone who believed in democracy and improving conditions for all the people, in order to preserve his governorship from innuendo and a secret campaign.

His memory would live on, despite a perceptible desire among many to forget the entire issue, on the grounds either that he was a homosexual, or that he was a socialist – the two issues which aroused opposition, prejudice, and fear. His socialism in the Leewards was of the mildest sort: basically it took the form of treating the black population as human beings, and enjoying their social events more than the company of the fastidiously class-conscious whites. (And who can blame him? For a man of his outlook and interests, an evening of small talk with the planters would have been quietly spirit-crushing.) As an industrial negotiator, he never favoured the workers, but rather sought only to broker a solution to a dispute. His great popularity in the islands, well captured in James Cameron's dispatch on his return, was the response of the majority community to his treatment of them, and to his concern for their economic prospects, their schools, their prisons and their homes for the elderly and for the lepers. Since the 1960s it has been taken for granted that these things belong to all the people, and not just one privileged race. The people of the Leeward Islands were fortunate that their governor was alert to the things that were theirs a decade or so before they were universally recognized to be so; but it was Lord Baldwin's misfortune, for the second time in his life (the first being his prescience of the end of communism), and unrecognized by himself, to have been prophetic of social and economic conditions, to have striven for a society taken for granted only a decade or so later, and to have been almost broken in that struggle.

CHAPTER 16

Retirement

Oliver Baldwin, home from the Leeward Islands, was only 51, but nevertheless facing retirement. On the voyage out, a little over two years earlier, as he had sung 'Sing hey to you, Good day to you' in duet with Ross Hutchinson, there had been an air of optimistic gubernatorial larkiness. It now seemed a lifetime away. The sense of fight had fled. His life in politics and public service was virtually over. It had been a shock to have been eased out of the governorship. His departure from the Caribbean had occurred partly through the authoritarian and secret nature of the British Empire's colonial culture, but partly too as a result of his own foolhardiness, shown in the unwise attempt to use the press to influence public opinion in his favour. The homecoming found him disillusioned. He put on a lot of weight; the Coronation photograph of 1953 shows a man unhealthily obese. It was as if his prison meditation upon ambition made thirty years earlier – that the urge to self-advancement leads only to spiritual hollowness and emptiness – had come true. He made no more discreet enquiries about serious employment, and took almost no part in public life. He was silent upon the benches of the House of Lords.

This was a sad contrast with 1948, a year defined by buoyancy and expectation. Until the return home was a fixed fact, this had continued to be the mood. The letters are filled with life and vigour, and a sense of fulfilment. The post had been a challenge, and he had risen to it. Here was the

satisfying job that he had been searching for all his life. Ross
Hutchinson's letters, and his elegant volume of unpublished
memoirs, concur here. Hutchinson had observed that the
responsibility was very congenial to Oliver.

Now that it was over, life became telescoped into the
parochial. In Oxfordshire, the Little Stoke House atmosphere
remained unbroken, and the genial social life continued to
prevail there. The tie with the house was too strong to be
severed. Despite the talk of selling, it remained in Oliver and
Johnnie's possession, as though they could not bear to part
with it. Money was managed without much competence.
Both Oliver and Johnnie appear to have lived largely by
selling shares, or by disposing of the odd picture or tapestry,
which in Oliver's case might have been an heirloom. An
economy drive resulted in the decision to stop taking the
Radio Times. Weekend parties continued as before, with continuing liveliness and good humour. At one of them,
Kenneth Williams – in his wildness, outrageousness and
camp theatricality a typical friend of theirs – was seen rolling
over and over with laughter down a bank in the garden. Sam
Phelips was another visitor; his father had been a canon of
Dudley, and for most weekend visits Sam would arrive with
a different girlfriend. Then there was Sir Campbell Mitchell-
Cotts, a tall man with a large frame, fond of wearing a
kimono, who was excellent as the butler in amateur
dramatics. He wrote poetry, and was remembered for having
phoned his dog, Daisy Jinks, from America. (This was most
unusual in the 1950s.) Major Patrick Uniacke and Richard
Baylis were a couple often down for the weekend – they were
still sharing a house in the 1990s; and Boldie's large writing
frequently adorns the visitors' books.

Tea was always taken punctually, and when Oliver and
Johnnie had no guests, two silver tea sets were set out in
opposite ends of the drawing room: one for Johnnie, in
which the teapot was filled with tea; while in the further
corner Oliver took tea from a pot half-filled with whisky. At

other times Mount Gay rum was consumed in heroic quantities. In London they rented a house at 42 Draycott Place, in Chelsea, having abandoned both the more exalted ambitions of Belgravia and the drop-out dreams of a boat at Hammersmith.

Some small activities kept alight a flickering candle of interest. The odd plan was set afoot, without much enthusiasm. In the search for a money-spinner, Oliver even got into negotiations about the manufacture and marketing of a kit-built bubble car, a three-wheeler, a kind of precursor of the Mini.[1] The prototype of this vehicle was the German Fuldamobile, and the British version was to be called the Nobel 200. But the plans reached a decisive stage just two months before his death. Oliver's writing, post-Leewards, lacked the earlier memorability: the unpublished memoirs ('Golden Rod', covering 1931 to 1948) occasionally flicker into life; a few articles (which included those for *Men Only*) were coaxed out of him by kind editors such as R. J. Minney. Otherwise, he seems to have churned on with Dickens dramatizations which no one wanted, and provided the inevitable final chapters to *The Mystery of Edwin Drood*.

Oliver did not entirely lose contact with politics; he was prepared to play a minor part at election time. In the 1951 general election campaign he spoke on behalf of Roy Jenkins. But the event ended in near farce, since the 2nd Earl, rather the worse for drink, fell over on the platform and had to be helped back to verticality.

Oliver Baldwin had a difficult personality; that cannot be denied. Whether it was through genetic predisposition, early experience or his own choice is a matter which can be disputed endlessly. Perhaps the experience of imprisonment and near-starvation in 1920–21 left its mark. But, besides his time in the West Indies, there were other times in his life when he turned round negativity, and swam with the current of the world: as a cadet, and in anything to do with the army (Oliver the soldier never once quarrelled with his admired

regiment, the Irish Guards), seeing communism crumble in
Armenia in 1921; in his life with Johnnie Boyle; and as a
socialist in the 1920s raising spirits amid the grime and
dehumanized work-places of British industrial practice. Few
other socialists showed his dedication in visiting industrial
centres – Burnley, Grimsby, Clitheroe, Swansea – and in
gaining smoke-choked insight into the lack of brotherhood
of humankind, and the world as it ought not to be.

In Little Stoke House there was, besides the hospitable
atmosphere, a rich and dark density of books, and Oliver had a
broad if somewhat haphazard knowledge of history, politics,
literature and science. His knowledge and his pursuit of
knowledge were undisciplined, in view of the unfortunate time
at Eton and his lack of any further academic training. He loved
art, he painted (and was painted), and he played the piano. His
fondness of music was genuine: beside the bluff extrovert
Gilbert-and-Sullivan type (as if appearing to conform to a
stereotype of liking nothing too deep in case it went beyond the
boundaries of permitted English whimsy), he was partial to
Schubert Lieder: how partial it is difficult to say, but since he
actually named the songs he loved – this was in 1933, two
decades before Fischer-Dieskau made Schubert really popular
– it is safe to say that there was genuine devotion to this pro-
foundest of musicians. The songs that he mentioned are
'Lachen und Weinen', 'Das Wandern' (from *Die schöne
Müllerin*), 'Das Fischermädchen' and 'Erlkönig'.[2] A letter to
Johnnie refers to the Goethe setting 'Heidenröslein', a song
where great depths are concealed beneath a light, almost banal
exterior.

Love of the theatre stayed with him all his life. But
somehow culture never became a touchstone to inner peace.
Stability came from his long and unquestioned relationship
with Johnnie – though even here, the references in the letters
to 'Mr Naggins' and 'Little Nag House' indicate occasional
temporary difficulties. But the idea of letting (say) music
afford him peace in retirement, rather than another bottle of

rum, seems not to have been possible. He had internalized some of the Edwardian suspicion of culture; the paradoxical attitude of hearty writers such as Kipling, Henty, Buchan and C. S. Lewis, that too much involvement in art or the written word (especially of a flowery nature) sapped the moral fibre, and was not right for a chap.

In public life, things had changed for him in the 1930s. The heights were not to be conquered. Parliament had been, and would be, only episodic. Oliver fell into a trap at this time. Some of the energetic idealism was lost, and he did not grasp the full meaning of developments on the international scene. The politics of the time became less clearly delineated, although he believed he saw what was going on with unclouded eyes. Despite having been a socialist in a communist prison, he failed for much of the 1930s to grasp the meaning of totalitarian politics. International politics at this time were not an arena where he could feel at home, although the editors for whom he wrote assumed that he had privileged knowledge. Although he wrote well from time to time, and his assault on the Blackshirts was magnificent, especially in the light of his former friendship with Mosley, his undercurrent of 'knowing it all from the inside' disguised a basic imperceptiveness, and often seems to have been passively derived from a vague grandiosity rather than actively to have been searched for in order to inspire those around him with truth and hope and idealism. An element of solipsism was present. Politics sometimes looked less like a dialogue than a semi-private language or coded communication. To unsympathetic souls, he could sometimes seem boring and self-obsessed.

He was also foolish enough to maintain a stand-off with his family, although there were temporary truces, as for example in the party given for his father in December 1938. Given his adoption of socialism, there were bound to be angry calls of betrayal from the family; but instead of facing them and discussing them in a mood of mature responsibility, he seems almost to have relished them, in the spirit of snubbing the bourgeoisie. Of his family, he only really sought to understand his father, and remained close to him till the end. His mother – complex, outspoken, theatrical, even operatic – he was fond of, but since she had indulged him as a child, and granted him favours above those granted to the rest of the family, he felt an ambivalence, maybe even seeking in democratic socialism an escape from the severe position of privilege to which she had raised him.

He never tried to develop any relationship with his brother or sisters at any level beyond the perfunctory, and after his mother's death, he picked an unnecessary dispute with them about the setting up of a memorial to her. It was as though he was still fighting old battles; as though, too, despite his departure from home aged 24, he had nevertheless remained enmeshed in rivalries with them. His principles of love and peace and forbearance were absent in dealings with his siblings. The high-minded utterances from the last act of *From the Four Winds* concerning the possibility of turning away from actions which were cruel or unspiritual vanished in the brotherly and sisterly context.

He remained friends with Violet and Clement Attlee, and he introduced Attlee into the Lords in January 1956.[3] But such events harked back to old days and old struggles. The present was not looked at. Of his few House of Commons friends, perhaps his closest was Seymour Cocks, with whom he exchanged volumes of comforting but depressing minor verse: a kind of verbal chemical substance, enabling the reader to function in the world without engaging in its processes.

At the same time youth and art could stir him into generosity. At the London opening of an art exhibition in 1952 dedicated to the work of George Warner Allen, son of his fellow journalist and Oxfordshire neighbour Warner Allen, Oliver was seen working the guests, and in a hushed voice saying to them, 'Buy, buy, buy!' as they viewed the new work.[4]

As a gay man, there was no hint of lavender about him – if

one discounts the passion for theatrical types. Except in the actual matter of sexual preference, he could really just as well have been straight. Any fussiness and dressiness were absent; maybe some vanity was present, even if it was cleverly concealed. Little Stoke House was famously unsmart, apart from the rigorous punctuality of meal-times. Johnnie would turn up looking like the gardener, with a piece of string holding up his trousers. In essence, the two of them found little need to pretend. Oliver could be what he was: an ordinary kindly socialist man, who hated class distinctions whether in private life or public, with some talent for words in public places, and a capacity to live a public life, and who in private happened to desire a man and not a woman as a partner. If he was a bore at dinner sometimes – then others were too.

Although he never embraced extreme dissidence, he made dissent possible to the many people he came into contact with, in a manner which a fully dissident person is less able to do. By his mild radicalism he made the radical option more accessible, where a dedicated radical might put off an interested party by strident militancy and hard-edged ideological commitment. Oliver remained human and humane to the end.

Oliver Baldwin died in the Mile End Hospital, Stepney, on 1 August 1958. He was 59. The cause of death was given as a chronic gastric ulcer. Johnnie Boyle was in Oxfordshire, and he lived on, first at Little Stoke House and then at The Giffords, Wallingford, until his own death on 24 February 1969. He was fortunate in his latter years to be looked after by the ever-attentive Dickie Payne. Dickie himself died quite suddenly in 1984.

Ultimately, Oliver did perhaps achieve what he wanted to be. The visions of high office had evaporated, the polished Rolls-Royce with liveried chauffeur was not waiting around the corner, the dramatizations of Dickens remained unperformed. What remained were the admirable ordinariness and uncommon virtues of being a Common Man.

References

Abbreviations: (n.b. all books are published in London unless stated)

6P: Oliver Baldwin, *Six Prisons and Two Revolutions*, 1925

CA: Oliver Baldwin, *The Coming of Aissa*, 1935

CRH: C. Ross Hutchinson

EK: Elsie Bambridge, née Kipling

GR: Oliver Baldwin, 'Golden Rod', unpublished, c. 1951

JPB: John Parke Boyle

LB: Lucy Baldwin

O: Oliver Baldwin, *Oasis*, 1936

ORB: Oliver Baldwin

QB: Oliver Baldwin, *The Questing Beast*, 1932

RK: Rudyard Kipling

SB: Stanley Baldwin

US: Oliver Baldwin, *Unborn Son*, 1933

Prologue

1. ORB papers, ORB to SB, 3 October 1918
2. The full names and ranks of those mentioned as killed or wounded in the action were: 2nd Lieut. AH O'Farrell; Lieut. BS Close; Capt. CWW Bence-Jones; Capt. BAA Ogilvy; 2nd Lieut AR Boyle; Lieut KR Mathieson; 2nd Lieut CS O'Brien

Chapter 1. 1899–1908: 'Amazement, Question and Indignation'

1. QB, p. 1
2. Angela Thirkell, *Three Houses*, 1932, p. 108
3. E. A. Ridsdale, *Cosmic Evolution*, 1889, p. 119
4. GR, pp. 85–6
5. Interview with the late Lady Lorna Howard, June 1988
6. QB, pp. 10, 11
7. QB, p. 3
8. QB, pp. 3, 7
9. QB, p. 17; Lily Whittington to ORB, 12 November 1918; interview with the late Lady Lorna Howard, November 1988
10. QB, p. 9
11. QB, pp. 13–14; papers of the late Lady Lorna Howard
12. QB, pp. 10–11
13. QB, p. 18
14. Angela Thirkell, *Three Houses*, p. 106
15. ibid., p. 105

Chapter 2. Schooldays: love and hate

1. Angela Thirkell, *Three Houses*, p. 127
2. ORB to SB, 10 May 1908
3. QB, pp. 21, 43
4. QB, p. 27
5. Angela Thirkell, *Three Houses*, p. 79
6. QB, pp. 25–6
7. ORB papers, juvenilia
8. QB, pp. 21–22
9. QB, p. 31
10. QB, pp. 32–3
11. QB, p. 35
12. QB, p. 42
13. QB, p. 37
14. Interview with CRH, April 1993
15. QB, p. 45–6

Chapter 3. War and Post-War

1. QB, p. 46
2. LB to ORB, 6 October 1915
3. QB, p. 62
4. Kipling Papers, Sussex University, RK to SB, 23 October, 20 November 1915
5. ibid., RK to ORB, 20 November 1915
6. QB, pp. 46–7
7. QB, p. 47
8. QB, pp. 47–8
9. QB, pp. 48–9
10. Kipling Papers, RK to SB, 22 October 1916
11. QB, 50–52
12. QB, pp. 54–5
13. QB, pp. 56–7
14. QB, pp. 58–60
15. QB, p. 62
16. ibid.
17. QB, p. 63
18. QB, p. 64
19. QB, p. 69
20. QB, p. 70; R. Kipling, *The Irish Guards in the Great War*, 1923, pp. 300–304
21. QB, p. 21
22. ORB to LB, 23 September 1918
23. R. Kipling, *The Irish Guards*, p. 177
24. QB, p. 73
25. ORB to SB, 25 October 1918. Full names are A E Hutchinson and C A Barnewall
26. QB, p. 75
27. QB, p. 76
28. QB, p. 77
29. ibid.
30. QB. p. 78
31. QB, p. 79; also Public Record Office, FO 369/1125.137890

32. QB, p. 80
33. QB, pp. 80–81
34. QB, p. 83

Chapter 4. Armenia I: 'Fate is a Sea without Shore'

1. QB, pp. 86–7
2. QB, p. 87; 6P, p. 9; also Alexander Khatisian, *Hayastani Hanrapetutian Dsagumn u Zargatsume* [*The Origin and Development of the Armenian Republic*], Beirut, 1968, pp. 238–9, French trans., Athens, 1989, pp. 221–2
3. 6P, p. 10
4. ibid.
5. 6P, p. 11
6. 6P, p. 13; QB, p. 90
7. 6P, p. 16
8. 6P, pp. 16–17
9. 6P, p. 18
10. 6P, p. 19
11. 6P, pp. 19–20
12. 6P, p. 21
13. 6P, p. 20
14. 6P, p. 23
15. 6P, pp 25–6
16. 6P, pp. 28, 38
17. 6P, pp. 28–9
18. ibid., pp. 29–30
19. ibid., p. 30
20. ibid., p. 31
21. ibid., p. 38
22. ibid., pp. 41, 43
23. ibid., p. 46
24. ibid., p. 49
25. ORB papers, 'Prison Diary', Erivan, 9 December 1920
26. ibid., 10 December 1920
27. ibid.; 6P, p. 54
28. 'Prison Diary', 12 December 1920

29. ibid.
30. 'Prison Diary', 13 December 1920
31. 6P, p. 56
32. 6P, p. 57
33. 6P, p. 58
34. 6P, pp. 59–60
35. 6P, pp. 61–3
36. 'Prison Diary', 11 January 1921
37. 6P, p. 85
38. 6P, p. 90
39. 6P, p. 91
40. 6P, p. 101
41. 6P, p. 103
42. ibid.
43. 6P, p. 105
44. 6P, p. 106
45. 6P, p. 114
46. 6P, p. 120
47. 6P, p. 121
48. ibid.
49. 6P, p. 127
50. 6P, pp. 133–5

Chapter 5. Armenia II: 'How completely can snow cover all traces of a stranger in a foreign land'

1. 6P, p. 136
2. 6P, p. 140
3. 6P, p. 142
4. 6P, p. 145
5. 6P, p. 146
6. 6P, p. 148
7. J. L. Barton, *Story of Near East Relief*, New York, 1930, p. 109
8. 6P, p. 150
9. 6P, p. 155
10. 6P, p. 158

11. 6P, p. 163
12. 6P, p. 167–8
13. 6P, p. 170
14. 6P, pp. 177–8
15. 6P, pp. 189–90
16. 6P, p. 193
17. 6P, pp. 194–5
18. 6P, p. 198
19. 6P, p. 206
20. 6P, pp. 207–8
21. 6P, p. 210
22. 6P, p. 219
23. 6P, p. 219–21
24. 6P, p. 226
25. 6P, p. 227
26. ORB papers, *Armenia: 'Au Commandant . . .'*
27. 6P, pp. 231–2
28. A. J. Smithers, *Toby: a Real-Life Ripping Yarn*, 1978, p. 185
29. 6P, p. 245
30. 6P, p. 251
31. 6P, pp. 268–71

Chapter 6. Recovery

1. QB, p. 131; interview with the late Lady Lorna Howard, July 1988
2. QB, p. 133; also *Burke, Peerage, Baronetage and Knightage*, 1923, p. 126, col. 2
3. QB, p. 144
4. QB, p. 145
5. QB, pp. 159, 164
6. QB, p. 164
7. QB, p. 170
8. A. Khatisian, *Hayastani Hanrapetutian Dsagumn u Zargatsume*, 1968, p. 380; French trans., Athens, 1989, p. 337
9. QB, p. 181

Chapter 7. The Break with Astley

1. QB, p. 205
2. *Westminster Gazette*, 25 May 1923, p. 1
3. *Justice*, 7 June 1923, p. 7
4. *Burke, Peerage, Baronetage and Knightage*, 1923, p. 585, col. 2
5. QB, p. 209
6. Stanley Baldwin papers, Cambridge University, SB to ORB, 23 August 1923
7. ORB to JPB, 1 August 1923
8. Alex Carlsen to JPB, 31 August 1923
9. *Justice*, 13 December 1923, p. 1
10. *Evening Standard*, 28 November 1923, p. 6
11. ibid, 1 December 1923, p. 6
12. *Westminster Gazette*, I December 1923, p. 3
13. LB to JPB, 7 Dec 1923
14. *Justice*, 31 January 1924, p. 6
15. QB, p. 215; information on chicken farming provided by James Knox
16. Lionel Fielden, *The Natural Bent*, 1960, p. 92
17. L. Fielden to JPB, 26 August 1958
18. Beverley Nichols to ORB and JPB, 10 October 1923; ORB to JPB, 19 August 1923; Beverley Nichols, *Twenty-Five*, 1926, pp. 183–5
19. Robert Byron archives
20. 'Martin Hussingtree', *Konyetz*, 1924, p. 12

Chapter 8. Dudley and Koot Farm

1. QB, p. 218
2. ORB to JPB, 15, 16 July 1924
3. *Dudley Chronicle*, 17 July 1924, p. 7
4. ibid., 24 July 1924, p. 5
5. ORB to JPB, 22 July 1924
6. ORB to JPB, 24 September 1924

7. *Dudley Chronicle*, 9 October 1924, p. 5

8. ORB to JPB, 29 September 1924

9. ORB to JPB, 30 September 1924

10. QB, p. 220

11. ORB to JPB, undated, c. 15 Oct 1924

12. ORB to JPB, 19 Oct 1924

13. ORB, 1924 election address, pp. 2–3

14. *Dudley Chronicle*, 23 October 1924, p. 5

15. ORB to JPB, 21 October 1924

16. ORB to JPB, 26 October 1924

17. *Dudley Chronicle*, 30 October 1924, p. 5

18. EK to JPB, 4 June 1924; GLB to ORB, 24 July 1924; EK to ORB, 2 August 1924

19. *The Social-Democrat*, May 1925, p. 3

20. ORB to JPB, 28 December 1925

21. ORB to JPB, 24 April 1926

22. ORB to JPB, undated, c. April 1926

23. *The Social-Democrat*, December 1926, p. 8

24. ORB to JPB, 19 August 1925

25. J.W. Drawbell to ORB, 12 June 1926; J.W. Drawbell to A.P. Watt, 30 August 1926

26. *Sunday Chronicle*, 18 July 1926, p. 3

27. *Sunday Chronicle*, 29 August 1926

28. Michael Baker, *Our Three Selves*, 1985, p. 231

29. *The Social-Democrat*, May 1927, p. 8

30. 'Janitor', *The Feet of the Young Men*, 1928, pp. 115–16

31. ORB to LB, undated, c. 1928

32. QB, p. 231

33. SB to ORB, 3 September 1928

34. *Dudley Chronicle*, 20 October 1928, p. 6

35. Beatrice Webb, Diary, 27 June 1927, p. 115

36. Beatrice Webb, *Letters*, ed. N. MacKenzie, vol. III, Cambridge, 1978, p. 289

37. *Daily Express*, 4 November 1926, p. 1

38. ORB to JPB, undated, ?January 1926

Chapter 9. Oliver Baldwin, MP

1. QB, p. 233
2. ORB, 1929 election address, pp. 2–3
3. *Dudley Chronicle*, 9 May 1929, p. 2
4. *Dudley Chronicle*, 16 May 1929, p. 2
5. ORB to SB, 3 June 1929
6. SB to ORB, 1 Jan 1930
7. *Hansard*, Commons, series 5, vol. 229, col. 658 (9 July 1929)
8. ibid., vol. 230, coi. 1121 (23 July 1929)
9. ibid., vol. 231, col. 879 (5 November 1929)
10. ibid., vol. 232, col. 2594 (5 December 1929)
11. ibid., vol. 233, col. 544 (24 January 1930)
12. QB, p. 241
13. QB, p. 239
14. W. J. Brown, *So Far...*, 1943, p. 154
15. ibid., p. 159
16. ORB papers, typescript of Mosley manifesto
17. GR, p. 90
18. GR, p. 91
19. *Manchester Guardian*, 20 August 1931, p. 16
20. GR, p. 94
21. *Chatham, Rochester and Gillingham Observer*, 16 October 1931, p. 9
22. ibid.
23. ORB to JPB, 10 August 1929
24. ORB to JPB, 17 January 1929
25. ORB to JPB, c.15 January 1929
26. ORB to JPB, 26 April 1930
27. ORB to JPB, 7 October 1930
28. John Drinkwater, *Summer Harvest*, 1933, p. 29
29. Michael Redgrave, *In My Mind's Eye*, 1983, p. 40
30. ibid., p. 49
31. ibid., p. 47
32. Lady Redgrave to the author, September 1992

33. Interview with Oswald Skilbeck, June 1992

34. ORB to JPB, 10? August 1928

35. Gwynne papers, ORB to Col. Gwynne, 10 September 1928

36. ORB papers, 'The Wrong Bus'

37. ORB papers, 'The Fog'

38. ORB papers, 'From the Four Winds', act II, p. 6

39. ibid., p. 8

40. ibid., p. 12

41. ibid., p. 26

42. ibid., act III, p. 3

43. ibid., p. 4

44. ibid.

45. ibid., p. 10

46. ibid., p. 33

47. ibid., p. 41

Chapter 10. Creatively Adrift in the Thirties

1. ORB papers, Colston Leigh contracts

2. GR, p. 100

3. GR, p. 103

4. ORB to JPB, 6, 15 Jan 1932

5. ORB to JPB, 21 January 1932

6. US, p. 57

7. ORB to JPB, 6 February 1932

8. GR, pp. 108–9

9. GR, p. 112

10. ORB to JPB, 16 February 1932

11. GR, p. 113

12. GR, p. 114

13. GR, p. 116

14. ORB, 'What I would like to hear broadcast through Europe', typescript, 28 November 1933, p. 2; ORB to JPB, 15 January 1932

15. ORB papers, account books

16. US, p. 246

17. ORB to JPB, undated, c. April 1932
18. London Film Productions to ORB, 13 July 1932
19. GR, 119–20
20. ORB papers, 'Films Worth Seeing' file
21. GR, p. 125. *On Moissi*, see also Stefan Zweig, *The World of Yesterday*, 1943, p. 138, and *The Oxford Companion to the Theatre*, 1951
22. Rosamond Lehmann to the author, August 1984
23. *Daily Mail*, 7 November 1935, p. 9
24. GR, p. 143
25. ORB, 1935 election address, pp. 2–3
26. C. Attlee to ORB, 26 November 1935
27. *Daily Telegraph*, 29 July 1936, p. 16
28. *Daily Telegraph*, 7 August 1936
29. *Daily Mail*, 23 March 1936, p. 14
30. *Daily Mail*, 18 April 1936, p. 8
31. ORB to JPB, 24 April 1936
32. ORB papers, Spain 1936 file
33. GR, p. 152
34. GR, p. 153
35. ORB to SB, 13 May 1937
36. SB to ORB, 16 May 1937
37. SB to ORB, 23 June 1937
38. *Daily Mail*, 27 April 1937, p. 6
39. GR, pp. 160–61
40. SB to ORB, 16 December 1938

Chapter 11. Tempted to Prolixity

1. US, p. 48
2. US, p. 53
3. US, p. 63
4. US, p. 85
5. US, p. 168
6. CA, p. 38
7. CA, p. 49

8. CA, p. 59
9. CA, p. 69
10. CA, p. 87
11. CA, p. 94
12. CA, p. 97
13. CA, p. 99
14. CA, p. 133
15. CA, p. 180
16. CA, p. 177
17. CA, pp. 210ff.
18. CA, p. 243
19. CA, p. 247
20. CA, p. 272
21. CA, p. 294
22. O, p. 51
23. O, pp. 311–18
24. O, p. 81
25. O, p. 85
26. O, p. 118

Chapter 12. The Discipline of Brevity

[ORB papers, Journalism file and loc. cit.]
1. *Daily Herald*, 17 January 1934, p. 8

Chapter 13. The Second World War: seeking service

1. GR, p. 163
2. GR, p. 165
3. GR, p. 169
4. ORB autograph diary, entries for 22 November, 13, 20 December 1939; GR, p. 170
5. GR, p. 172
6. GR, p. 173
7. ibid.
8. ORB to JPB, 13 June 1940

9. GR, p. 182
10. ORB to JPB, 5 October 1940
11. I. S. O. Playfair, *The Mediterranean and the Middle East,* 1954–66, vol. I, p. 432
12. *Daily Telegraph,* 4 April 1941
13. GR, p. 190; Alan Moorehead, *African Trilogy,* 1944, p. 118
14. ORB papers, verse file
15. GR, p. 192
16. GR, p. 193
17. GR, pp. 195, 194
18. GR, p. 199
19. GR, pp. 200–201
20. GR, pp. 203, 207
21. GR, p. 209; also ORB papers, Brismis document
22. GR, p. 222
23. GR, p. 229
24. GR, p. 240
25. GR, pp. 243–8
26. ORB to JPB, 21 April 1942
27. ORB to JPB, 18 June 1942
28. ORB to JPB, 13 and 21 July 1944, and undated (1945)
29. ORB to JPB, 31 August 1940, 9 August 1942
30. SB to JPB, 8 July 1943
31. ORB to JPB, 4 August 1944
32. ORB to JPB, 16 March 1945
33. ORB to JPB, 29 June 1945
34. LB to JPB, 20 June 1939
35. LB to JPB, 8 April 1939
36. LB to JPB, 29 December 1939
37. LB to JPB, 5 July 1940
38. LB to JPB, 7 November 1940
39. LB to JPB, 17 October 1940
40. LB to JPB, 9 March 1941
41. LB to JPB, 5 May 1943
42. LB to JPB, 27 August 1943

43. LB to JPB, 18 January 1945

Chapter 14. Viscount Corvedale

1. ORB, 1945 election address autograph notes, pp. 1–2
2. *Paisley and Renfrewshire Gazette*, 16 June 1945, p. 2
3. ORB to JPB, ?late May 1945
4. ORB to JPB, 12[?] June 1945
5. GR, p. 251
6. ibid.
7. *Hansard*, Commons, 5th series, vol. 415, col. 875 (2 November 1945)
8. ibid., vol. 417, col. 1641 (20 December 1945)
9. ibid., vol. 418, col. 59 (written), (23 January 1946)
10. ibid., vol. 431, col. 59 (written), (3 December 1946)
11. ORB to JPB, 15 October 1946
12. ORB to JPB, 10 November 1947
13. Fred Bellenger to ORB, 8 October 1947
14. GR, p. 256
15. GR, p. 256
16. SB to ORB, 23 June 1946
17. GR, p. 260

Chapter 15. A Most Unconventional Governor

1. ORB papers, Leewards file, A. Creech Jones to ORB, 20 January 1948
2. GR, p. 261
3. CR Hutchinson, 'Leeward Letters', unpublished, [1951], pp. 1–2
4. ORB to JPB, 13 March 1948
5. ORB to JPB, 28 March 1948
6. CRH, 'Leeward Letters', p. 16
7. ORB to JPB, 16 May 1948
8. ORB to JPB, 4 April 1948
9. ORB to JPB, 11, 18 April 1948; CRH to JPB, 20 April 1948

10. ORB to JPB, 19 June 1948, also 26 September 1948
11. CRH to JPB, 20 June 1948
12. ORB to JPB, 30 May 1948; CRH to JPB 30 May 1948
13. CRH to JPB, 2 May 1948
14. ORB to JPB, 11, 18 April 1948
15. ORB to JPB, 16 May 1948
16. ORB to JPB, 6 June 1948; CRH to JPB, 6 June 1948
17. ORB to JPB, 11 July 1948
18. *The Times*, 20 August 1948, p. 4
19. *The Times*, 20 September 1948, p. 7; ORB to JPB, 26 September 1948
20. CRH, 'Leeward Letters', p. 132
21. ORB papers, speech of 8 December 1948
22. Public Record Office, CO 537/3788, letter from Jim Burns, 3 December 1948
23. *The Times*, 29 January 1949, p. 4; ibid, 3 February 1949, p. 4
24. *Daily Express*, 2 February 1949, p. 1
25. *News Chronicle*, 3 February 1949, p. 4
26. *The Times*, 8 February 1949, p. 4
27. *Hansard*, Commons, 5th series, vol. 561, cols. 362–6 (9 February 1949)
28. CO 537/4884, letter of 29 December 1948
29. ibid., from SNIPE, 15 February 1949
30. See reference in *Daily Mail*, 21 February 1949, p. 1
31. CO 537/4884, letters of 4 March, 14 February, 1949
32. ibid.
33. *Sunday Dispatch*, 13 February 1949, p. 1
34. *The People*, 13 February 1949, p. 6
35. *Daily Herald*, 14 February 1949, p. 1
36. *News Chronicle*, 14 February 1949, p. 1
37. *Daily Express*, 14 February 1949, p. 1
38. *Daily Mirror*, 15 February 1949, p. 4
39. *Manchester Guardian*, 15 February 1949, p. 4
40. Attlee papers, Bodleian Library, dep. 79, pp. 76–9

41. *Daily Express*, 16 February 1949, p. 4
42. *Daily Mirror*, 17 February 1949, p. 2
43. *Daily Express*, 17 February 1949, p. 1; *Manchester Guardian*, 17 February 1949, p. 3
44. *Sunday Express*, 20 February 1949, p. 7; *The People*, 20 February 1949, p. 2
45. *Daily Mail*, 21 February 1949, pp. 1, 3
46. Attlee papers, loc. cit.
47. *News of the World*, 6 March 1949, p. 4
48. ORB to JPB, 6 March '1948' (i.e. 1949)
49. *The Times*, 9 March 1949, p. 4
50. *Daily Mirror*, 9 March 1949, p. 1
51. *Hansard*, 5th series, vol. 462, cols. 1178–80 (9 March 1949); *The Times*, 10 March 1949, p. 4
52. *Daily Express*, 10 March 1949, p. 4
53. *Daily Mirror*, 11 March 1949, p. 12
54. *Daily Mail*, 14 March 1949, p. 1
55. *Daily Express*, 24 March 1949, p. 1
56. ORB to JPB, 17 April 1949
57. ORB to JPB, 31 July 1949
58. ORB to JPB, 4 September 1949
59. ORB to JPB, 1 May 1949
60. ORB to JPB, 2 October 1949
61. ORB to JPB, 18 December 1949
62. CRH to JPB, 19 June 1949
63. ORB to JPB, 27 December 1949
64. ORB to JPB, 21 August 1949, 18 September 1949
65. ORB to JPB, 28 August 1949
66. ORB to JPB, 7/8 January 1950
67. ORB to JPB, 19 March 1950
68. ORB to JPB, 21 May 1950
69. ORB to JPB, 14 May 1950
70. ORB to JPB, 23 April 1950
71. ORB to JPB, 14 May 1950
72. ORB to JPB, 7 May 1950
73. Charlesworth Ross to ORB, 10 April 1956

Chapter 16. Retirement

1. *Evening Standard*, 19 June 1958, p. 9; *Manchester Guardian*, 20 June 1958, p. 11
2. 'The World is Calling', *World-Radio*, 22 December 1933, p. 811
3. *The Times*, 26 January 1956, p. 6
4. Personal interview with Dr J. G. P. Delaney, May 2003

Acknowledgements

I am grateful for the help and patience of the librarians of the London Library, the British Library and Lambeth Palace Library (the latter for kindly identifying Thomas Becon's Prayer), and of my local Hammersmith Public Library. The keepers of the Kipling Archive at Sussex University were generous with their time and information.

For permission to reproduce published works, my thanks are due to Associated Newspapers for quotations from the *Daily Mail*, *Evening Standard* and *Sunday Dispatch*. Also grateful thanks to Trinity Mirror for permission to quote from the *Daily Mirror*. To Express Newspapers the same for permission to use the *Daily Express* and *Sunday Express*. To the Hollinger Group for the use of material from the *Daily Telegraph* and the *Spectator*. To News International for permission to quote from the *Daily Herald*, *The Times* and the *News of the World*. To the Guardian Group for permission to quote from the *Manchester Guardian* and the *Observer*. I must express thanks to the Oxford University Press for permission to quote from Angela Thirkell's *Three Houses*, and to Messrs Sidgwick & Jackson for allowing me to reproduce John Drinkwater's Sonnet from *Summer Harvest*. I am also grateful to the Keeper of Public Records for permission to reproduce material in the Public Record Office, which is Crown Copyright, and my thanks are due to the Publishers of *Hansard* for permission to quote from Commons proceedings. If I have overlooked any copyright owners, I would be glad to hear from them, so that they may be credited in any future edition.

Bibliography

Oliver Baldwin, *Konyetz*, 1924 (published under the pseudonym 'Martin Hussingtree')
——, *Six Prison and Two Revolutions*, 1925
——, (with Jean Ouvret), *Socialism and the Bible*, 1928
——, (with Roger Chance), *Conservatism and Wealth*, 1929
——, *The Questing Beast*, 1932
——, *Unborn Son*, 1933
——, *The Coming of Aissa*, 1935
——, *Oasis*, 1936
Collin Brooks, *Fleet Street, Press Barons and Politics*, 1998
W. J. Brown, *So Far . . .*, 1943
John Drinkwater, *Summer Harvest*, 1933
Lionel Fielden, *The Natural Bent*, 1960
'Janitor', *The Feet of the Young Men*, 1928
Alexander Khatissian, *Eclosion et Développement de la République arménienne*, Athens, 1989
Rudyard Kipling, *The Irish Guards in the Great War*, 1923 and reprint
Alan Moorehead, *African Trilogy*, 1944 and reprints
Beverley Nichols, *Twenty-Five*, 1926
I. S. O. Playfair, *The Mediterranean and the Middle East*, 1954–88
Michael Redgrave, *In My Mind's Eye*, 1983
A. J. Smithers, *Toby: a Real-Life Ripping Yarn*, 1978
Angela Thirkell, *Three Houses*, 1932
Beatrice Webb, *Letters*, 1978
Philip Williamson, *Stanley Baldwin*, 1999

Index